PRIVACY IN EMPLOYMENT: CONTROL OF PERSONAL INFORMATION IN THE WORKPLACE

KRIS KLEIN

VIVIAN GATES

NATASHA BEZNOSOVA

CARSWELL®

A cataloguing record for this publication is available from Library and Archives Canada.

Composition: Computer Composition of Canada Inc.

 THOMSON REUTERS

CARSWELL, A DIVISION OF THOMSON REUTERS CANADA LIMITED

One Corporate Plaza
2075 Kennedy Road
Toronto, Ontario
M1T 3V4

Customer Relations
Toronto 1-416-609-3800
Elsewhere in Canada/U.S. 1-800-387-5164
Fax: 1-416-298-5082
www.carswell.com
Online www.carswell.com/email

Foreword

The relationship between employers and workers is complex, characterized often by competing interests, and always by an inherent imbalance of power. Of the many factors that contribute to this complexity, one of the most important is privacy, an issue on which employers and employees often hold divergent views. Consider, for example, the employer's interest in information about staff. Does the job applicant have a poor credit rating or a criminal record? Are there substance abuse issues among the employees? Do workers fritter away time on personal e-mails or social networking sites? Do they steal or commit fraud? Workers, meanwhile, do not expect to trade their personal autonomy and dignity for a pay cheque. As such, they retain a certain expectation of privacy when they apply for a job, enter the office or step onto the shop floor. They may, for instance, wonder whether their personal financial situation is relevant to the duties of the job they are applying for, or whether the boss has a right to monitor their off-duty activities.

Striking the right balance between competing interests is undeniably difficult, but it is essential to a successful and modern enterprise. And never has it been more urgent than now, against the backdrop of challenging economic times and the unprecedented reach of technology. Economic pressures are pushing employers to explore new efficiencies, some of which could threaten the privacy rights of workers. And there is no shortage of tools at their disposal, from new surveillance and tracking technologies to biometrics, genetic testing and the monitoring of electronic correspondence.

Privacy in Employment: Control of Personal Information in the Workplace, explores the many legal and ethical dimensions of privacy in the employer/employee relationship. Fully updated and practical, it is the kind of resource that will help human resources professionals, lawyers and academics better understand a uniquely challenging issue at a uniquely challenging time.

Elizabeth Denham
Assistant Privacy Commissioner of Canada

February, 2009

Preface

Whereas the notion of privacy has been around for centuries, it has gained a certain degree of significance since the advent of the "information age". The struggle to control personal information is emerging as individuals, corporations, associations, unions and lawmakers place a newfound value on information that reveals details about people. Nowhere is this struggle more evident than in the workplace. The obvious tension between employer and employee is the perfect arena for two players to spar over who should have control over personal information. As in many relationships, employers and employees need and depend on each other. Nonetheless, there exists within this symbiotic agreement a constant struggle to "get more" from the relationship. Each party partakes. Management wants to improve efficiency, promote the right people, cut costs, prevent theft and harassment, etc. Employees want to remain autonomous human beings, be treated with dignity, be promoted fairly, and reveal only that information about themselves that will aid their cause. It is inevitable for the two sides to eventually clash over privacy rights.

The law of privacy in Canada is admittedly in its infancy. Jurisprudence is far from complete and it is not even entirely clear where and how the law protects privacy. A myriad of provincial, federal and common laws do provide a patchwork of helpful guidelines, but uncertainty remains. Determining when exactly one interest will prevail over the other remains a difficult task. Continuing technological advances, varying degrees of employee organization, changing economic pressures and continued expectations to create profit and efficiency come together every day in new ways creating new contexts and new tensions. From the traditional "hiring of a private detective to determine if an employee's allegations of injury are valid", to the futuristic "genetic testing of employees to determine long term suitability for employment", to the perpetually controversial practice of monitoring employees' use of email or internet - what is certain is that the tug-o-war over workplace privacy continues to broaden and take on new significance.

The employment context does provide, because of the particular differences in interests amongst the parties, a clear window into how the law is answering questions about which contexts will allow certain interests to prevail. This book looks through that window and explores the debate raging in the workplace. We have endeavoured to provide a no-nonsense look at what questions have been asked and how they were answered, and combine it all into a useful tool for those who need to know the jurisprudence to date.

By studying how the law has currently tackled the issues, some predictions might be made for the situation the reader might find themselves in presently or in the future. While uncertainty remains, we hope this study of what has been decided up until now will prove a useful mechanism to guide employers and employees alike through the emerging privacy-related problems they may face in the workplace.

Kris Klein
Vivian Gates

July 2005

Privacy in Employment – 3 years later

When we started to write the update for this handbook, we knew that within the three years since writing the first edition, a fair amount of cases, work and thinking had taken place within the area of employment privacy. We feel that this second edition captures these events in the similar nononsense manner that we used the first time around. Upon writing the new preface, we looked at what had been discussed in the first edition and the information seemed as relevant today as it did three years ago. Notwithstanding the substantial changes in law, the cases that have come and gone, and the growing range of academic discussion on the topic, there still remain important questions that have not been answered; for example, issues relating to drug and alcohol testing as privacy interests, genetic testing, the use of biometrics, and the use of information found online at social network sites, all of which encompass only the "tip of the iceberg". It is our belief, however, that the last three years have provided us with guidance that will be helpful to privacy professionals as they navigate through the ongoing challenges that continue to arise.

This edition is substantially more comprehensive than the previous and we hope it proves useful to those of us trying to find answers in our day-to-day work. We also hope that practitioners will continue to benefit from any future insights concerning employment privacy, and in another three year's time, we expect to have the benefit of even more new material to help guide us as we move forward in our information age.

Kris Klein & Vivian Gates

December 2008

Table of Contents

Table of Cases

TABLE OF CASES

1

Data Protection and Privacy Legislation – Generally

1.1 OVERVIEW

Canada's legal framework for privacy issues in relation to employment and the workplace comprises a wide scope of legislation and jurisprudence. This spectrum includes constitutional law (i.e. the *Canadian Charter of Rights and Freedoms*[1]), quasi-constitutional law (i.e. Quebec's *Charter of Human Rights and Freedoms*[2]), federal and provincial/territorial human rights codes, federal and provincial/territorial data protection and privacy statutes, provincial health information protection legislation, laws governing professional confidentiality, workers' compensation law, employment standards legislation, the criminal law (i.e. protections against physical intrusion), statutory privacy torts in certain provinces, and the emerging common law tort of invasion of privacy. Against this backdrop, it should be noted that the *Canadian Charter of Rights and Freedoms* applies only to governments and private sector bodies acting as agents of government, and any provision within federal, provincial or territorial legislation that is inconsistent with the Charter is of no force or effect.

While all of these laws combined play a vital role in balancing the competing interests of employees and employers with respect to privacy issues at work, depending on the nature of each circumstance, it is beyond the scope of this book to conduct an in depth study of each legislative area. The foregoing statutes and common law are briefly addressed in relation to specific topics throughout this book; therefore, the discussion will be limited to a general overview of federal and provincial/territorial data protection and privacy legislation in Canada as it applies to employees and employers in the workplace.

---

[1] *Charter of Rights and Freedoms*, Part I of the *Constitution Act, 1982*, being Schedule B to the *Canada Act 1982* (U.K.), 1982, c. 11.

[2] *Charter of Human Rights and Freedoms*, R.S.Q. c. C-12.

1.2 FEDERAL LEGISLATION

1.2.1 Public Sector

The federal *Privacy Act*[3] of 1982 regulates the collection, use and disclosure of personal information by federal government institutions, including government employers, and controls the rights of individuals to access personal information held by those agencies. "Personal information" under this Act is broadly defined as "information about an identifiable individual that is recorded in any form", subject to certain exclusions. Most of the *Privacy Act*'s protection does not apply to personal information that is publicly available, to personal information placed in the National Archives of Canada or other federal public libraries by persons or organizations other than government institutions.

Government institutions may only collect personal information which relates directly to an operating program or activity and is intended to be used for an administrative purpose.[4] Wherever possible, personal information should be collected directly from the individual to whom it relates, and the individual should be informed of the purpose for which their personal information is being collected, unless there is a concern that informing the

---

[3] *Privacy Act*, R.S.C. 1985, c. P-21.

[4] See for example *Cash Converters Canada Inc. v. Oshawa (City)*, 2007 ONCA 502, 2007 CarswellOnt 4229 where the Ontario Court of Appeal endorsed the interpretation by various provincial privacy commissioners of the necessity requirement for the collection of personal information. The Court said:

Again, the jurisprudence developed by the Privacy Commissioner interpreting this provision is both helpful and persuasive of the proper approach to be taken by the courts as well. In cases decided by the Commissioner's office, it has required that in order to meet the necessity condition, the institution must show that each item or class of personal information that is to be collected is necessary to properly administer the lawfully authorized activity. Consequently, where the personal information would merely be helpful to the activity, it is not "necessary" within the meaning of the Act. Similarly, where the purpose can be accomplished another way, the institution is obliged to choose the other route.

Further, in its Order F07-10, the Information and Privacy Commissioner for British Columbia said that necessity is both case-specific and the decision-maker's interpretation of the notion of "necessity"; each particular case is fully reviewable by privacy offices. In determining whether personal information is necessary, three aspects must be looked at: the sensitivity of the personal information, the particular purpose for the collection and the amount of personal information collected, assessed in light of the purpose for collection.

individual might result in the collection of inaccurate personal information, or defeat the purpose or prejudice the use for which the information is collected. Personal information must be retained by an institution for such period of time after its use to ensure that the individual to whom it relates has a reasonable opportunity to obtain access to that information. The institution must take reasonable steps to ensure that the personal information used for an administrative purpose is as accurate, complete and up-to-date as possible.

Personal information under the control of the government may be used by the institution without the consent of the individual to whom it relates if it is used for the purpose for which the information was compiled, or for a use consistent with a that purpose. The government institution may not disclose the personal information without the consent of the person to whom it relates unless the disclosure falls within the specified exceptions under section 8(2) of the Act. The head of a government institution must retain a record of any use or disclosure by the institution of personal information contained in a personal information bank, except where such use is in connection with an investigative body specified in the regulations for the purpose of enforcing any law of Canada or carrying a lawful investigation, where the investigative body provides a written request identifying the purpose and describing the information to be disclosed. Each government institution must also publish at least once a year a comprehensive index of personal information banks maintained by the institution, and make the publication available throughout Canada via Canadian Government Publishing (commonly referred to as InfoSource) and the Internet.

The *Privacy Act* also grants Canadian citizens and all individuals present in Canada a mandatory right of access to their personal information upon request to a government institution. To access non-personal information controlled by a government institution, individuals may apply via the provisions of the federal *Access to Information Act*[5] provided that the institution is subject to this Act. Following an individual's request for access to personal information under the *Privacy Act*, a government institution has 30 days after receiving the request to respond to the applicant, with the option to extend the response time to an additional 30 days if reasonably necessary. Where an individual is refused access, the head of the government institution must justify the basis upon which access had been denied. The head of the institution may also refuse to indicate whether or not the personal information actually exists, in which case, the applicant must be informed of the provisions of the *Privacy Act* that would allow for an exemption if the personal information did in fact exist.

---

[5] *Access to Information Act*, R.S.C. 1985, c. A-1.

Pursuant to the exemption provisions of the *Privacy Act*, an applicant may be denied access to personal information where the head of the institution has a reasonable expectation that the use of this information would cause probable harm or another consequence specified in the exempting provision. In addition, certain personal information banks may be designated as exempt banks to which a head of government may also refuse right of access where disclosure may be injurious to international affairs and defence, national security, the conduct of police investigations and other lawful inquiries, and the enforcement of any law in Canada.

Privacy regulation in Canada with respect to health information is both complex and controversial due to the sensitive nature of this personal information. A myriad of other laws in Canada also protect personal health information and regulate health information "custodians" in addition to specific federal and provincial health information protection legislation. In the federal domain, the *Privacy Act* broadly extends to protect personal information relating to an individual's medical history and the blood type of an individual.

1.2.2   Private Sector

The federal *Personal Information Protection and Electronic Documents Act*[6] (*"PIPEDA"*) came into effect on January 1, 2001 and regulates how private sector organizations (including associations, partnerships, persons, and trade unions) may collect, use or disclose personal information in the course of commercial activities that fall within federal jurisdiction. The Act also applies to personal information about employees of organizations that the organization collects, uses or discloses in connection with the operation of a federal work, undertaking or business. Health data, specifically, information about an individual's mental or physical health, including information concerning health services provided and information about tests and examinations, is also covered under *PIPEDA*. *PIPEDA* permits the collection, use or disclosure of personal information by these organizations "for purposes that a reasonable person would consider appropriate in the circumstances". Exceptions to its scope include personal information collected, used or disclosed for personal, domestic, journalistic, artistic, literary or non-commercial purposes.

Part 1 of the Act establishes parameters for the collection, use, disclosure, retention, and disposal of personal information.[7] *PIPEDA* broadly

---

[6] *Personal Information Protection and Electronic Documents Act*, S.C. 2000, c. 5.
[7] Parts 2 through 5 deal with the use of electronic transactions and documents to facilitate business with the federal government electronically, assist electronic

4

defines "personal information" as information, recorded or otherwise, about an identifiable individual, with the exception of the name, title, business address, or business telephone number of an employee of an organization. To constitute personal information, the data must be linked to a specific, natural person. While personal information need not be recorded to be protected under the Act, records include any correspondence, memorandum, book, plan, map, drawing, diagram, pictorial or graphic work, photograph, film, microform sound recording, videotape, machine-readable record, and any other documentary material, regardless of physical form or characteristics, and any copy of any of those items.

Part 1, which is where privacy protection is found, reflects 10 core principles from the Canadian Standards Association's "Model Code for the Protection of Personal Information" that organizations must comply with when processing personal information, namely, identification of purposes, accountability, openness, consent, limiting collection, limiting use, disclosure and retention, individual access, security safeguards, accuracy, and compliance.

PIPEDA requires organizations to identify the purposes for which personal information is collected, at or before the time the information is collected, and ensure that the knowledge and consent of the individual has been obtained for the collection, use or disclosure of personal information, except where inappropriate as specified under the legislation. Further, an organization must limit the collection, use and disclosure of personal information to that which is necessary for the purposes identified, unless it obtains the express consent of the individual, or is required to provide the information by law. Organizations are obliged to retain personal information only for as long as is necessary to fulfill those purposes, and personal information must be kept as accurate, complete, and up-to-date as is necessary for the purposes for which it is to be used. Personal information must also be protected by security safeguards appropriate to the sensitivity of that information.

An organization is required to adhere to principles of openness and accessibility by making available to individuals specific information about its policies and practices relating to the management of personal information. The organization must inform an individual of the existence, use and disclosure of his or her personal information upon written request, and must give the individual access to that information. An individual may challenge the accuracy and completeness of the information and have it amended as appropriate. The organization must provide a mechanism by which an in-

---

communication and submission of records in judicial proceedings, and disseminate federal government publications by electronic means.

dividual may address a challenge concerning compliance with the afore-mentioned principles. Finally, the CSA Model Code emphasizes account-ability of organizations responsible for personal information under their control, thus, an organization should designate a Chief Privacy Officer, or the equivalent, to be accountable for the organization's compliance with its privacy policies and the fundamental principles of *PIPEDA*.

1.2.3   Office of the Privacy Commissioner of Canada

The Office of the Privacy Commissioner is an independent body which oversees both the *Privacy Act* and *PIPEDA* and reports to Parliament on an annual basis. The Commissioner has broad powers to investigate, compel evidence, issue subpoenas, access internal documents (though limited in the power to access documents protected by solicitor-client privilege[8]), mediate, and make recommendations regarding a complaint of invasion of privacy. However, he/she does not have the authority to issue orders or penalties to remedy the alleged violation, or to initiate a Charter challenge in relation to a breach of privacy.[9] Investigations must be conducted by the Commissioner in confidence, and evidence provided thereof is not admissible against the parties in Court or in any other proceeding. However, the Commissioner may, on reasonable notice and at any time, conduct audits of an organiza-tion's personal information management practice if he/she has reasonable grounds to believe that the organization has contravened a provision in Part 1, and may reveal to the public details of an organization's practices where he/she determines that it is in the public interest to do so.

The complainant is entitled to a report of the Commissioner's findings following the completion of an investigation, and if a complainant is dis-satisfied with the Commissioner's decision, he or she has the right to seek judicial review of the matter by the Federal Court of Canada. Where the Court deems it appropriate, it may, in addition to providing other remedies, order an organization to correct its practices in order to comply with the legislation; order an organization to publish a notice of any action taken or proposed to be taken to correct its practices; and award damages to the complainant, including damages for humiliation. The Commissioner can

---

[8] See, however, *Blood Tribe Department of Health v. Canada (Privacy Commis-sioner)*, 2005 FC 328 (F.C.), reversed 2006 FCA 334 (F.C.A.), affirmed 2008 SCC 44 (S.C.C.).

[9] *Canada (Privacy Commissioner) v. Canada (Attorney General)*, 2003 BCSC 862 (B.C. S.C.). *Murdoch v. Canada (Royal Canadian Mounted Police)*, 2005 FC 420, 2005 CarswellNat 800.

also initiate a review by the Federal Court of Canada in limited circumstances involving denial of access to records.

1.3 PROVINCIAL LEGISLATION

1.3.1 Public Sector

All provincial and territorial legislatures have enacted general data protection and privacy legislation to regulate the collection, use and disclosure of personal information by public sector bodies, although these laws and the levels of privacy protection vary significantly from one jurisdiction to another. Unlike the federal regime, the provinces and territories address access to information rights and privacy rights under the same statute in the respective jurisdictions, New Brunswick being the exception. Quebec in particular has enacted a broad range of privacy laws which cover both the public and private sectors. Most notably in the public sector, section 5 of the province's *Charter of Human Rights and Freedoms* enshrines the right to privacy as a fundamental individual right by prescribing that "Every person has a right to respect for his private life".

The privacy train of thought in other provinces is moving in the same direction. While considering whether an information request by a Prince Edward Island newspaper publisher must prevail over public servants' privacy protection with respect to their names, job titles and salaries, the Chief Justice of the provincial Supreme Court ruled that "one must start the balancing in favour of privacy of personal information not in favour of disclosure of personal information".[10] The foundation for this decision was found in the ruling by the Nova Scotia Court of Appeal in *Dickie v. Nova Scotia (Department of Health)*.[11]

Noteworthy is the fact that unlike the *Privacy Act*, some of the counterpart provincial privacy laws do not distinguish between ordinary individuals and "individuals who [are or were] an officer or employee of a government institution".[12] As a result, public servants are entitled to the same protection of personal information as any other residents of these provinces. This means that disclosure of governmental employees' names along with

---

[10] *MacNeill v. Prince Edward Island (Information & Privacy Commissioner)*, 2004 PESCTD 69 (P.E.I. T.D.).

[11] (1999), [1999] N.S.J. No. 116, 1999 CarswellNS 97 (N.S. C.A.).

[12] See for example, *Freedom of Information and Protection of Privacy Act*, S.P.E.I. 2001, c. 37, *Freedom of Information and Protection of Privacy Act*; R.S.A. 2000, c. F-25.

their particular salary, as opposed to salary range, and job title constitutes an unreasonable invasion of their privacy.[13]

(For additional case law discussing the interrelation between personal information and professional information, see Chapter 4.2 – *Professional Information*.)

1.3.2   Private Sector

As of January 1, 2004, *PIPEDA* was extended to every organization which collects, uses and discloses personal information in the course of any commercial activity, including provincially regulated organizations, unless the province which regulates the organization enacts laws "substantially similar" to *PIPEDA*. To date, only Ontario's health-related law, and the private sector laws of Quebec, British Columbia and Alberta have been determined to be substantially similar in privacy legislation in the private sector. Therefore, all other provincial organizations that collect, use and disclose personal information in the course of any commercial activity fall within the purview of *PIPEDA*. Personal information controlled by agents of the provincial Crown and by private sector organizations conducting activities *other than* commercial enterprise in provinces without substantially similar legislation is not protected under *PIPEDA*, thereby leaving certain individuals susceptible to violations of privacy. With respect to provincial health privacy legislation, Quebec was the first Canadian jurisdiction to introduce privacy legislation governing the private sector by enacting the *Act Respecting the Protection of Privacy in the Private Sector* in 1994. The Act has been deemed substantially similar to *PIPEDA* and applies to all private sector organizations with respect to the collection, use and disclosure of personal information, including health information, in all contexts, rather than strictly in relation to commercial activities as per *PIPEDA*. Notably, while Quebec's Act also contemplates the protection of employee information, *PIPEDA* does not apply to organizations in relation to their employees unless the organizations are federal works, undertakings or businesses.

Alberta, Saskatchewan, Manitoba and Ontario have enacted specific health information protection legislation applicable to private and public sector "custodians" or "trustees" and professionals in the health sector. The following health privacy laws apply within these provinces to specific entities such as health care providers, health care practitioners and hospitals: the Alberta *Health Information Act* ("*HIA*"), the Saskatchewan *Health Information Protection Act* ("*HIPA*"), the Manitoba *Personal Health Infor-*

---

[13] *Supra*, note 1.

mation Act ("*PHIA*") and the Ontario *Personal Health Information Protection Act* ("*PHIPA*").

The scope of application of these statutes to health sector bodies is similar because they contain similar definitions relating to these bodies as well as personal health information. Ontario's *PHIPA* applies to "health information custodians", Alberta's Act applies to "custodians" and the Acts in Saskatchewan and Manitoba apply to "trustees". The definitions of "personal health information" have a wide application and all of the statutes require custodians and trustees to exercise some level of supervision over service providers and agents.

Only Ontario's health information protection legislation has been declared "substantially similar" to *PIPEDA* in 2006; therefore, both *PIPEDA* and the health information statutes in Alberta, Saskatchewan and Manitoba may apply to private sector organizations in those provinces with respect to personal health information. *PIPEDA* does not apply to businesses, organizations, hospitals or practitioners in Ontario defined as "health information custodians" under *PHIPA*, except in relation to interprovincial and international disclosures of personal health information. However, since many private organizations operate in more than one province and across numerous provinces, they are likely subject to a blend of provincial and federal privacy laws.

In provinces where specific health information legislation has not been enacted, namely British Columbia, Quebec, the four Atlantic provinces, and Canada's three territories, a combination of public sector and private sector privacy and health care regulatory legislation will apply. Because many hospitals and health care institutions in Canada are governed by a public health care system, these entities are subject to public sector privacy statutes or health care regulatory statutes for the purpose of protecting patient privacy. However, private health care providers such as pharmacies, diagnostic facilities, laboratories and private practitioners may be subject to the general private sector privacy laws. Health care providers in Quebec and British Columbia would fall within the purview of the privacy legislation enacted within those provinces, while *PIPEDA* would apply to health care providers in the Atlantic provinces and Canada's three territories since these provinces and territories have not yet enacted privacy legislation applicable to the private sector.

1.3.3 Regulatory Bodies

Oversight bodies range widely in scope and powers between the provinces, from simply providing an Ombudsman for the entire region to the establishment of a dedicated office with a Privacy Commissioner and trained staff. Unlike the *Privacy Act*, some provincial data protection legislation, such as that of British Columbia, Alberta, Ontario, and Quebec, prescribes powers for adjudicators to make enforceable orders. However, the decisions of adjudicators are subject to judicial review by the provincial trial and appeal courts.

2

Hiring Procedures

2.1 INTERVIEWING

Human rights legislation provides the legal framework that proscribes practices by employers in all matters relating to prospective employment which may deprive individuals of employment opportunities on the prohibited grounds of discrimination enumerated in respective federal and provincial human rights statutes. Such practices may include inappropriate questioning on an application for employment or during a job interview which directly or indirectly classifies or indicates qualifications by a prohibited ground of discrimination. The same line of questioning, though not designed to discriminate or exclude, could arguably extend to invasion of a candidate's privacy as well, and may not necessarily be relevant to the position sought by the applicant.

Federal and provincial privacy legislation makes clear that employers may collect personal information only for purposes that relate directly to an operating program or activity of the institution, or that a reasonable person would consider appropriate in the circumstances. The federal *Privacy Act* regulates the collection, use and disclosure of personal information of any individual by the federal government institutions, which are defined as all of the government departments, bodies and offices listed under the schedule of Government Institutions.

The *Privacy Act* protects an employee's personal information from unauthorized collection, use and disclosure. For a government employer to collect personal information, that personal information must relate directly to an operating program or activity of the institution and where possible, the employer must collect the personal information from the employee directly. In accordance with section 8(1) of the *Privacy Act*, when information is collected without the employee's consent, disclosure of that personal information is restricted to the purposes for which it was collected, or to use consistent with that purpose, unless it falls under the exceptions in section 8(2) of the *Privacy Act*.

Currently, *PIPEDA* applies to every employer that collects, uses and discloses personal information in the course of a commercial activity unless those employers are located in a province that has enacted legislation

11

deemed substantially similar to *PIPEDA*.[1] *PIPEDA*, however, would still be applicable to employers in those provinces when personal information crosses provincial borders or, arguably, when it passes to federal bodies and to federal works.

Personal information means any information about an identifiable individual, but does not include the name, title or business address or telephone number of an employee of an organization. Unlike the *Privacy Act*, *PIPEDA* does not include an enumerated list to illustrate the specific meaning of personal information, therefore, one could infer that all information "about an identifiable individual" would be considered personal information for the purposes of *PIPEDA*. In other words, personal information should be given a broad and liberal meaning.

The purpose of *PIPEDA* is similar to that of the *Privacy Act*, except that the activity in question is between an employee and an employer in the private sector. The purpose is defined under section 3 which can be distilled to mean that rules that govern the collection, use or disclosure of personal information balances the interests of the employee's right to privacy with those of the employer's need to collect, use or disclose personal information for purposes that a reasonable person would consider appropriate.

One example of personal information that may not be collected by potential employers from candidates being interviewed for available vacancies is the candidates' social insurance numbers. In his Order F07-10, the Information and Privacy Commissioner for British Columbia said:

> Social insurance numbers are only required for the purposes of federal programs such as income taxation and employment insurance. An employer is required to collect the social insurance numbers of employees for such programs, but it need not collect them from mere job applicants. This personal information cannot be said to be related directly to and necessary, within the meaning of s. 26(c), for the hiring process at the stage of processing or considering applications.

Additionally, the Canadian Human Rights Commission has established comprehensive guidelines for employers regarding the type of information obtainable from applicants during the interview process without inviting a

---

[1] Currently, only Alberta (*Personal Information Protection Act*, S.A. 2003, c. P-6.5), British Columbia (*Personal Information Protection Act*, S.B.C. 2003, c. 63), and Quebec (*An Act Respecting The Protection Of Personal Information In The Private Sector*, R.S.Q. c. P-39.1) have enacted legislation that has been deemed substantially similar to *PIPEDA*.

human rights complaint or possibly one of invasion of privacy.[2] These guidelines specifically caution employers from eliciting extraneous information from applicants to assess their candidacy for a position.

2.2 RÉSUMÉS/PORTFOLIOS/DOCUMENTATION

Employers regularly collect from prospective employees various types of documentation, such as résumés, portfolios, and university transcripts, which are considered personal information protected by privacy statutes if these relate to an identifiable individual. Employers also often receive unsolicited documentation from eager applicants, implying collection with consent since the information is voluntarily submitted to the employer. Arguably, candidates who are asked to provide specific documentation prior to or in conjunction with being interviewed consent to divulging their personal information in part as a condition of employment.

Privacy legislation prescribes that such information may only be used for the purpose for which it was collected, that is, one which relates directly to an operating program or activity of the institution or that a reasonable person would consider appropriate in the circumstances, such as considering an individual for a position within the organization.

Recently, in a unionized workplace, these questions along with the issue of the extent to which personal information collected during the hiring process may be disclosed to a union have turned into a real battlefield. A bus company (the employer) and the respective union differed on the interpretation of a provision in the collective agreement that addressed hiring, promotions, transfers and demotions and the impact the British Columbia *Freedom of Information and Protection of Privacy Act* (*"FOIPPA"*)[3] has on that interpretation.[4] In particular, the disputed provision stated that the employer was required to provide the union, upon the union's request, with copies of applications for vacancies advertised by the employer. While the union contended that the collective agreement was not limited by *FOIPPA*, the employer's position was that it could not disclose any personal information of applicants unless they consented in writing. The union submitted its grievance under the collective agreement.

---

[2] Canadian Human Rights Commission, "Guide to Screening and Selection in Employment", March 2007, online: Canadian Human Rights Commission <http://www.chrc-ccdp.ca/publications/screening_employment-en.asp>.

[3] R.S.B.C. 1996, c. 165.

[4] *C.O.P.E., Local 378 v. Coast Mountain Bus Co.* (2007), 165 L.A.C. (4th) 141, 2007 CarswellBC 3258 (B.C. Arb. Bd.).

The arbitrator upheld the employer's position with respect to disclosure, under the collective agreement, of personal information about an identifiable individual. The union appealed this decision to the British Columbia Court of Appeal. This time, the scales tipped against the employer who was ordered to disclose the requested information to the union, albeit after having eliminated all personal identifiers. The Court of Appeal further recommended that the employer expressly notify candidates that their personal information may be disclosed to the union for the purpose of ensuring compliance with the collective agreement. To finally clarify and resolve the issue of the scope of the employer's obligation to disclose under the collective agreement, both the employer and the union agreed to submit the question to the British Columbia Arbitration Board. The Board agreed with both authorities previously trying to resolve the matter that "the union's use of the information for the purpose of assessing the employer's hiring decision is . . . a purpose consistent with the purpose for which the information was obtained namely, seeking a suitable candidate for a job with the employer through a job competition governed by a collective agreement". It therefore identified three specific issues to be determined: (1) what documents typically generated in the job selection process are included in "copies of applications"; (2) what personal information must be disclosed to meet the union's purpose of ensuring the employer's hiring decision complies with the collective agreement; and (3) what personal information typically collected in the job selection process is not related to the ability to perform the vacant job or to seniority?

In determining the first issue, the Board looked at two other cases involving disputes over the interpretation of similar disclosure provisions in two other collective agreements. The Board noted that in both reference cases, *University of Alberta v. University of Alberta Non-Academic Staff Assn.*[5] and *Chilliwack School District No. 33 v. Chilliwack Teachers' Assn.,*[6] the respective provisions were drafted to cover all possible disputes arising from the collective agreements. As a result, the wording of the provisions was intentionally of generic application and broad. In the case before the Board, on the other hand, the provision concerned exclusively disputes in relation to employer job selection decisions. Therefore, an "application" was held to include "all the information the applicant gives and all the information the employer asks the applicant to supply to assess his or her ability and seniority". More particularly, "'copies of applications' includes any electronic or other form the employer requires applicants to use to make

---

[5]　(2006), 2006 CarswellAlta 1532, 151 L.A.C. (4th) 365, 56 Admin. L.R. (4th) 259 (Alta. Arb. Bd.).

[6]　(2004), 2004 CarswellBC 3470 (B.C. C.A.A.).

timely applications; resumes; any document voluntarily supplied by an applicant; interview questions and responses; score sheets; written tests; criteria used to evaluate candidates and the weight given to each; score sheets; seniority dates; and overall scores achieved".

In providing a response to the second question before it, the Board stated that personal information required for the union's purpose of ensuring compliance of the employer's hiring procedures with the collective agreement should include all personal information in complete "applications" of the successful candidate and union members. Two exceptions to this requirement, according to the Board, are: (1) personal information not related to an applicant's ability to perform the job or seniority; and (2) the limited class of information that qualifies as a personal identifier. A "personal identifier" was in turn interpreted by the Board as information that is specific to a unique individual, more particularly, names and contact information, such as postal, email and other addresses and telephone numbers; passwords, social insurance numbers, drivers licence, care card and financial numbers; and biometrics.

In its attempt to clarify what information should be considered as not related to the ability to perform the job or seniority, the Board said once again that neither applications of unsuccessful candidates nor personal identifiers of all applicants should be disclosed to the union. It was also noted that there may be further information falling under this rubric, but which should be determined on a case-by-case basis. Once ruled out as not related, such information may not be used by the employer to support its decision to select a particular candidate over the others.

The decision in the *Coast Mountain Bus* case is consistent with two other earlier awards made by arbitration boards. In *S.G.E.U. v. Saskatchewan*,[7] the arbitrator held that the grievor's employment references must be disclosed to the union. The reasoning was that there was no evidence that the references had been provided in confidence. While not necessary for the disposition of this grievance, the arbitrator further ruled that the information requested fell within the provisions of the *Freedom of Information and Protection of Privacy Act* that provided that the Act "does not limit the information otherwise available by law to a party to litigation".

By the same token, the award made in Chilliwack School District No. 33, referred to in Coast Mountain Bus, stands for the proposition that personal information of job applicants may be disclosed under the B.C. FOIPPA if it constitutes information "available by law to a party to a proceeding" (section 3(2)) or when "a disclosure of personal information is not an unreasonable invasion of a third party's personal privacy if . . . an

---

[7] (2007), 164 L.A.C. (4th) 129, 2007 CarswellSask 755 (Sask. Arb. Bd.).

enactment of British Columbia or Canada authorizes the disclosure" (section 22(4)(c)). In this case, the authorizing legislation was the B.C. Labour Relations Code, which obligates employers to do everything which is required to ensure compliance with collective agreements.

The bottom line of this series of arbitration awards appears to be that in a unionized setting: (1) disclosure, under collective agreements containing provisions similar to the one in dispute in this case, of personal information of successful candidates for vacancies as well as personal information of union members applying to respective unions is considered to be consistent with a purpose for which such information was obtained, thereby removing any allegations of privacy legislation violations; and (2) such disclosure is also supported by relative provisions in privacy legislation stating that whenever a disclosure is authorized by a provincial or federal enactment, subject to the relevancy of the information to be disclosed, privacy acts cannot shield employers from disclosing the requested information.[8]

Similar issues were raised and considered in relation to staffing competitions within the realm of the federal *Privacy Act*. In one case, the applicant competed for a position with the Canadian Food Inspection Agency ("CFIA") as a Regional Operations Coordinator[9]. When he failed to pass one of the selection process phases, he expressed concerns regarding the process. In particular, he doubted that the successful candidates had the required minimum qualifications. Therefore, the applicant requested copies of the successful candidates' applications. The CFIA selection board refused to disclose the requested records as they contained personal information about the successful candidates' education and employment, and section

---

[8] Contrast with *University of British Columbia v. C.U.P.E., Local 116* (2005), [2005] B.C.C.A.A.A. No. 166, 2005 CarswellBC 2683 (B.C. C.A.A.). In that case the union requested that the employer provide it with "résumés of all candidates, applications for each, names of interviewers, questions, answers and marking guide for the interviews and the weighting and scoring for each factor for each candidate". The arbitrator held against the union. The reasoning was that firstly, the collective agreement did not contain a provision entitling the union to the requested information. Secondly, since at the time of the request the union had not commenced any actual grievance arbitration, section 3(2) of the B.C. *FOIPPA*, which provides that information may be disclosed if it is "available by law to a party to a proceeding", was of no assistance to the union in this case. For the purpose of section 3(2) of the Act, the arbitrator distinguished "grievance process" from a "grievance arbitration". Only the latter falls under the category of a "proceeding" as referred to in the Act.

[9] *Forsch v. Canadian Food Inspection Agency*, 2004 FC 513, 2004 CarswellNat 4134 (F.C.).

8(1) of the federal *Privacy Act* prohibits disclosure of such information without the consent of the individual in question.

When the dispute reached the Federal Court, the judge presiding over the case ruled that under these circumstances the employer could not be exempted from disclosing the successful candidates' applications. A number of reasons were given for this decision. Firstly, section 8(2)(a) of the Act allows disclosure of "personal information" where such disclosure is "consistent with the purpose for which it was obtained." According to the Court, "disclosure of the successful candidates' applications within the staffing complaints process is a purpose consistent with the purpose for which the information was obtained, that is, in seeking an appointment with the CFIA through a staffing competition". Secondly, the Court held that the principles of procedural fairness would be violated if the applicant were deprived of access to the requested information, and thereby precluded from fully and fairly presenting his complaint. Finally, disclosure was also permissible under section 3(j) of the Act, where the material in the candidates' applications related to their "past employment positions and duties . . . while employed at a 'government institution'".

The outcome of this case is consistent with the ruling of the Supreme Court of Canada in *Canada (Information Commissioner) v. Royal Canadian Mounted Police Commissioner.*[10] In that case, the Court held that section 3(j) of the *Privacy Act*, which authorizes the release of "information about an individual who is or was an officer or employee of a government institution, applies retrospectively. As a result, information about both the past and current positions held by a government employee may be disclosed. The Court noted, however, that only information "relating to the position or functions of the employee" is covered by the section 3(j) exception. Thus, information such as "the evaluations and performance reviews of a federal employee and notes taken during an interview. . . are aspects of employment history that are not related to functions or past positions".

When it comes to selecting a contractor to undertake a project instead of hiring a new individual employee to fill a vacancy, personal information used in the selection process appears to be guarded more zealously. For example, the Ontario Information and Privacy Commissioner upheld the decision of the Town of Richmond Hill, which had invited submissions for a Request for Proposals made by the Town, to deny a requester access to résumés of employees of the winning bidder.[11] In issuing this order, the Commissioner relied on prior similar orders made by the Office. The reasoning was that the *Municipal Freedom of Information and Protection of*

---

[10] 2003 SCC 8, 2003 CarswellNat 448 (S.C.C.).
[11] Order MO-2176, March 27, 2007.

17

Privacy Act,[12] under which the request for the information was made, defines such information as personal (section 2(1)) and prohibits its disclosure without the consent of the affected party (section 21). The requester could not even get access to the résumés with the names of the respective individuals severed. According to the Office, "the résumés contain sufficiently detailed information about the individuals such that . . . it is reasonable to expect that each of the individuals may be identified" even if their names have been removed from the résumés. The employer is also obligated to secure the information in an appropriate manner, which might entail placing the documentation in a personnel file for new hires, or perhaps destroying it within a reasonable time frame if the candidate is not selected for employment.

2.3   STAFF INPUT/CONSULTATION

Privacy legislation clearly outlines an employer's obligations to collect, use, disclose, and secure the personal information of employees and potential employees only for purposes that a reasonable person would consider appropriate in the circumstances, or for a purpose that relates directly to an operating program or activity of the institution. This raises questions of propriety regarding access by non-management colleagues to an applicant's personal information (for example, résumés, portfolios, and other documentation) in the hiring process. Moreover, should non-supervisory colleagues participate in or conduct job interviews, and be consulted in the hiring of candidates? Generally, non-management colleagues play a lesser role or no role after hiring with regard to coworkers' performance reviews, pay raises, promotions, discipline, and termination, which supports the view that the employer-employee relationship is highly personal and usually exclusive of others not privy to a respective employment contract. Interestingly, these principles appear to be more flexible in the hiring process, despite the fact that candidates may consider their preliminary documentation to be no less personal and no less worthy of privacy protection from coworkers who may be their professional equals in the workplace.

The following case illustrates one example of an employee's personal information being exposed to co-workers by the employer, albeit legitimately, but without the employee's consent. The team manager at a telecommunications company shared a telemarketer's sales figures with coworkers without her consent, prompting her to file a complaint with the Privacy Commissioner. The employee considered her work performance and sales commission to be confidential and had not received any expla-

---

[12] R.S.O. 1990, c. M.56.

nation regarding the purpose of collecting and displaying employees' sales statistics. The company alleged that all new employees were informed of this practice and that the purpose of this practice, which was to motivate employees and encourage competition in order to increase sales, had been reiterated at numerous staff meetings. The company maintained that this was a proven and accepted practice in sales and that the posting of employee sales results was also a widely accepted practice among telemarketers. Further, the company did not consider sales figures to be personal information since they were produced in the course of business activities, and even if it was found to be personal information, reasonable use of such information in the workplace should not require the express consent of employees.

The Commissioner found that sales statistics are personal information pursuant to *PIPEDA*, as they constitute information about an identifiable individual. However, although the complainant did not expressly consent to the practice of displaying sales statistics, the complainant had implied her consent by willingly participating in a business environment where the practice of disclosing employees' personal sales results could reasonably be expected. The Commissioner did recommend that the company take steps to ensure that all telemarketing employees were clearly informed of the company's practices and its purposes for disclosing personal sales records.[13]

2.4 BACKGROUND CHECKS

Employers generally use background checks to verify the accuracy of information provided to them by job seekers, and to uncover information not acquired in the application or interview. However, such investigations are subject to various federal and provincial statutes designed to protect an individual's privacy rights.

Credit checks may be conducted both on potential and current employees where the employee is or will be performing their duties in a position of trust or financial responsibility. In these circumstances, employers must notify the individual in writing that they are conducting a credit check and identify the consumer reporting agency that will be providing the credit check, pursuant to section 10(2) of the *Consumer Reporting Act*, R.S.O. 1990, c. C.33.[14] Some consumer reporting agencies have access to infor-

---

[13] Privacy Commissioner of Canada, September 15, 2003, Summary #220.

[14] See *Somwar v. McDonald's Restaurants of Canada Ltd.*, 263 D.L.R. (4th) 752, 2006 CarswellOnt 48. In that case, the Court had an opportunity to discuss the availability of a civil remedy when a breach of a statute also constitutes a tort.

mation regarding, for example, a person's character, reputation, health, physical or personal characteristics and lifestyle. Thus, employers must be mindful to not use such information in a way that may discriminate against or invade an individual's privacy.[15]

Recently, the office of the Alberta Information and Privacy Commissioner held that pursuant to the Alberta *Personal Information Protection Act*, an employer violated the privacy rights of its potential employee by having conducted a credit check for the position of an administrative assistant/receptionist.[16] Following her interview, the candidate was required to consent to a background check. Having received the results of the check, the employer decided not to hire the candidate. The Senior Portfolio Officer reasoned that the "nominal value" of petty cash flow to be managed by the nominee, and the lack of previous issues with petty cash theft at the company rendered the credit check unreasonable. Further, it was noted that the employer should have considered "whether there are other, possibly more effective and/or less intrusive, means" to assess the applicant's suitability to manage finances in an employment context.

A complaint brought before the Privacy Commissioner of Canada by a bank customer further illustrates the point that employers do not have unlimited entitlement to an employee's credit information. The employer in this case had not acted inappropriately, rather, a collections officer contracted by a bank allegedly disclosed a customer's credit card and outstanding debt to her employer, though the officer swore an affidavit that she had never spoken to the employer. Instead, the officer accused the employer of covering for the complainant with regard to the outstanding debt. When the Commissioner's office investigated the matter, the employer corroborated

---

The statute in question was the *Consumer Reporting Act*. The plaintiff sued his employer alleging that the latter had violated the plaintiff's privacy by conducting a credit check on him without his permission. In particular, the defendant argued that while the Act makes it an offence in certain circumstances to conduct unauthorized credit checks, it does not, confer any civil remedy for its breach. Having analyzed the jurisprudence coming out of the Supreme Court of Canada, as well as commentary by leading academics in this field, the Court concluded that while a statutory breach per se cannot give rise to civil liability, liability may attach if the plaintiff succeeds in showing that in addition to the statutory breach, the required "constituent elements of tortious responsibility" have also been satisfied.

[15] Ogilvy Renault, "Employee Background Checks", October 2002 [*Ogilvy Renault*]; McCarthy Tétrault LLP, "Privacy in the Workplace" (McCarthy Tétrault Publication, January 2002) online: McCarthy Tetrault <http://www.mccarthy.ca/article_detail.aspx?id=650>.

[16] Investigation Report P2005-IR-008.

the employee's accusations against the officer and the Commissioner determined that the bank had not conducted a proper investigation, having failed to consult with the complainant's employer. The bank indicated numerous ways in which the agency had not met its contractual obligations to the bank with respect to the bank's privacy and confidentiality policy, which was to inform an employer of an employee's financial problems, in accordance with the section 7(3)(b) debt collection provision of PIPEDA, only when legal action was required to garnish an employee's wages.[17] The bank subsequently implemented punitive measures and subjected the agency to a detailed audit.[18]

Employers may ask for references and undertake employment history checks, however, those who do ask for references can incur liability for failing to check those references in the event of an employee's improper acts.[19] Security checks, which often also encompass criminal record checks, may be done where an employer can establish that they are reasonable and relevant to the position, and where the prospective employee consents to the check. Employers can ask on an application form whether the applicant has been convicted of a criminal offence for which a pardon has *not* been granted, however, prior to the interview stage employers may not ask about the applicant's record of offences regarding provincial statutes. While an employer can refuse to hire an applicant based on their criminal record if no pardon has been granted, human rights legislation prohibits against discrimination in employment on the grounds of conviction for a provincial offence or for an offence for which pardon has been granted.[20]

The Privacy Commissioner has heard numerous complaints against employers regarding security checks. In one case, 35 employees of a company's nuclear products division filed a complaint after the Canadian Nuclear Safety Commission ordered its licensed companies to ensure that all persons who entered a licensed facility first had security clearance. The employees each received an information package that included consent forms describing the type of information being collected, the purpose for the collection, and details of a confidentiality agreement between the collection firm and the company. However, the employees complained that their consent to the security check was not meaningfully voluntary since employees who consented and failed the security check would likely be reassigned, and those who refused consent could lose their job.

---

[17] See also, Privacy Commissioner of Canada, October 24, 2005, Summary # 317, Privacy Commissioner of Canada, October 21, 2004, Summary # 282.

[18] Privacy Commissioner of Canada, April 24, 2003, Summary #168.

[19] *Ogilvy Renault, supra,* note 15.

[20] *Supra,* note 2.

The Commissioner determined that the company had ensured that it would not collect personal information without the employees' express consent, and despite the possibility of negative consequences with or without consent, the security check was still voluntary as the employees always had a choice. The security check was deemed appropriate by a reasonable person in the circumstances due to the Canadian Nuclear Safety Commission notification that it would revoke its companies' licences if they did not comply, and due to increased concern over terrorist attacks against nuclear facilities.[21]

The Privacy Commissioner Office relied on its reasoning in the above case when considering another case dealing with a nuclear installation.[22] In this case, a facility employee complained that his employer was requiring employees to provide personal information of spouses or common-law partners for the purpose of a security clearance check without the spouse's or partner's consent. The Commissioner once again analyzed whether a reasonable person in those circumstances would find such a requirement appropriate. The question was answered in the affirmative. According to the Office, as "it is assumed that spouses or common-law partners have intimate knowledge of each other, and share common goals, as well as income and expenses," it was concluded that not only would it be inappropriate not to perform a security check on the spouse/common-law partner of the employee, but that no separate consent is required. It was held that the onus to discuss these issues with his or her spouse or common-law partner was on the employee.

Very similar facts were before the Ontario Arbitration Board when the Society of Energy Professionals tried to dispute the validity of enhanced security checks required by Ontario Power Generation Inc. ("OPG") on its nuclear division employees with access to areas designated as protected areas.[23] The enhanced security checks, including detailed personal information of current spouses or common-law partners of employees with access to protected areas, were performed by OPG upon the instructions received from its regulatory body, the Canadian Nuclear Safety Commission ("CNSC"). These enhanced security requirements were implemented as a response to the concerns raised by the events of September 11, 2001. While CNSC decided that the information in question was required for "national security reasons" and directed OPG to collect the same from employees

---

[21] Privacy Commissioner of Canada, August 14, 2002, Summary #65.
[22] Privacy Commissioner of Canada, October 1, 2003, Summary # 232.
[23] *Ontario Power Generation Inc. v. Society of Energy Professionals* (2004), 2004 CarswellOnt 4296 (Ont. Arb. Bd.).

who had access to designated areas, OPG went further by extending this requirement to cover all its employees.

The Arbitrator ruled that OPG was entitled to collect detailed spousal information only from its nuclear division employees who had access to protected areas. The Board was of the view that OPG acted reasonably when it complied with the direction of its regulatory authority. He also rejected the argument that by collecting such information, OPG violated *PIPEDA*. His reasoning was that under section 7(3)(c.1)(i) of the Act, disclosure of personal information to a government agency is allowed without the individual's knowledge or consent if the government agency "suspects that the information relates to national security, the defence of Canada or the conduct of international affairs."

Interestingly, while the Arbitrator acknowledged the existence of decisions made by the Privacy Commissioner of Canada in this respect, he did not feel that those were of any assistance to him as they were not binding authority.

Another complaint involved allegations by an employee that his employer had forced him to consent to a security check enabling him to work in a restricted area at an airport. The security check was required in accordance with federal government policy, which necessitates all persons working in restricted areas in all of its airports to submit to a security check. The employee had signed a form when first hired acknowledging the possibility of a security clearance and the possible repercussions should an employee refuse. However, the employee claimed that his subsequent consent was neither informed nor voluntary since he had signed the consent form after being suspended for three days and being threatened with dismissal. The Commissioner found that the company had initially informed the employee at the time of hiring that a security check may be required and that failure to consent could result in dismissal; that the employee did have a choice in the matter despite the potentially negative consequences; that it was reasonable for the airport to require security clearance given the increased threat of terrorism; and that a reasonable person would deem it appropriate for a company to comply with federal requirements.[24]

The issue of airport security has been considered from a different angle in another reliability check case.[25] A complaint was lodged by an employee of the Canada Customs and Revenue Agency ("CCRA") who was required by the airport authority to undergo an enhanced security check that was allegedly duplicative of a security clearance program under the federal Government Security Policy ("GSP"). Initially the Canadian government

---

[24] Privacy Commissioner of Canada, March 4, 2003, Summary #127.
[25] Privacy Commissioner of Canada, December 24, 2003, Summary # 255.

created a security clearance program called the Airport Restricted Area Access Clearance ("ARAAC") program. Any airport employee who required access to airport restricted areas or sensitive information had to have an ARAAC certificate which could be issued upon completion of a background check involving fingerprint verification, a Canadian Security Intelligence Services check, a criminal record check, a check against the databank of lost or stolen passports, and a confirmation of the applicant's 'landed immigrant' status, if necessary. Prior to September 2001, those individuals who held Level II (Secret) and Level III (Top Secret) security clearances were not required to undergo additional clearance procedures for obtaining an ARAAC certificate. As a result of the September 11, 2001 events, this provision has been repealed.

During its investigation, the Privacy Commissioner compared the two clearance programs and found a high degree of resemblance between them. Moreover, the Level II (or higher) security checks exceeded the scope of the ARAAC clearance program. The Commissioner was concerned that the duplicative practices unjustifiably intrude upon the privacy rights of individuals with Level II or higher screening as they allow for more people to have access to those individuals' personal information.

Another problem revealed by the investigation was that the airport authority in question had failed to institute a personal information retention policy. As a result, the Commissioner found the airport authority in contravention of Principle 4.5 of *PIPEDA* which provides that personal information shall not be kept longer than it is required by the purpose for which it was collected.

Transport Canada's experience in conducting background checks for airport employees has been used recently to develop a similar clearance program for the marine industry. The Marine Transportation Security Clearance Program, which requires workers who have access to certain restricted areas of ports as well as workers occupying certain positions to undergo a transportation security clearance, was announced to start on December 15, 2007. This date is the start date of the first phase of the program that covers the ports of Montreal, Halifax, Vancouver, Fraser River, North Fraser River, and the control centers of the St. Lawrence Seaway Management Corporation. The second phase, scheduled to be complete by December 15, 2008, will include the ports of St. John's, Newfoundland and Labradour; Saint John, New Brunswick; Quebec, Quebec; Toronto, Hamilton and Windsor, Ontario; and Prince Rupert and Victoria, British Columbia.

According to the Ministry, the clearance program is designed to reduce the risk of security threats, and prevent unlawful interference with the marine transportation system. To this end, designated marine personnel will be subjected to four types of security checks. These are a criminal record check, a check of the relevant files of law enforcement agencies, including intelligence gathered for law enforcement purposes, a Canadian Security Intelligence Service ("CSIS") check and, if required, a CSIS assessment and verification of an applicant's immigration and/or citizenship status.

Transport Canada stated that extensive consultations had been conducted with numerous stakeholders before the final version of the program was approved. One of the goals of the consultation process was to balance the security for the Canadian ports with individual privacy rights.

Another significant feature of the newly implemented program is the availability of re-consideration. Any marine worker whose security clearance has been refused or cancelled may apply to the Office of Reconsideration, which is independent of the office that conducts the initial evaluation. The Office will perform its own assessment of the application and make a recommendation.[26]

In *O.P.S.E.U. v. Ontario (Management Board Secretariat)*,[27] the union applied for interim relief in connection with two other grievances relating to the employer's plans to implement employee security checks. The purpose of the security checks was to establish the same level of security certification of employees as that existing federally in connection with information that was exchanged between the two levels of government. The union sought an order prohibiting the employer from proceeding with the process until the Grievance Settlement Board had disposed of the grievances. The grievances dealt with the unilateral implementation of security checks by the employer without consultation with the bargaining agent, despite documentation indicating that consultation meetings were planned to discuss bargaining agent feedback to the proposed policy and implementation.

The draft policy stated that an employee who refused to consent to a security check would be removed from the position requiring security clearance, and if security clearance was not granted, the employee would not be able to remain in that position. In balancing the convenience to the employer against the potential harm to employees, the arbitrator ruled that there was no indication that the province's ongoing relationship with its federal counterparts was in jeopardy if things remained *status quo* pending the resolution of the grievances. Conversely, the questioned integrity of employees who might be displaced because of an unsatisfactory security check could not be undone. Thus, the union was granted interim relief as the privacy interests

---

[26] For more information regarding the Marine Transportation Security Clearance Program, visit online: Transport Infrastructure and Communities Portfolio <http://www.tc.gc.ca/MarineSecurity/implementationMTSCP.htm>.

[27] (2003), 117 L.A.C. (4th) 128 (Ont. C.E.G.S.B.).

of the employees outweighed those of the employer in the particular circumstances of this case.

At issue in a case involving a commercial airline pilot was a request by the pilot's employer that pilots sign an authorization form, required by the United States government, to disclose personnel information of Canadian pilots to the U.S. government indicating that the pilots had received requisite training on aircraft simulators twice a year to maintain their professional certification. The Privacy Commissioner held that the form did not meet fair information principles and the airline's reasons for requiring its pilots to sign the form were unreasonable. It was inappropriate to require pilots to consent to collection and disclosure practices that contravened Canadian law, and since Canadian pilots had already received security clearance, a reasonable person would be unlikely to find it appropriate to force pilots to disclose their personal information at the request of a foreign government.[28]

2.5 PSYCHOLOGICAL & APTITUDE TESTING

In Canada, the use of psychological tests is not prohibited and is popular amongst employers to screen prospective employees or assess the suitability of an employee to a particular job. These tests include a wide range of instruments, such as general intelligence tests, aptitude tests, performance tests, personality tests, honesty tests, handwriting analysis. Pre-employment testing is permitted if the purpose of the test is to measure the individual's inherent ability to perform certain job requirements. However, the validity of such tests has been questioned due to possible built-in cultural and gender biases.[29] Human rights legislation prohibits testing that is linked to an individual's characteristics rather than to specific ability to perform job functions. For example, the *Canadian Human Rights Act*[30] states:

> 8. It is a discriminatory practice
>
> . . .
>
>> (b) in connection with employment or prospective employment, to publish any advertisement or *to make any written or oral inquiry*

---

[28] Privacy Commissioner of Canada, December 19, 2002, Summary #106.

[29] Information and Privacy Commissioner of Ontario, "Workplace Privacy: The Need for a Safety-Net", November 1993, online: <http://www.ipc.on.ca/scripts/index_.asp?action=31&P_ID=11439&N_ID=1&PT_ID=11351&U_ID=0#testing>.

[30] *Canadian Human Rights Act*, R.S.C. 1985, c. H-6.

that expresses or implies any limitation, specification or preference based on a prohibited ground of discrimination.

9. (1) It is discriminatory practice for an employee organization on a prohibited ground of discrimination

. . .

(c) to *limit, segregate, classify* or otherwise act in relation to an individual in a way that would deprive the individual of employment opportunities, or limit employment opportunities or otherwise adversely affect the status of the individual, where the individual is a member of the organization or where any of the obligations of the organization pursuant to a collective agreement relate to the individual.

Aptitude tests, for example, must be appropriately connected to the position in question that the individual has applied for and must not violate human rights law. However, because aptitude tests are not reliable indicator of the quality of future job performance, it is very difficult for an employer to demonstrate a valid and useful relationship between the test results and the performance of a particular job function. Further, aptitude tests are often discriminatory, therefore, by implementing these tests, employers risk making hiring decisions based on unreliable information and may be exposing themselves to claims of human rights violations.[31]

Likewise, the use of psychological testing requires employers to show that the test results are linked to specific job requirements and must not include extraneous, irrelevant, or discriminatory information relating to the individual's psychological make-up. Studies indicate that the most important and useful role for pre-employment psychological testing is that it can expose a candidate's character as honest or dishonest.[32]

In its Order F07-10, the Office of the Information and Privacy Commissioner of British Columbia had the opportunity to comment on one type of assessment of potential employees that, in the opinion of the Office, contained elements of both aptitude and psychological testing. At issue was whether the "Gallup TeacherInsight Assessment" developed and administered in the United States infringed upon privacy rights of candidates for teachers' positions. The Assessment was introduced by the Board of Education of School District No. 75 in 2004. Every candidate was required by the Board to take the test as a pre-requisite for being short-listed for the subsequent interviewing process. Gallup used the responses to prepare a report, which included a numeric score that Gallup claims is predictive of an

---

[31] McCarthy Tétrault LLP, "Privacy in the Workplace", *supra*, note 15.
[32] *Ibid.*

applicant's potential for teaching success in the classroom. The British Columbia Teachers' Federation ("BCTF") and the Mission Teachers' Union ("MTU") took the position that this screening requirement violated the B.C. *Freedom of Information and Protection of Privacy Act ("FIPPA")* and filed the respective complaint with the Office. One of the major issues raised in the complaint was whether the Board was authorized to collect the personal information through the Assessment.

Before addressing the substantive issues, the Information and Privacy Commissioner discussed the issue of standing and noted that *FIPPA* does not extend its protection to public bodies and organization. Nonetheless, it was decided that in light of the seriousness of the issues raised and the broad discretion under section 42(1)(a) of the Act, it was appropriate to proceed with the inquiry regardless of whether an individual had complained.

During the discussion of the first substantive issue, the Commissioner made a number of interesting observations and conclusions. Pursuant to section 26(c), personal information of an individual may be collected if it relates directly to or is necessary for an operating program or activity of the public body. Therefore, the notion of "necessity" in this context required further clarification. Having applied relevant statutory interpretation techniques, the Commissioner concluded that necessity is both case-specific and the decision-maker's interpretation of the notion of "necessity"; each particular case is fully reviewable by privacy offices. In determining whether personal information is necessary, three aspects must be looked at: the sensitivity of the personal information, the particular purpose for the collection and the amount of personal information collected, assessed in light of the purpose for collection.

Replying to the BCTF's contention that collecting psychological testing information goes beyond the collection of personal information that is necessary for the program in question, the Commissioner drew a parallel between the disputed screening techniques and more conventional methods of collecting similar information during an interviewing process:

> Certainly, questions in the Assessment draw out individuals' attitudes about the nature of teaching, ascertain how they would react to certain scenarios in the classroom or with their teaching colleagues, elicits how they perceive themselves in terms of attributes such as honesty and emotional control, and draws out how they believe others see them. To some extent, one could say that the answers, and the scores that Gallup assigns and reports to the Board, or applying the results of Gallup's research methods, reveal something about the 'psychological' make-up of respondents. Put another way, however, it is reasonable to infer that the Assessment tells the Board something about the

character and aptitude of those who apply to teach children for whose education the Board is responsible.

I take notice of the fact that employers, including this Office, may ask questions intended to elicit information about candidates' character and aptitude for the position and that the Assessment includes questions much like those one encounters during face-to-face job interviews. Employers may ask questions similar to those found in the Assessment, although this may be done during face-to-face interviews (perhaps with applicants who have passed first-cut screening of some kind). Even using this method, candidates' answers will be noted and assessed by the employer or its consultants, enabling the employer to assess and rank, with varying degrees of formality, competing candidates' competencies across a range of job and personality attributes.

In conclusion, the Commissioner found that in this particular situation, the collection of personal information through the Assessment was authorized by section 26(c) of *FIPPA*.

The Office of the Alberta Information and Privacy Commissioner was asked on a number of occasions to look at another aspect of these types of testing used for employment purposes, specifically the disclosure of testing materials themselves. In two Orders made by the Office, the Calgary Police Service refused to provide the requesters with materials used for testing job applicants.[33] The employer was concerned with the utility and efficacy of its testing methods if they became available to potential employees. The Commissioner agreed with the Police Service. The same conclusion was made by the Office in another Order dealing with test answers and psychological assessment tools.[34] The same argument, that disclosure would hinder the future use of the testing methods, was successful. The Commissioner, however, held that the scoring sheets would not jeopardize the hiring procedures and had to be disclosed.

---

[33] Information and Privacy Commissioner for Alberta, Order F2003-020, April 15, 2004; Information and Privacy Commissioner for Alberta, Order F2004-022, November 28, 2005.
[34] Information and Privacy Commissioner for Alberta, Order F2004-015, May 10, 2005.

3

Employment Records

3.1 INTRODUCTION

Federal and provincial labour/employment standards legislation requires employers to keep and maintain employee records for varying periods, depending on the jurisdiction, statute, and the type of information placed in the record. Privacy legislation generally prohibits collection, use and disclosure of personal information, including the personal information contained in employee records, without the knowledge and consent of the individual, unless it relates directly to an institution's operating program or activity or to a purpose which a reasonable person would consider appropriate in the circumstances.

3.2 WORK PERFORMANCE

Decisions by the Privacy Commissioner of Canada suggest that personal information of employees and company information are not always mutually exclusive. However, these decisions emphasize that while *PIPEDA* recognizes the needs of organizations to use personal information in the workplace, the Act does not allow for uses that are unreasonable, unnecessary or poorly defined.

A telemarketer at a telecommunications company filed a complaint with the Commissioner that her team manager had shared her personal information, specifically, her sales figures, with co-workers without her consent. She considered her work performance and sales commission to be confidential and had not received any explanation regarding the purpose of collecting and displaying employees' sales statistics. The company alleged that all new employees were informed of this practice and that the purpose of this practice, which was to motivate employees and encourage competition in order to increase sales, had been reiterated at numerous staff meetings. The company maintained that this was a proven and accepted practice in sales and that the posting of employee sales results was also a widely accepted practice among telemarketers. Further, the company did not consider sales figures to be personal information since they were produced in the course of business activities, and even if it was found to be personal information, reasonable use of such information in the workplace should not require the express consent of employees.

The Commissioner found that sales statistics are personal information pursuant to *PIPEDA*, as they constitute information about an identifiable individual. However, although the complainant did not expressly consent to the practice of displaying sales statistics, the complainant had implied her consent by willingly participating in a business environment where the practice of disclosing employees' personal sales results could reasonably be expected. The Commissioner did recommend that the company take steps to ensure that all telemarketing employees were clearly informed of the company's practices and its purposes for disclosing personal sales records.[1]

In another case involving a telecommunications company, two former employees complained that their employer had collected statistics about their work without their consent and had subsequently used this personal information to assess their work performance. The company asserted that it was company practice to collect information regarding the volume, duration, and type of call received by its operators to manage individual work performance, and that this practice was communicated to employees in a variety of ways, including disclosure of individual statistics each month. The Commissioner determined that a reasonable person would conclude that it is proper for a company to monitor and assess its employees' work performance and that it is proper to use statistical information in connection with the calls to measure their performance. The employer had informed the employees and by virtue of working for a company, the employees had given implicit consent to work performance evaluations.[2]

Information on the daily movements of work vehicles operated by a company's in-field employees that is collected through the use of Global Positioning System ("GPS") was found to constitute "personal information" under section 2 of *PIPEDA*.[3] Employees of a telecommunications company affected by the use of this technology became concerned that the employer would be using GPS to monitor their performance and punish them if they were not sufficiently productive. The company, on the other hand, argued that it had other valid and serious purposes served by the installation of the positioning devices. Among others, the employer cited the need to manage workforce productivity, ensure safety and development, and protect and manage assets as legitimate purposes. The company also emphasized that GPS allowed it to locate a vehicle and not an individual. Anyone using the

---

[1] Privacy Commissioner of Canada, September 15, 2003, Summary #220.
[2] Privacy Commissioner of Canada, April 14, 2003, Summary #153.
[3] Privacy Commissioner of Canada, November 9, 2006, Summary # 351.

system would see the vehicle identifier rather than the driver's name. Therefore, the employer argued that this was information related to the location of a vehicle and not to that of an individual. The Assistant Commissioner disagreed with the company's position, stating that because the information could be linked to specific employees driving the vehicles, the employees were identifiable even if they were not identified at all times to all users of the system.

While the company lost this argument, it managed to persuade the Assistant Commissioner that even if the information in question is personal, in collecting and using it the employer had not violated any provisions of the Act. The Assistant Commissioner deliberated that the company was obliged to obtain employee consent prior to collection of the information and that in this case, the consent could be implied as the data collected was not viewed as sensitive. It was further noted that in examining the reliance on implied consent, an individual's expectations must be considered, as required by principle 4.3.5 of the Act. This means that if implied, the consent should only be used for the purposes for which the employee could reasonably expect the information would be used. To assess the appropriateness of installing GPS for the purposes stated by the company, the Assistant Commissioner stressed that four questions must be considered: (1) is the measure demonstrably necessary to meet a specific need; (2) is it likely to be effective in meeting that need; (3) is the loss of privacy proportional to the benefit gained; and (4) is there a less privacy-invasive way of achieving the same end?

Having assessed all the purposes of GPS use in accordance with the foregoing questions, the Assistant Commissioner concluded that workforce productivity improvement and safety and assets management met the test. As a result, she found that implied consent was present for these purposes. Regarding the use of GPS for employee management purposes, the Assistant Commissioner noted that the technology should only be used this way when employees have been clearly notified beforehand of such purposes and provided with the company's policies outlining an appropriate process of warnings and progressive monitoring. The company provided the Office with such a policy, which emphasizes that where performance management is concerned, GPS will be used for investigating a complaint from a member of the public, investigating concerns raised internally, and addressing productivity issues. In her final comments, the Assistant Commissioner underscored that "the purposes and uses of a particular technology should be precisely specified, and that technology should be restricted to its intended purposes."

Another example of what is considered to be "personal information" within the rubric of "employment history" is detailed scheduling information of an employee's shifts at his or her workplace. This question was determined by the Prince Edward Island Privacy and Information Commissioner in a case involving the collection of an employee's personal information by one of his employers, the Office of the Attorney General, from another public body, the Department of Health, where the employer held his second job.[4] The employee had called in sick to the OAG for two consecutive nights. The operations manager at the OAG contacted the Department of Health with a view to finding out whether the employee had worked his shifts there while he was absent from his job at the OAG due to his alleged illness. A Department of Health employee informed the operations manager that the employee had worked his shifts during the nights concerned. As a result of this telephone conversation, the employee was formally disciplined.

The Office of the Information and Privacy Commissioner rejected the OAG's position that the personal information was collected without violation of P.E.I.'s *Freedom of Information and Protection of Privacy Act* (*"FOIPP"*) because it was a necessary requirement for an operating program or activity of a Public Body pursuant to section 31(c) of the Act. While the Commissioner accepted that managing employees is an activity of the OAG, the collection of the personal information from a third party, especially in the absence of any prior concerns about the employee's actual work performance, was deemed unnecessary.

In response to the submissions of the OAG and the Department of Health, that an employer requires some means of monitoring its employees and ensuring proper compliance with benefits such as sick leave, and that such collection of employee information had been routinely used before, the Commissioner stated that "privacy sometimes overrides human resources desires." As the Commissioner could not order these public bodies to cease collecting or disclosing the employee's personal information because the investigation had been conducted after the fact, the Commissioner invoked section 66(3)(f) of the Act. In accordance with this section, the Office of the Attorney General was ordered to destroy the improperly collected information as if the collection had never occurred.

At issue in another case concerned with collection of employees' personal information for the purpose of monitoring employees' work performance and administering the employment relationship, was an employee's non-work-related use of the internet during his working hours.[5]

---

[4] *Prince Edward Island (Attorney General), Re* (2006), 2006 CarswellPEI 60 (P.E.I. I.P.C.).

[5] Information and Privacy Commissioner for British Columbia, Order F07-18, September 24, 2007.

The employee was employed by the University of British Columbia as an Engineering Technician and had almost exclusive access to his work computer which he needed for job-related purposes. After the employee's supervisor shared with the Administration Manager his concerns about the employee's productivity and his use of non-work-related websites during University time, the manager directed the supervisor to take appropriate measures to determine whether the hours spent on the Internet were excessive. To do this, the supervisor had the Golden Eye Spy Software installed, which enabled the employer to fully monitor the employee's computer activity and print out related reports. They, in turn, were used to terminate the employee's job for cause. The employee's union grieved that termination and the employee made a request under B.C.'s *Freedom of Information and Protection of Privacy Act* (*"FOIPP"*) for access to information relating to his job performance and computer use. The University provided the employee with, among other documents, the reports generated from his computer with respect to his Internet use. The employee filed a complaint with the Office of the Information and Privacy Commissioner alleging that his employer had collected his personal information in violation of the Act.

Among other issues, the Adjudicator had to determine whether the information in question constituted personal information as defined in *FOIPP* and if so, whether its collection was authorized by the Act. On the first issue, the Adjudicator found that the reports containing information with respect to the employee's internet use did constitute the employee's personal information. The Adjudicator therefore dismissed the employer's argument that the information about the websites visited was not the employee's personal information, as it related not to an identifiable individual but rather to the computer. The Adjudicator reasoned that the employee's exclusive access to the computer qualified the information in question as belonging to an easily identifiable individual. Further, the employer's very reliance on the computer use reports for the purpose of terminating the employee's job contradicted its submission. In responding to the employer's statement that it did not collect such information as it was automatically registered by the computer itself, the Adjudicator commented that while it was arguable whether the recording of the internet websites amounted to collection of the information, the employer's printing out of such data did.

Next, the Adjudicator considered whether the collection of the information was "directly related to and necessary for an operating program or activity" of the University. She agreed that managing its human resources and workplace behaviour was part of an operating program or activity of the University. In that sense, the information collected related to the stated program or activity. However, the Adjudicator questioned the necessity of the collection by reasoning that in this case there were less intrusive, "reasonable and viable alternatives to the surreptitious collection of personal information" available, such as first warning the employee of the concerns raised by his supervisor. This position was supported by the findings that the employee made no attempt to conceal his personal use of the computer and that he was fully aware that his supervisor knew of that use, yet never raised that issue with the employee.

By contrast, the Privacy Commissioner of Canada's earlier decision in *IMS Health Canada* (see Chapter 5 – ***Personal Opinions***), suggests a lack of consistency in assessing what specifically constitutes personal information in relation to the professional information of employees obtained by employers as compared to the foregoing cases. In response to a complaint filed by a physician against IMS Health Canada alleging that the company was selling information about the prescribing patterns of physicians without their consent, the Privacy Commissioner held that the prescribing patterns of physicians did not comprise personal information about the physician. Rather, the Commissioner stated that a prescription in relation to an identified patient is personal health information about that patient, and not the physician. Further, a prescription is the outcome of professional interaction between the physician and patient and thus is more appropriately regarded as work product. With regard to the bodies covered by *PIPEDA*, the Commissioner stated that "to interpret personal information so broadly as to include work products could allow for the inclusion of documents written by employees in the course of employment, reports prepared by employees for managers' use, or legal opinions, and would therefore be inconsistent with the stated purpose of *PIPEDA*". However, the issue of the appropriate place for work product within the privacy legislation framework remains subject to debate and can hardly be seen as settled.[6]

---

[6] For example, while British Columbia has excluded "work product" from the definition of "personal information" in its privacy legislation, Alberta hesitated to follow suit reasoning that "the current contextual approach allows for greater flexibility than a categorical exclusion" (Final Report, dated November 2007, of the Alberta Select Special Personal Information Protection Act Review Committee, p. 25, 26). The federal legislature does not seem to feel comfortable about categorical exclusion either. In response to the recommendation by the Standing Committee on Access to Information, Privacy and Ethics, in its Fourth Report tabled in the House of Commons on May 2, 2007, that *PIPEDA* be amended "to include a definition of 'work product' that is explicitly recognized as not constituting personal information for the purposes of the Act", the Government took a more cautious position and decided to hold consultations with all stakeholders. Recognizing the significance of the issue as well as the general approach of the Act, the Government endeavoured to strike a balance between "a business-friendly

The *IMS Health Canada* line of thought appears to prevail in the decision of the Federal Court of Appeal in *Rousseau v. Wyndowe*.[7] This time it was an insured person who wanted to get access to his personal information in the file created by a doctor who performed an independent medical examination of the insured at the request of his insurer. As a result of the doctor's report, the insured's benefits were terminated. The doctor refused the insured access to the requested file. The case went up to the Federal Court of Appeal which decided that "personal health information" is a subset of "personal information" for the purposes of *PIPEDA*. It further ruled that the insured had a right of access to his file held by the doctor to the extent that the file contained the insured's personal information, in particular, details provided to the doctor by the insured along with the doctor's final opinion regarding the insured's medical condition. At the same time, the Court noted that the process of formulating that final medical opinion from initial information provided by the insured belonged to the doctor.

3.3   PERSONNEL FILES

Privacy legislation and decisions by the Privacy Commissioner indicate that requests by individuals to access their personal information should not be unreasonably withheld, and that reasons for denying access should be limited and specific.

Two employees who unsuccessfully competed for another position at an airport requested a copy of their personnel files to determine why they did not win the competition. The employer initially denied their request to see the files but eventually allowed them access five months after the request, which was well beyond the 30-day time limit prescribed in *PIPEDA*. When the individuals complained to the Privacy Commissioner, the Commissioner determined that the employer had contravened the Act. The employer agreed to place scores obtained in a job competition in the employee file, and retain the file for a period of six months following the competition.[8]

In another private sector case, an individual suing his former employer for wrongful dismissal and breach of contract complained that the employer did not respond to his request within the 30-day time-limit. Further, though the company released some of the documents, it failed to provide him with all of his personal information. The employer claimed that the cost of

---

privacy regime with the need for maintaining the existing level of privacy protection currently provided by the Act."

[7] 2008 FCA 39, 2008 CarswellNat 246 (F.C.A.).

[8] Privacy Commissioner of Canada, October 22, 2002, Summary #87.

responding to the request was too costly and likened the former employee's request to a "forensic audit". The company opposed granting access because the employee was suing the employer and believed that his request was directly linked to the lawsuit. The company did provide the employee with some of his personal information several months after the access request, however, the Assistant Privacy Commissioner found that the employer failed to provide the employee with information about him contained in minutes from meetings of the board of directors around the date of his dismissal. The company argued that the employee was seeking the documents in question to circumvent the disclosure and production rules under the *Rules of Civil Procedure*, and that the minutes from board meetings were confidential and should not be made available.

The Assistant Privacy Commissioner determined that since nearly six months had passed since the initial access request, the employer was deemed to have refused access contrary to *PIPEDA*. The Assistant Privacy Commissioner also found that the company had contravened the Act by imposing a $1,500 access fee, which was not a minimal amount pursuant to requirements under the Act, and that some of the complainant's personal information had in fact not been provided to him. Moreover, in differentiating the scope of discovery from the scope of an access to personal information request, the Assistant Privacy Commissioner informed the employer that with respect to their claim regarding the employee's attempts to circumvent the legal process, whereas discovery requires each party to disclose all facts and information before trial, *PIPEDA* grants a right of access to all personal information which an employer retains about an individual whether the information is relevant or not.[9]

One significant exception to this all-encompassing right of access to an individual's personal information under the control of that individual's employer has been dealt with recently in the case of *Blood Tribe Department of Health v. Canada (Privacy Commissioner)*[10] In that case, an employee of the Blood Tribe Department of Health (Blood Tribe) was dismissed and requested access to her personal employment information. Her personnel file contained, among other things, correspondence between Blood Tribe and its solicitors that was covered by solicitor-client privilege. The Assistant Privacy Commissioner ordered Blood Tribe to forward all documents in the file to their attention to enable the Office to investigate the employee's complaint. Blood Tribe disclosed all requested documents save those that

---

[9] Privacy Commissioner of Canada, December 21, 2004, Summary #285.

[10] 2006 FCA 334, 2006 CarswellNat 3294 (F.C.A.), leave to appeal allowed (2007), 2007 CarswellNat 681 (S.C.C.), affirmed (2008), 2008 CarswellNat 2244 (S.C.C.).

were privileged. In response, the Assistant Privacy Commissioner invoked section 12(1)(a) and (c) of *PIPEDA*, which enables the Commissioner to compel the production of any documents the Commissioner considers necessary to investigate a complaint in the same manner and to the same extent as a superior court. Blood Tribe appealed this decision to the Federal Court of Canada, which upheld the decision of the Information and Privacy Commissioner Office. The Federal Court of Appeal, however, disagreed with the approach taken by the lower authorities with respect to privileged documents. In its unanimous decision, the Court noted that section 12(1) powers of the Commissioner were not the same as those of superior court judges. The powers were purely procedural and only applied to matters that otherwise fell within the jurisdiction of the Commissioner, the production of documents shielded by solicitor-client privilege not being one of them. The Court referred to recent discussions by the Supreme Court of Canada regarding the interaction between privileged documents and a statutory power to compel the production of records in *Descôteaux c. Mierzwinski*[11] and *Pritchard v. Ontario (Human Rights Commission)*.[12] The upshot of these decisions is that express statutory language is required to abrogate solicitor-client privilege because such privilege is deemed to be presumptively inviolate. *PIPEDA*, however, lacks the requisite express language.

In conclusion, the Court noted that section 15 of *PIPEDA* allows the Commissioner to apply to the Federal Court in relation to matters concerned with, in particular, solicitor-client privilege. The three-step test for determining whether privileged information should be disclosed was set out in the Supreme Court of Canada's decision in *R. v. McClure*.[13] In the first two stages, the party seeking privileged material must establish that there is no other compellable source for the privileged information, as well as an evidentiary basis upon which to conclude that the information would be legally useful. At the third stage, the judge must then examine the documents and must not release them unless satisfied that they would likely give rise to an issue of relevance pertinent to the ultimate disposition of the case.

In this case, the Court was of the opinion that non-disclosure of the privileged materials did not affect the Commissioner's ability to investigate the complaint. Therefore, the Orders of the Commissioner and the Federal Court for production of privileged records were set aside. The Supreme Court of Canada affirmed the decision of the Federal Court of Appeal that

---

[11] [1982] 1 S.C.R. 860 (S.C.C.).
[12] [2004] 1 S.C.R. 809 (S.C.C.).
[13] 2001 SCC 14 (S.C.C.).

PIPEDA does not contain clear enough language to abrogate solicitor-client privilege.[14]

In *MacNeil v. R.*,[15] the Federal Court ruled that providing poor references does not constitute a breach of an employee's privacy. In this case, an RCMP officer who had resigned from the force filed an action against the RCMP for damages for malicious conspiracy and breach of privacy following his unsuccessful application to six other police forces and for re-engagement with the RCMP, and the placement of assault charges against him in his personnel file. The officer claimed that he had been promised a positive reference by his RCMP supervisor upon his resignation, however, the supervisor denied he had made such an offer because of the officer's poor performance. Although the officer had authorized the other police forces to contact the RCMP for employment references, his RCMP supervisor provided him with poor references when contacted by the forces because the officer had not fulfilled his commitment to serve anywhere in Canada and had never completed his field training.

The Court held that there was no defamation or malicious conspiracy by the RCMP to ruin his career. The officer had failed to appreciate that other police forces did not find him to be an attractive candidate given his poor performance and his criticism of the RCMP during his interviews. Moreover, all negative notes had been removed from the officer's personnel file before his application for re-engagement with the RCMP was considered. The supervisor had not breached the officer's privacy rights since the officer had authorized the other police forces to contact the RCMP for references.

The Supreme Court of Canada has emphasized that while information about government employees may be considered personal information as defined by the *Privacy Act*, such information must be disclosed if it directly relates to the general characteristics associated with the position or function of a federal employee and to understanding the functions performed by those employees.

The issues in *Canada (Information Commissioner) v. Canada (Commissioner of the Royal Canadian Mounted Police)*[16] pertained to freedom of information and the right to inspect public documents containing personal information. In connection with litigation against four RCMP officers, an individual had requested information from the RCMP about the officers, including a list of the officers' historical postings, their status and date, the

---

[14] *Blood Tribe Department of Health v. Canada* (Privacy Commissioner), 2008 SCC 44, 2008 CarswellNat 2244 (S.C.C.).

[15] [2002] FCT 277, [2002] F.C.J. No. 363 (Fed. C.A.).

[16] [2003] 1 S.C.R. 66 (S.C.C.).

list of ranks and when they achieved those ranks, their years of service, their anniversary dates of service, and any public complaints made against the officers. The RCMP refused the request on the basis that the records constituted "personal information" as defined under section 3 of the *Privacy Act*, and therefore were exempt from disclosure pursuant to section 19(1) of the *Access to Information Act*, R.S.C. 1985, c.A-1.

The Federal Court of Appeal held that only information regarding a public servant's current or most recent position had to be released, however, on appeal to the Supreme Court of Canada, the Supreme Court ruled that although the information did qualify as "personal information" pursuant to the Act, the RCMP must disclose all of the information requested by the individual. The exception under section 3(j) of the *Privacy Act* applied, allowing disclosure because the information was directly related to the general characteristics associated with the position or function of a federal employee. The information did not reveal anything about the competence of the officers or divulge any personal opinion given outside the course of employment, rather it provided information relevant to understanding the functions performed by the officers. The Court also held that the information applied retroactively and was not limited to an employee's most recent position.

In another case involving public body employees, an applicant made a request under Alberta's *Freedom of Information and Protection of Privacy Act* for access to severance arrangements as well as all employment-related benefits for all managerial employees of the City of Calgary.[17] In response to the request, the City released a number of agreements but refused to provide four supplementary pension agreements, invoking section 17(1) of the Act, which requires a public body to refuse to disclose personal information "if the disclosure would be an unreasonable invasion of a third party's personal privacy." The applicant filed a complaint with Alberta's Information and Privacy Commissioner. The Adjudicator ordered the City to provide the applicant with the requested agreements. While acknowledging that all of the information contained in the supplementary pension benefit agreements was "personal information" within the meaning of the Act, the Adjudicator held that the City was obliged, under section 17(2) of the Act, to disclose all but the names, signatures, and retirement dates of the affected individuals. Section 17(2) states that "disclosure of personal information is not an unreasonable invasion of a third party's personal privacy if . . . (e) the information is about the third party's classification, salary range, discretionary benefits or employment responsibilities as an

---

[17] Information and Privacy Commissioner for Alberta, Order F2003-002, June 16, 2003.

officer, employee or member of a public body . . . or (h) the disclosure reveals details of a discretionary benefit of a financial nature granted to the third party by a public body."

The City argued that section 17(2) did not apply to the supplementary pension agreements because the supplementary pension benefits were not discretionary as the City had no authority to approve or withhold the pension. The Adjudicator did not accept this argument stating that the City Council had a choice as to whether, or how, to grant the benefit and that City Council had exercised its discretion on behalf of the public body to grant the supplementary pension benefits to the affected retirees.

The Federal Court of Canada issued a decision along the same lines when it dealt with performance bonuses awarded to certain National Research Council ("NRC") employees.[18] An Officer of the Research Council Employees' Association requested a list of recipients under the federal *Access to Information Act* in order to determine how the bonuses were distributed across the NRC's various branches. The NRC refused to provide this information citing section 18 of the Act, which prohibits the head of a government institution from disclosing any record that contains personal information as defined in section 3 of the *Privacy Act*. The applicant complained to the Office of the Privacy Commissioner of Canada who ordered the NRC to provide a somewhat limited list of bonus recipients. This decision was judicially reviewed by the Federal Court. The presiding judge agreed with the applicant that full disclosure must be made and accepted her argument that the names of the employees fell within the exception in section 3(1)(1) of the *Privacy Act*, which provides that "information relating to any discretionary benefit of a financial nature . . . conferred on an individual, including the name of the individual and the exact nature of the benefit" does not constitute personal information. The Court opined that while the employees' names alone were their personal information within the meaning of the *Privacy Act*, the exception in the Act mandating disclosure of discretionary financial benefits applied as "everything about the program was discretionary". In addition, the judge ruled that the information requested may have been disclosed based on the public interest exception "given that the information [the Officer] sought was of a general nature and the purpose for which she was seeking it was to undertake a legitimate analysis of the expenditure of public funds."

Noteworthy is the fact that unlike the *Privacy Act*, some of the counterpart provincial privacy laws do not distinguish between ordinary individuals and "individuals who [are or were] an officer or employee of a govern-

---

[18] *Van Den Bergh v. National Research Council of Canada*, 2003 FC 1116, 2003 CarswellNat 3034 (F.C.).

ment institution."[19] As a result, public servants are entitled to the same protection of personal information as any other residents of these provinces. This means that disclosure of government employees' names, along with their particular salary (as opposed to salary range) and job title constitutes an unreasonable invasion of their privacy. This supports the outcome in *MacNeill v. Prince Edward Island (Information & Privacy Commissioner)*.[20] In this case, a newspaper publisher made a request to obtain a list of employees including their names, positions/titles and salary from Prince Edward Island's Workers' Compensation Board. The request was rejected. Instead, P.E.I.'s Information and Privacy Commissioner ruled that under the provincial *Freedom of Information and Protection of Privacy Act*, an individual's name constituted personal information, the disclosure of which represents an unreasonable invasion of the employee's privacy when combined with actual salary earned and job title. The P.E.I. Supreme Court upheld the Commissioner's decision, commenting in particular, that even if public servants were previously thought to forfeit their privacy protection, it was no longer the case after the coming into force of the Act.

3.4 DISCIPLINARY RECORDS

Arbitration decisions indicate that all prior incidents of discipline can form part of an employment record, unless the collective agreement contains a sunset clause requiring the expunging of such incidents after a specified period of time. Prior acts of misconduct that are unrelated to a particular disciplinary action can also be considered in determining the penalty for a subsequent act of misconduct or a culminating incident.[21]

Despite the foregoing principles, however, the arbitrator in *SKF Manufacturing of Canada Ltd. v. I.A.M., Local 901*[22] ruled that while prior acts of unrelated misconduct can be considered in determining the penalty for subsequent misconduct, those acts must have been documented in the employee's disciplinary record. The employee in this case was discharged for consuming alcohol at work, although his discipline records consisted of only three warnings that were unrelated to the alcohol incident. Relying on the warnings in the employee's disciplinary record and other incidents which were never formally recorded, the employer argued that this was a culmi-

---

[19] See for example, *Freedom of Information and Protection of Privacy Act*, S.P.E.I. 2001, c. 37, *Freedom of Information and Protection of Privacy Act*; R.S.A. 2000, c. F-25.

[20] 2004 PESCTD 69 (P.E.I. T.D.).

[21] *Calgary (City) v. A.T.U., Local 583* (1997), 61 L.A.C. (4th) 317 (Alta. Arb. Bd.).

[22] (1975), 9 L.A.C. (2d) 139 (Ont. Arb. Bd.).

nating incident for which dismissal was the appropriate penalty. The arbitrator reduced the discharge to a one-month suspension and ruled that it would be unfair to base the penalty on incidents for which the employee had not been formally disciplined; formal disciplinary measures informs an employee that further misconduct may result in dismissal and allows him or her to either correct the alleged conduct or challenge the allegations through the grievance process.

An exception to the rule that an employer cannot use prior non-disciplined misconduct to discipline or discharge an employee was established in *Air Canada v. C.A.L.E.A.*,[23] where a passenger agent was suspended for poor customer service following 13 prior non-disciplined incidents. The arbitrator reduced the suspension from 10 days to five, however, he stated that the employer can rely on non-disciplined matters that are not "stale", which combined with subsequent incidents demonstrate a pattern of carelessness or poor attitude merit discipline. The arbitrator held that some of the incidents taken together with the incident in question indicated a pattern of unacceptable performance warranting discipline.

In subsequent decisions more favourable to employees, arbitrators have recognized an additional exception to the general rule against considering previous non-disciplinary misconduct in a culminating incident. The ruling in *Newfoundland Light & Power Co. v. I.B.E.W., Local 1620*[24] established that incidents of misconduct can be considered in determining whether there are mitigating circumstances, such as an employee's good employment record, which might support a lesser penalty than the dismissal of an employee following a culminating incident.

The employee in this case was discharged due to employer concerns over his antagonistic and uncooperative attitude, his reluctance to follow safety procedures after having been spoken to about it on numerous occasions, violations of safety regulations, and a suspension following a violation, however, not all of these incidents were formally made part of a disciplinary record. The arbitrator held that the discharge must stand on those incidents which formed part of the formal disciplinary record, in accordance with provisions of the employee's collective agreement and with previous arbitral decisions.

The arbitrator also ruled that where an incident warranted the penalty of discharge, an arbitrator could consider an employee's good record in assessing things such as an employee's attitude, remorse and credibility and mitigating the penalty. While the arbitrator would not allow the employer to present prior incidents of the employee's non-disciplined misconduct to

---

[23] (1981), 4 L.A.C. (3d) 68 (Can. Arb. Bd.).
[24] (1990), 13 L.A.C. (4th) 341 (Nfld. Arb. Bd.).

support its discharge penalty, the employer was permitted to provide such evidence to argue that mitigation of the discharge should not be ordered by the arbitrator.

3.5 CRIMINAL RECORDS

Third party access provisions in privacy legislation emphasize that employers can only access an employee's criminal record if the employee consents in writing, and employers must inform the employee of the type of criminal record information being sought. Once a pardon has been granted to an individual, however, employers receive no evidence that an employee's criminal record existed or that the employee was pardoned.[25] Human rights legislation prohibits against discrimination in employment on the grounds of conviction for a provincial offence or for an offence for which pardon has been granted.

In *MacNeil v. R.*,[26] the Federal Court ruled that placing criminal charges in an employee's personnel file does not constitute a breach of an employee's privacy, as defined by the *Privacy Act*. In addition to having a poor performance record, the officer had a criminal record in connection with assault charges involving a former girlfriend. The individual who had placed the criminal record in the officer's file did not intend to undermine the officer's re-engagement application with the RCMP or invade his personal privacy; he simply did not believe that the former employee had the potential to be rehired and determined that the employee would have had to disclose the criminal charges regardless of their placement in his file. Additionally, the Court ruled that the prohibition in the *Privacy Act* against disclosing personal information to third parties only applies to documents in the control of a government institution, and that criminal record documents do not belong to a government institution (or in this case, the RCMP).

---

[25] John Howard Society of Alberta, "Understanding Criminal Records", 2000.
[26] *Supra*, note 15.

4

Work Product & Professional Information

4.1 WORK PRODUCT

Following the decisions of the Supreme Court of Canada and the Privacy Commissioner of Canada, work product or tangible information resulting from an employee's work activity is not "personal information" as defined under privacy legislation.[1] Work product is not information *about* an employee, rather, it is information *in association with* or *in relation to* an employee.[2] However, the issue of the appropriate place for the definition "work product" within the privacy legislation framework remains subject to debate and can hardly be seen as settled.[3]

---

[1] See for example, Information and Privacy Commissioner for British Columbia, Order P06-05, December 14, 2006. In that case, three independent contractors of an organization complained to the Information and Privacy Commissioner that their privacy had been invaded by the organization when the latter hacked into their e-mails without their knowledge or consent. The materials submitted to the Information and Privacy Commissioner Office revealed that the complainants' e-mails in question contained the exchange of ideas with respect to setting up a new competing business of their own. As a result, the Commissioner concluded that first, information about other business activities, which had nothing to do with the complainants' business responsibilities in relation to the organization, did constitute "work product information." As the British Columbia *Personal Information Protection Act* excludes work product information from the definition of "personal information", there was no merit to the complaints. Second, the Commissioner noted that even if the information in question was seen as personal, the organization was authorized to collect this information without the complainants' knowledge or consent as it had serious grounds to investigate an alleged breach of the confidentiality clause of the Independent Contractor Agreements that it had concluded with the complainants.

[2] *Dagg v. Canada (Minister of Finance)*, [1997] 2 S.C.R. 403 (S.C.C.); Privacy Commissioner of Canada, October 2, 2001, Summary #15.

[3] For example, while British Columbia has excluded "work product" from the definition of "personal information" in its privacy legislation, Alberta hesitated to follow suit, reasoning that "the current contextual approach allows for greater flexibility than a categorical exclusion" (Final Report, dated November 2007, of

A decision following a complaint filed with the Privacy Commissioner against IMS Health Canada indicates that little protection is afforded under *PIPEDA* to the work product of employees in the private sector.[4] The complainant here alleged that the company was selling information about the prescribing patterns of physicians without their consent. The information was gathered from Canadian pharmacies and comprised specifics such as the store number, drug identification number, drug name, form, strength, quantity, cost, doctor's first and last name, identification number, phone number, manufacturer, selling price, patient gender, and date of birth.

The Commissioner defined "personal information" as that information about an identifiable individual, meaning a natural person, which did not include legal persons such as corporations, partnerships or associations. The Commissioner held that a prescription in relation to an identified patient is personal health information about that patient, however, anonymized prescription information did not constitute personal information about the prescribing physician. Rather, a prescription is the outcome of professional interaction between the physician and patient and thus is more appropriately regarded as work product. With regard to the bodies covered by *PIPEDA*, the Commissioner stated that to interpret personal information so broadly as to include work products could allow for the inclusion of documents written by employees in the course of employment, reports prepared by employees for managers' use, or legal opinions, and would therefore be inconsistent with the stated purpose of *PIPEDA*. Striking a proper balance involves determining whether the information is about the individual or is simply about the results of his or her work product.

The *IMS Health Canada* line of thought appears to prevail, as indicated in the decision of the Federal Court of Appeal in *Rousseau v. Wyndowe*.[5] This time it was an insured person who wanted to get access to his personal

---

the Alberta Select Special Personal Information Protection Act Review Committee, p. 25, 26). The federal legislature does not seem to be comfortable with a categorical exclusion either. In response to the recommendation by the Standing Committee on Access to Information, Privacy and Ethics in its Fourth Report tabled in the House of Commons on May 2, 2007, that *PIPEDA* be amended "to include a definition of 'work product' that is explicitly recognized as not constituting personal information for the purposes of the Act", the Government took a more cautious position and decided to hold consultations with all stakeholders. Recognizing the significance of the issue as well as the general approach of the Act, the Government endeavoured to strike a balance between "a business-friendly privacy regime with the need for maintaining the existing level of privacy protection currently provided by the Act."

[4] Privacy Commissioner of Canada, *ibid.*
[5] 2008 FCA 39, 2008 CarswellNat 246 (F.C.A.).

information in the file created by a doctor who performed an independent medical examination of the insured at the request of his insurer. As a result of the doctor's report, the insured's benefits were terminated. The doctor refused the insured access to his file. The case went to the Federal Court of Appeal, which held that "personal health information" is a subset of "personal information" for the purposes of *PIPEDA*. It further ruled that the insured had a right of access to his file to the extent that the file contained personal information that he had provided to the physician, along with the doctor's final opinion regarding the insured's medical condition. At the same time, the Court noted that the *process* of getting to that final opinion from the initial information provided by the insured belonged to the doctor.

Opponents of this approach argue that the work product of professionals should first be acknowledged as personal information belonging to them. Then a determination should be made as to whether its collection, use or disclosure is permitted by law, for example, in an instance where it may be in the public interest to disclose such information. The initial recognition of work product as an individual's personal information, realizing that it may not be afforded the same protection as other types of personal information, would allow for a balancing of interests between the holder's right to control the information and a body's right to collect, use and disclose the information. *PIPEDA* expressly excludes some, but not all, aspects of professional information, such as the employee's name, title, business address and business telephone number. Thus, if the drafters of the Act had intended to exclude an employee's work product or the manner in which an employee performs their job, they would have included this in the exclusion to the definition of "personal information". Instead, the drafters chose the broadest possible language to define personal information about an identifiable individual. The proper approach should be to recognize professional information as a subset of personal information under privacy legislation and then weigh any competing interests. If the law does not deal adequately with the collection, use or disclosure of such information, amendments should be made to the legislation in question, rather than removing all protections to which may attach to the information.

Since the decision in IMS Health Canada, there appears to have been a shift in the Privacy Commissioner's thinking as to what specifically constitutes personal information in relation to the professional information derived from an employee at work. In subsequent decisions, the Privacy Commissioner has held that an employee's work performance and sales statistics comprised personal information, although the employees were deemed to have implicitly consented to the collection, use and disclosure of this information by willingly participating in a business environment where the practice of disclosing employees' personal sales results could reasonably be expected.[6]

In the public sector, the ruling in *Canada (Information Commissioner) v. Canada (Commissioner of the Royal Canadian Mounted Police)*[7] affirms that the *Privacy Act* affords no protection for the work product of public service employees.[8] In this case, the Supreme Court of Canada held that the information about four RCMP officers sought by an individual who had commenced litigation against them was information that fell within the exemption of the general definition of "personal information" under section 3(j) of the *Privacy Act* with regard to an individual who is an officer or employee of a government institution that relates to the position or function of the individual. The litigant sought personal information *about* the officers under the *Access to Information Act*,[9] including a list of the officers' historical postings, their status and date, the list of ranks and when they achieved those ranks, their years of service, their anniversary dates of service, and any public complaints made against the officers. The RCMP refused the request on the basis that the records constituted "personal information" as defined under section 3 of the *Privacy Act*, and therefore were exempt from disclosure pursuant to section 19(1) of the *Access to Information Act*, which prohibits a head of a government institution from disclosing any record that contains personal information pursuant to section 3 of the *Privacy Act*. The Federal Court of Appeal held that only information regarding a public servant's current or most recent position had to be released.

On appeal to the Supreme Court of Canada, the Court ruled that the two Acts must be read jointly and harmoniously, and that neither takes precedence over the other. Although the officer's information did qualify as "personal information" pursuant to section 3 of the *Privacy Act*, the section 3(j) exception of the *Privacy Act* applied, allowing disclosure because the information was directly related to the general characteristics associated with the position or function of a federal employee. The infor-

---

[6] Privacy Commissioner of Canada, April 14, 2003, Summary #153; Privacy Commissioner of Canada, September 15, 2003, Summary #220.

[7] [2003] 1 S.C.R. 66 (S.C.C.).

[8] As the *Privacy Act* applies to public servants (or contractors working for government), logic dictates that the work product of people who are not public employees should be considered their personal information and protected under the Act. See, however, *Geophysical Service Inc. v. Canada Newfoundland Offshore Petroleum*, 2003 FCT 507 (CanLII), (2003), 26 C.P.R. (4th) 190, wherein it was suggested that the professional opinion of a non public servant was not considered to be personal information under the *Privacy Act*.

[9] *Access to Information Act*, R.S.C. 1985, c. A-1, s. 4(1).

mation did not reveal anything about the competence of the officers or divulge any personal opinion given outside the course of employment so as to exempt it from disclosure, rather, it provided information relevant to understanding the functions performed by the officers. The Court held that the RCMP must disclose all of the information requested by the individual, and that the information applied retroactively and was not limited to an employee's most recent position.

Though the information sought was not work product *per se*, the Supreme Court's decision signals that any information related to the general characteristics associated with the position or function of a federal employee, including work product and certain information *about* a federal employee, is exempt from the purview of the *Privacy Act* and does not constitute "personal information" pursuant to the *Access to Information Act*, thereby making work product accessible to the public.[10]

4.2 PROFESSIONAL INFORMATION

Jurisprudence establishes that not only is work product accessible to the public in accordance with access to information and privacy legislation, but so is certain work-related information. At issue in *Dagg v. Canada (Minister of Finance)*[11] was whether the information in logs signed by employees entering and exiting the workplace on weekends constituted "personal information" as defined by section 3 of the *Privacy Act*, and whether the information should be disclosed pursuant to section 19(2)(c) of the *Access to Information Act* and section 8(2)(m)(i) of the *Privacy Act*. Section 19(2)(c) of the *Access to Information Act* permits the head of a government institution to disclose any record requested under the Act that contains personal information if the disclosure is in accordance with section 8 of the *Privacy Act*. In turn, section 8(2)(m)(i) of the *Privacy Act* provides that personal information under the control of a government institution may be disclosed for any purpose where, in the opinion of the head of the institution, the public interest in disclosure clearly outweighs any invasion of privacy that could result from the disclosure.

The logs were kept by security personnel only for safety and security reasons. Dagg filed a request with the Department of Finance for copies of the logs for the purpose of presenting the information to the union to assist them in the collective bargaining process, hoping that the union would be inclined to retain his services. While the logs were disclosed, the names, identification numbers and signatures of the employees were deleted, thus,

---

[10] *Supra*, note 7.
[11] [1997] 2 S.C.R. 403 (S.C.C.).

Dagg unsuccessfully filed a complaint with the Information Commissioner, arguing that the deleted information should be disclosed in accordance with the section 3(j)(iii) exception of the *Privacy Act,* which provides for the disclosure of information about a federal employee in relation to their position and functions including the classification, salary range, and responsibilities of the their position. While the Federal Court, Trial Division ruled that the information did not constitute personal information, this decision was reversed by the Federal Court of Appeal.

On appeal to the Supreme Court of Canada, the Court interpreted the *Privacy Act* and *Access to Information Act* together to determine that the number of hours spent at the workplace was information relating to the position of function of federal employees, as it allowed for assessment of the amount of work required for a particular employee's position or function. As such, the information did relate to the "responsibilities of the position held by the employee" pursuant to section 3(j)(iii) of the *Privacy Act* and was accessible to the applicant under *the Access to Information Act.*

A recent decision by the Assistant Privacy Commissioner of Canada indicates that an individual business e-mail address falls within the definition of "personal information" under section 2 of *PIPEDA*, and therefore may not be collected, used or disclosed by organizations without the individuals' knowledge and consent.

A University of Ottawa law professor received unsolicited commercial email at his business e-mail address from the Ottawa Renegades marketing season tickets, despite his having made an opt-out request. The team had collected his work e-mail address from the University of Ottawa website and his law firm website, and continued to send him e-mail without his consent, even after he indicated that he did not wish to be marketed further. Email addresses of staff were posted on the University Ottawa website to meet the university's expectation that employees be easily accessible.

The Assistant Commissioner held that section 4.3 in Schedule 1 of *PIPEDA* states that organizations may only collect and use personal information under section 7(1)(d) and section 7(2)(c.1) without the knowledge and consent of an individual if the information is publicly available in a professional or business directory, listing, or notice and is specified by the regulations. Further, such collection, use, disclosure must be conducted for the purpose for which the information appears in a directory, listing or notice. The Assistant Commissioner emphasized that *PIPEDA* defines "publicly available information" as an individual's name, title, business address and phone number; business e-mail addresses are not considered publicly available information since they are not specifically enumerated under the Act. Further, although the professor's personal information was publicly available, the purpose for which the Ottawa Renegades collected and used the email address was unrelated to the intent of the listing on U Ottawa website. It is believed that the intent of this decision is to protect individuals at work from spam and mass marketing that is not work-related.[12]

The calling history of an employee is another example of personal information, according to the Assistant Privacy Commissioner of Canada, who came to this conclusion following an investigation of complaints against several major Canadian telecommunications companies. The complaints were prompted by the publication in *Maclean*'s magazine of telephone calls made by one of the magazine's senior editors as well as the Privacy Commissioner of Canada. The investigation revealed that the records in question had been purchased from a U.S. data broker and that the information had been collected due to poor identification and authentication techniques employed by the companies.

In an attempt to defend itself, one of the telecommunications companies contended that the history of work-related telephone calls made by an employee using a phone provided by the employer should be viewed as the employer's business information, rather than as the employee's personal information. It further argued that a list of numbers called was associated *with* an employee rather than *about* an employee. As such, the company claimed that the information in question was a work-product.

The Assistant Privacy Commissioner rejected these arguments. Her reasoning was that *PIPEDA* did not draw the line between personal and business information. Thus, any calls made by an employee while at work, including his or her personal calls, constitute that employee's personal information. In addressing the second argument, the Assistant Commissioner noted that an employee's "calling history is not the tangible result of his or her work but represents manner in which that employee does his or her work in order to achieve a work-product." Therefore, an employee's calling history is his or her personal information.

The recent decision of the Federal Court of Appeal in *Rousseau v. Wyndowe*[13], may be viewed as an attempt to protect an individual's professional knowledge and information, as well as the method of its application during the work towards the final product, from being disclosed to third parties. In this case, an insured person wanted to get access to his personal information in the file created by a doctor who performed an independent medical examination of the insured at the request of his insurer. As a result of the doctor's report, the insured's benefits were terminated. The doctor also refused the insured access to his file. While the Court agreed with the complainant that he had a right of access to his file to the extent that the file

---

[12] Privacy Commissioner of Canada, December 1, 2004, Summary #297.

[13] 2008 FCA 39, 2008 CarswellNat 246 (F.C.A.).

contained personal information that the insured had provided to the doctor, along with the doctor's final opinion with respect to the insured's medical condition, the process of getting to that final opinion from the initial information provided by the insured was determined to belong to the doctor.

5

Personal Opinions in Employment

5.1 INTRODUCTION

In the employment context, individuals adopt views and form opinions in the course of their work and in regards to their colleagues, employees or employers on a regular basis. Once collected or divulged, issues may arise as to whom the information belongs to and what may legitimately be done with it pursuant to privacy legislation. In making their rulings on privacy and access to information issues, the Courts and Commissioners must frequently perform a balancing act between each party's interests, including the public's interest, to determine whose situation would be most adversely impacted by the decision.[1]

For the purposes of this chapter, the *Privacy Act* recognizes that the recorded personal opinions or views of public service employees are their personal information. However, an individual's views or opinions about *another* individual belong to that other individual, rather than to the one

---

[1] Jurisprudence also indicates that the personal opinions of union officials representing employees are protected as well by privacy legislation *vis-à-vis* the employer. In *Robertson v. Canada (Minister of Employment & Immigration)* (1987), 13 F.T.R. 120 (Fed. T.D.), an application by the Trenton Public Utilities Commission for a Canada Works Grant required the Commission to include a letter in its application from any union which represented their employees. After the application was denied, the Commission learned that the selected union had expressed opposition to the grant application. A Commissioner requested access to the letter under section 4(1) the *Access to Information Act* and was advised that certain parts of the information in the letter were exempt under the Act. The Commissioner filed a complaint with the Information Commissioner to argue for access to the severed portions of the record. The Information Commissioner informed the complainant that section 19(1) allowed a government institution to refuse to disclose any record containing personal information as defined under section 3 of the *Privacy Act*. An application for review of the Information Commissioner's decision was subsequently brought before the Federal Court. The Federal Court held that the official's general comments in the letter should be made public, however, the introduction of the term "personally" accompanying the impugned paragraphs clearly illustrated the author's own observations based on personal experiences and opinions, thereby constituting personal, confidential information which were properly withheld from disclosure.

holding those views or opinions. "Personal information" under the Act does not include a government officer's or employee's opinions or views given in the course of employment, or the opinions or views of individuals given in the course of performing services under contract for a government institution.

In the private sector, *PIPEDA* broadly defines personal information as information in any form about an identifiable individual, which may include the foregoing classifications in the *Privacy Act* but does not similarly enumerate specific examples. As the former Privacy Commissioner stated in a 2002 decision regarding a bank's refusal to allow a customer access to her credit score, "since *PIPEDA* is virtually limitless as to what can constitute 'information about an identifiable individual', its scope includes opinions. *PIPEDA*, after all, seeks to avoid limiting the definition of what personal information can be."[2]

The provisions of the *Privacy Act* and decisions pursuant to *PIPEDA* clearly emphasize that personal opinions given by employees in the course of employment or via work product do not constitute "personal information" of employees protected by the Acts. Like the *Privacy Act*, which considers the personal opinions or views of public servants about another individual to be personal information belonging to the *object*, rather than the *holder* of the opinion, *PIPEDA* has been construed by the Privacy Commissioner to prescribe corporate opinions about other individuals as personal information belonging to those individuals.

One distinguishing feature of *PIPEDA* is that in its present form, the Act is silent as to the manner in which an opinion about another individual may be held. The *Privacy Act* specifies that personal information in the form of opinions must be recorded, whereas *PIPEDA* simply refers to "personal information" as information about an identifiable individual, including opinions. This suggests that where an employee or employer has formulated an opinion about another individual without actually expressing

---

[2] Privacy Commission of Canada, February 27, 2002, Summary #39; This finding contradicts a prior decision in the *IMS Health Canada* case (see c. 4, 4.1 – **Work Product**) suggesting that *PIPEDA* does in fact limit the scope of personal information. In that case, the Privacy Commissioner held that letters written by employees in the course of employment, reports prepared by employees for managers' use, and legal opinions (all of which arguably would comprise the personal opinions of employees), do not constitute "personal information" falling under the purview of *PIPEDA*. Thus, these decisions indicate an inconsistent interpretation and application of the definition of "personal information" in the handling of privacy complaints by the Privacy Commissioner, which may lead to confusion as to the actual scope of "information about an identifiable individual".

that opinion, the other individual may seek to be informed whether the employer or employee in fact holds an opinion about them and may be granted access to this information. The notion of a body being statutorily required to disclose an unexpressed opinion conjures up rather absurd and controversial scenarios, and does not necessarily guarantee the disclosure of accurate information. It also raises the question whether forcing the holder of an opinion about another person to divulge their thoughts may be invasive of the holder's personal privacy instead.

5.2   PERSONAL OPINIONS IN THE PUBLIC SECTOR

5.2.1   Opinions and Views viz. the Employer

The following case law illustrates the balancing act which decision-makers must carry out in considering the competing interests of employees and employers when privacy-related conflicts arise between these parties in the workplace. This process necessarily involves weighing an employee's rights to privacy at work against an employer's right to carry on business in an efficient and productive manner.

In *Lavigne v. Canada (Commissioner of Official Languages)*,[3] a federal public servant complained to the Commissioner that his rights regarding language of work, and employment and promotion opportunities had been violated. Employees of the Commission were interviewed by investigators and assured that the interviews would remain confidential pursuant to the *Official Languages Act*. The complainant requested access to the notes of the interview with his supervisor and to non-personal information in the investigators' interview notes. On the basis that disclosure could reasonably be expected to be injurious to the conduct of lawful investigations as per section 22(1)(b) of the *Privacy Act*, the Commissioner refused to disclose the information to the complainant.

The Supreme Court of Canada affirmed the Federal Court of Appeal's decision to order disclosure of the personal information, but not the non-personal information, in accordance with section 12(1) of the Act. Section 22(1)(b) could apply to future investigations, as well as those that were ongoing, however, the Court ruled that in this case, disclosure of the interview notes could not reasonably be expected to be injurious to the conduct of future investigations. The Commissioner had not established that it was reasonable to maintain confidentiality. His decision was based on the fact that the supervisor had not consented to disclosure of the information ac-

---

[3] [2002] 2 S.C.R. 773 (S.C.C.).

quired during his interview; however, he had not determined what risk of injury to investigations might be caused by the disclosure.

Decisions by Canadian information and privacy commissioners indicate that notes, comments, opinions or views made in relation to an employee's references are the personal information of the employee, unless that information was provided by the referee to the prospective employer in confidence.[4]

An employee for the City of Calgary applied for another employment opportunity with a different department of the City. The employee requested access to the reference notes created by the person conducting the interview, along with the names of the referees and the specific comments made by the referees. The department holding the job competition denied the request on the grounds that the two-page record contained confidential evaluations and opinions for the purpose of determining the candidate's suitability, eligibility or qualifications for employment, as defined by section 19(1) of the *Freedom of Information and Protection of Privacy Act*. The complainant subsequently asked the Information and Privacy Commissioner to review the department's decision to withhold access to the records.[5]

The Commissioner determined that the record containing third party opinions about the complainant's character and personality, as well as competence and skills in an employment situation comprised personal information belonging to the complainant. However, as the word "CONFIDEN-TIAL" appeared prominently on the record and as the interviewing party's affidavit stated that he believed that the discussion he had with the referee was implicitly confidential, the Commissioner held that the opinions of the referee had been provided in confidence and therefore, the content of the records came within the ambit of section 19(1) of the Act. Additionally, because the department had released 15 pages of records to the complainant, most of which had little or no severing, the Commissioner was satisfied that the department had properly exercised its discretion to not disclose the information.

The interpretation of an individual's "personal information" as inclusive of reference information related to that individual is further supported

---

[4] See Information and Privacy Commissioner for Ontario, May 20, 1993, Order M-132; Information and Privacy Commissioner for Ontario, October 18 1995, Investigation 195-045P; Information and Privacy Commissioner for Alberta, June 8, 1998, Order 98-008; *Inquiry Regarding Ministry of Social Development and Economic Security Records*, Information and Privacy Commissioner for British Columbia, October 5, 2000, Order 00-44.

[5] Information and Privacy Commissioner for Alberta, December 20, 2002, Order F2002-008.

by a decision of the Saskatchewan Grievance Arbitration Board.[6] In this case, an employee who had unsuccessfully applied for a position as a Highway Traffic Officer with the Saskatchewan Department of Highways and Transportation challenged the selection process. In particular, the grievor sought information regarding the names of the individuals the employer had contacted, copies of the questions asked of the referees, and a copy of the reference checker's notes. The employer refused to disclose the requested details, arguing that they constituted confidential information and accordingly were shielded by section 31(2) of Saskatchewan's *Freedom of Information and Protection of Privacy Act*. This provision allows the government to "refuse to disclose to an individual personal information that is evaluative or opinion material compiled solely for the purpose of determining the individual's suitability, eligibility and qualifications for employment or for the awarding of government contracts and other benefits, where the information is provided explicitly or implicitly in confidence."

The Board agreed with the grievor that the information in question fell under the purview of section 24(1)(h) of the Act, which defines "personal information" as "personal information about an identifiable individual that is recorded in any form, and includes . . . the views or opinions of another individual with respect to the individual." The employer's section 31(2) argument was rejected by the Board since there was no evidence to indicate that the information was provided by the references explicitly or implicitly in confidence. Consequently, the Board ruled that the section did not operate to shield the government from having to make the disclosure.

A decision by the Information and Privacy Commissioner for Ontario indicates that notes taken by an employer during a meeting with an employee which contain the opinions and views of that employee are personal information according to section 2(1)(e) of the *Freedom of Information and Protection of Privacy Act*. An employee at one of the detention centres of the Ministry of Community and Social Services complained to the Commissioner that the Ministry had improperly destroyed handwritten notes created by a human resources staff member during a meeting held to discuss correspondence from the employee about his concerns regarding the sexual identity group and workplace harassment at the detention centre. The notes were used to compose a memo which was later sent to the complainant with a copy also put on file.[7]

---

[6] *S.G.E.U. v. Saskatchewan* (2007), 164 L.A.C. (4th) 129, 2007 CarswellSask 755 (Sask. Arb. Bd.).

[7] Information and Privacy Commissioner for Ontario, October 18, 1995, Investigation I95-045P.

The complainant subsequently requested that corrections be made to the handwritten notes, maintaining that the notes comprised his personal information pursuant to section 2(1)(e) and (h) of the Act, but was informed that they had been destroyed after the memo was written. The complainant contended that this was a contravention of section 5(1) of Regulation 460 of the Act, which requires that personal information used by an institution must be retained by the institution for at least one year after use, unless the person to whom the information relates consents to its earlier disposal. The Ministry stated that keeping the notes was unnecessary as they were a duplicate of the information in the memo, however, the Commissioner held that the memo appeared to be a summary of the issues discussed at the meeting and concluded that notes likely contained more specific information than the memo itself and therefore the memo was not a duplicate. Further, the fact that the employee wanted corrections to be made to the notes but not to the memo suggested that the information contained in the notes was not the same as that produced in the memo.

The Commissioner agreed that the notes consisting of the employee's name and his views about sensitive issues met the definition of personal information under section 2(1)(e) and (h) of the Act, and since this information was used to prepare the memo and since the complainant did not consent to the disposal of the notes, the Ministry was required to retain the notes for the prescribed period of one year after writing the memo. Thus, the employee's personal information was not retained in accordance with section 5(1) of Regulation 460 of the Act.

Another complaint against the Ontario Ministry of Community and Social Services by a former employee of another government agency, which was funded and supervised by the Ministry, prompted an investigation of the Ministry's disclosure of information that had been provided by the former employee and some co-workers. During her employment with the Agency, the complainant and co-workers had significant concerns about the Agency's operations and subsequently met with the Ministry to convey their concerns. The complainant asserted that the Ministry was aware of longstanding complaints about the Agency and encouraged her and her co-workers and ex-coworkers to state their concerns in writing, in order to assist the Ministry with its pending negative review of the Agency. The complainant and nine other employees agreed and wrote a letter to Ministry expressing their concerns adding their signatures to the letter.[8]

When the Ministry conducted its review of the Agency, it disclosed the letter to a member of the Agency's Board of Directors, who then attached

---

[8] Information and Privacy Commissioner for Ontario, August 16, 1996, Investigation I96-016P.

the letter to the review and distributed copies of it to other members, Agency staff, other Agencies in the community, and to a local newspaper. The signatories' names were then published in the local newspaper. The complainant alleged that the signatories were later harassed at the Agency and that the Minister had to issue a "no harassment" directive to the Agency. She also alleged that the disclosure of the letter to the Agency eventually led to her dismissal and that of some of the other signatories to the letter. The complainant further contended that the contents of the letter were their personal information pursuant to section 2(1)(e) of the *Freedom of Information and Protection of Privacy Act*, which defines personal information as recorded information about an individual, including the personal opinions or views of the individual except if they relate another individual. Since neither she nor the other signatories consented to the Ministry's release of the letter to the Agency, the employee submitted that the disclosure of her personal information contravened their rights under section 42(c) of the Act, which states that an institution shall not disclose personal information in its custody or control except for the purpose for which it was obtained or compiled or for a consistent purpose.

The complainant maintained that she and the other signatories did not agree to sign a consent for the Ministry to disclose the letter to the Agency, and that none of them expected the contents to become public information in this manner. The Information and Privacy Commissioner determined that as the information in the letter contained the opinions and views of the complainant and other colleagues about the Agency's operations, it satisfied the definition of personal information under the Act. Further, the Commissioner held that the employees' concerns could have been brought to the attention of the Board without the disclosure of any names and that the Ministry should have severed the names from the review before its release. As such, the Ministry's disclosure of the complainant's name and opinion was not for the same or consistent purpose for which it was obtained or compiled, and therefore was not disclosed in compliance with section 42(c) of the Act.

The rationale of this decision is echoed in the ruling of the Federal Court in *Canadian Imperial Bank of Commerce v. Canada (Human Rights Commission)*.[9] One of the issues in this case was whether personal opinions, provided anonymously by visible minority senior managers of the bank for the purposes of an audit by the Canadian Human Rights Commission ("CHRC") of CIBC's compliance with the *Employment Equity Act*, were exempt from disclosure under section 19 of the federal *Access to Information*

---

[9] 2006 FC 443, 2006 CarswellNat 1063 (F.C.), reversed (2007), 2007 CarswellNat 4584 (F.C.A.).

Act (ATIA). The CHRC released its final report on the bank's compliance, including the managers' opinions, in response to a request made under *ATIA*.

The bank argued that since the total number of the visible minority senior managers employed by the bank was only seven, those of them who provided their personal opinions were "reasonably identifiable". As a result, the paragraph containing this information should be redacted from the report before its disclosure.

The Court did not find this argument persuasive, however. Rather, the Court concluded that as long as any given opinion cannot be attributed to any specific individual, section 19 of the Act is of no assistance. In the words of the Court, the information disclosed in this case represented "a collective opinion of a group of visible minority senior managers who have self-identified as such for the purpose of the employment equity compliance review audit." The Court further emphasized the fact that the report revealed neither the number of visible minority senior managers interviewed for the "opinion", nor the total number of the visible minority senior managers employed by the bank.

While the Federal Court of Appeal reversed this ruling on other grounds, it approved the approach taken by the Federal Court in the resolution of this issue.[10]

5.2.2 Opinions and Views viz. Colleagues

Privacy-related conflicts can also arise between colleagues over whose proprietary interests should prevail where information may be personal to more than one individual. This is particularly prevalent in instances where an employee is seeking to access personal information, such as opinions expressed about them by colleagues which might identify those colleagues. The case law is clear that colleagues' opinions about another employee belong to that employee; therefore, an employee's access rights to opinions expressed about him or her override the proprietary and confidentiality interests of those who offered the opinions.

At issue in *Canada (Information Commissioner) v. Canada (Minister of Citizenship & Immigration)*[11] was whether the names of employees interviewed, who had expressed personal opinions or views about their Director in the course of an administrative review, and portions of their interviews which would identify them constituted personal information that belonged to the employees or to the Director.

---

[10] *Canadian Imperial Bank of Commerce v. Canada (Chief Commissioner, Human Rights Commission)*, 2007 FCA 272, 2007 CarswellNat 2588 (F.C.A.).

[11] [2003] 1 F.C. 219 (Fed. C.A.).

Allegations of discrimination and harassment by the Director of the Alberta Department of Citizen and Immigration Case Processing Centre prompted the Department to conduct an independent investigation of the corporate culture at the Centre. Employees, but not managers, who were interviewed were informed that their disclosures would be confidential and that notes taken by the Investigator would not be divulged to the Department. Following the review, the Director of the Centre was relieved of his duties and denied access to the interview notes. On complaining to the Information Commissioner of Canada, limited information was disclosed to him but the names of the employees interviewed and information regarding the position they held were excluded. Additionally, in keeping with section 3(i) of the *Privacy Act*, the views and opinions of the employees about the Director were severed from the report where the employees' identity would be indirectly revealed by the disclosure.

Interpreting the *Access to Information Act* and the *Privacy Act* together, the Federal Court of Appeal undertook to balance the privacy interests of the employees against the Director's access rights and the impact of the report on his career. The Court also considered the public interest in ensuring fairness in the conduct of administrative inquiries, which entails allowing an individual the opportunity to be informed of unfavourable views against them, challenge their accuracy, and correct them if necessary. While both the employees and the Director had proprietary interests in the personal information in question, the Court determined that the promise of confidentiality made by the Department to the interviewees could not override the Director's statutory right to access the information and respond to their allegations. Without full disclosure and proper context, much of the information would be incomprehensible to the Director. The employees' interests in maintaining a good working relationship with the Director and avoiding legal action were minimal; they had no reason to fear full disclosure of the interview notes if their testimony was justified. Lastly, the Court dismissed the argument that disclosure might have a chilling effect on possible future investigations as one that has consistently been denied as a valid ground for refusing disclosure.

The case of *French v. Dalhousie University*[12] involved personal opinions of colleagues and students in relation to the department head of physiology and biophysics at the University of Dalhousie medical school. Colleagues and students ("authors") were asked to complete a survey and participate in interviews to evaluate the department head and make recommendations as to whether or not he should continue as head for another five-year term. The survey committee's report was critical of the department

---

[12] (2003), 2003 CarswellNS 40, [2003] N.S.J. No. 44 (N.S. C.A.).

head and his management style and recommended a second term of only 18 months. The department head requested and was granted copies of the report by the Nova Scotia Supreme Court, and the University appealed this decision to the Court of Appeal.

The Court of Appeal, in determining whether the authors' submissions constituted personal information as defined by Nova Scotia's *Freedom of Information and Protection of Privacy Act*, upheld the lower court's decision that the views and opinions about the department head in the submissions were his personal information and not that of the authors, and should be disclosed. Such disclosure was not an unreasonable invasion of the authors' privacy on the basis that the overwhelming focus of the case was on the department head, the report caused him financial loss, and the authors' understanding regarding the confidentiality of the survey and their submissions diverged from that of the department head. The decision required disclosure of the opinions expressed about the department head, their assertions of fact as to his behaviour or action, and ancillary information necessary for his full understanding of the opinions and assertions, which included the authors' names and comments on the present or past operation of the school, the department or any part of it.

In *C.U.P.E., Local 82 v. Windsor (City)*[13], the Ontario Arbitration Board relied upon the same principles of fairness outlined in the above-mentioned cases, and the right of an employee who is subject to certain disciplinary measures to provide a full answer and defence against allegations of misconduct, ruling that confidential opinions about the grievor supplied by his colleagues were subject to disclosure. This arbitration concerned a grievance filed by an employee alleging that the employer violated the 'just cause' provisions of the collective agreement by issuing a two-week suspension without pay to the employee. The grievor had worked as a seasonal employee in the City's ice arenas and discipline was issued following an investigation by the employer into allegations that the grievor had made threatening statements on two occasions after learning that he had been unsuccessful on a job posting for a more secure, non-seasonal position. The employer's designate took the decision to impose these sanctions on the grievor after considering the report summarizing the witness interviews.

The Union, acting on behalf of the grievor, requested production of a list of documents which included, among other things, the notes taken during the interviews. The employer refused to provide the interview notes arguing that the requested information had been provided by the employees interviewed in accordance with the employer's Workplace Violence Prevention

---

[13] (2006), 151 L.A.C. (4th) 184, 2006 CarswellOnt 6827 (Ont. Arb. Bd.).

Policy ("WVP Policy") which, in turn, assured the interviewees that their opinions would be kept in confidence. Specifically, it stated that "all reports of violence shall be handled in a confidential manner, with information released only on a 'need to know' basis." The employer therefore contended that the disclosure of the notes would undermine the WVP Policy. In particular, the employer emphasized that the investigators of the workplace violence allegation had given the interviewed employees assurances of confidentiality.

The Union's position was that without the disclosure of the requested documents, the grievor would be deprived of his right to make a full answer and defence to the allegations. The Union further argued that their request for the information did not necessarily contradict the WVP Policy provision allowing release of information on a "need to know" basis. The Board agreed with the Union. They reasoned that it was hard to imagine documents that could be of more "arguable" or "potential" relevance to the grievor's case, alleging that the employer had violated the 'just cause' provisions of the agreement by issuing a suspension for making threats of violence in the workplace. The Board commented as follows:

> Given the importance of the fairness interests at stake in the right to pre-hearing production of documents of the type at issue herein, we find that this right should only be overridden in the interests of confidentiality interests where there is a clear statutory basis for such an override or the common law *Wigmore* criteria are clearly met, and in particular where the fourth *Wigmore* criteria is met by demonstrable proof of an injury to the relationship that would result from production that clearly outweighs the harm to fairness interests that would result from non disclosure.

As such, the Board turned to consider the *Wigmore* criteria adopted by the Supreme Court of Canada in *Slavutych v. Baker*,[14] which consists of four conditions:

1. The communications must originate in a confidence that they will not be disclosed;

2. The element of confidentiality must be essential to the full and satisfactory maintenance of the relationship between the parties;

3. The relation must be one which in the opinion of the community ought to be sedulously fostered; and

4. The injury that would inure to the relation by the disclosure of the

---

[14] (1975), [1976] 1 S.C.R. 254 (S.C.C.).

'communications must be greater than the benefit thereby gained for the correct disposal of litigation.

Having analyzed all of the material before them, the Board concluded that "the potential prejudice and detrimental impact to the rights of the Union and the grievor to a fair hearing and the right to make full answer and defence that would result from a failure to provide pre-hearing disclosure outweighs the potential injury to the operation of the WVP Policy and the interests it protects that could result from production." In the opinion of the Board, the principles of fairness that underlay the pre-hearing production also warranted disclosure of interviews conducted with employees whom the employer does not intend to call to testify. It was also persuaded by the Union's argument that their request for the information fell within the WVP Policy which allows for release of information on a "need to know" basis.

While the Board's decision is ostensibly pro-Union, the employer's confidentiality concerns were not completely ignored. To strike a balance between the employer's desire to maintain confidentiality of the collected information and the Union's need to prepare for a grievance hearing, the Board suggested that at some reasonable time before the hearing, the Union be given access to the documents arising from the investigation into the alleged misconduct. The Union's representative would review the documents and determine which of them were relevant and had sufficient probative value to justify their pre-hearing production. Only disclosure of those documents could subsequently be requested and released to the grievor and used for the hearing purposes. The Board intended that this arrangement would facilitate the employer's operation of the WVP program by reassuring employees reporting incidents of workplace violence that the information they share will not be disclosed unnecessarily. At the same time, the Board recommended that employees should be made aware that their reports may become subject to the employer's obligation with respect to pre-hearing production of documents of sufficient relevance and probative value should these reports result in a grievance proceeding.

Current jurisprudence appears to indicate that the approach towards disclosure of information obtained by employers of the unionized workplace in return for reassurances of confidentiality hinges on the purpose for which the information has been collected. As discussed above, once confidential information is used by an employer to discipline existing employees, courts and arbitration boards allow significant latitude in terms of circumstances warranting disclosure as well as the extent thereof.

However, the need to exercise caution becomes more acute when deciding whether to compel the release of reference information provided in confidence if collected for the purposes of filling a vacancy. In one decision, the Alberta Arbitration Board had opportunity to comment on the potential chilling effect caused by allowing the disclosure of confidential reference information.[15] The Board stated the following:

> One particular concern expressed by the University is the chilling effect the potential disclosure of confidential references solicited from third parties might have on the frankness of future references. We accept that this is a real risk, and one that therefore calls for prudence by both parties before seeking or disclosing such references. While allegations may arise in an unusual case where disclosure would be justified by the nature of those allegations, we think this will be rare, and we urge caution by both parties in this respect. We remind the parties as well, when they are considering the potential for creating a chilling effect, that the difference may only be between early and discreet disclosure and later and perhaps less discreet disclosure during an arbitration proceeding.

In *Board of School Trustees of School District No. 84 (Vancouver Island West)*,[16] an employee requested copies of records made pursuant to an investigation by the School District of the employee's complaint about a manager. The records contained the investigation report, a list of witnesses, the employee's submissions and interview notes, the manager's submissions and interview notes, and the investigator's rough notes of witness interviews.

The Information Commissioner held that any evidence of, or statements made by witnesses about the manager's workplace behaviour or actions (including any opinions or views expressed by them about the manager), the investigator's views or opinions, evidence given or statements made by the complainant and any findings or conclusions made by the investigator all constituted personal information of the manager according to section 22(3)(d) of British Columbia's *Freedom of Information and Protection of Privacy Act*. As such, disclosure of this information presumed an unreasonable invasion of personal privacy under the Act's provision. Therefore, the School District was required to withhold the manager's employment history, which included the statements made by witnesses and the observations of the investigator about the manager's workplace behaviour actions, as well as information that would identify witnesses who supplied, in confidence, personal information of the complainant and the manager. The School District was not required to withhold information that

---

[15] *University of Alberta v. University of Alberta Non-Academic Staff Assn.* (2006), 151 L.A.C. (4th) 365, 2006 CarswellAlta 1532 (Alta. Arb. Bd.).

[16] Information & Privacy Commissioner for British Columbia, December 21, 2001, Order 01-53.

would identify the manager complained about or the complainant's allegations, or the investigator's findings that the allegations were not substantiated, since this was information about which the complainant was already aware.

5.2.3   Third Party Access to Opinions of Employer/Employees

Third party access to the personal opinions of employers or employees involves weighing the privacy rights of employees or employers against an individual's access to information rights. While the law favours disclosure generally, personal information such as an employee's employment history, job performance, competence and characteristics, and an employer's opinions and recommendations regarding the employee is beyond the scope of information which may be disclosed to third parties.

The decision in *Canada (Information Commissioner) v. Canada (Immigration & Refugee Board)*[17] involved balancing the privacy rights of Board employees against an individuals' access to information rights, as well as the public interest in ensuring the integrity of future investigations. Following the publication of two articles in a Vancouver newspaper, which apparently were based on incidents that occurred during in camera hearings at the Refugee Division of the Immigration and Refugee Board, the Chairperson of the Board ordered an independent investigation into the leak giving rise to the newspaper articles. The investigator was unable to determine who leaked the information and turned her notes and report over to the Board. Two requests for access to the information and two privacy requests for disclosure of compiled information were filed with the Board.

The Board decided not to disclose the notes and the report since the interviewees were promised by the investigator that their interview information would remain confidential. The Board also contended that labour relations compelled it to uphold the investigator's promise and that disclosing the information would hinder its ability to conduct similar investigations in the future. The Information and Privacy Commissioners argued that the report and notes should be disclosed as they did not contain information that was injurious to the conduct of lawful investigations in the future. In turn, the Federal Court granted the application for disclosure, stating that the Board did not have reasonable grounds to refuse to disclose the information. The investigator's promise to the employees interviewed could not override the obligation to release information under the *Access to Information Act* and the *Privacy Act*, which were designed to facilitate disclosure. The Court held that the board was not entitled to refuse disclosure to protect

---

[17] (1997), 1997 CarswellNat 2436, [1997] F.C.J. No. 1812 (Fed. T.D.).

unspecified future investigations, and there was no evidence that disclosure would in fact impair future investigations.

The decision in *Canada (Information Commissioner) v. Canada (Solicitor General)*[18] established that certain opinions expressed about the training, personality, experience or competence of individual employees do not fall under the seciton 3(j) exception of the *Privacy Act*, which allows for the disclosure of personal opinions or views of individuals given in the course of employment as an officer or employee of a government institution. The Court ruled that section 3(j) should only apply when the information requested is sufficiently related to the general characteristics associated with the position or function held by a federal employee, and not when it concerns the competence and characteristics of an identifiable employee.

This case involved an application by the Information Commissioner for judicial review following the Solicitor General's refusal to disclose certain portions of a report on the Food Services Operations at the Regional Psychiatric Centre in Saskatoon, on the basis that the author's opinions and the information which identified certain employees were protected from disclosure under the *Privacy Act* and the *Access to Information Act*. The report contained personal opinions of the author about specific employees and supervisors regarding their level of training and comparisons of their actual job function with the job descriptions which accompanied the positions. The Information Commissioner argued that the report itself was a publicly funded study by a public institution and ought to be available to the public.

However, the Court held that while the definition of personal information in the *Privacy Act* was deliberately broad and that contrary to the applicant's arguments, the effect of section 3(j) was not to create an exception to the general rule of privacy where government employees were concerned. There was no indication that qualitative evaluations of a government employee's performance were ever intended to be made public, and it would be unjust to consider an employee's job performance to be public information simply because the individual is employed by the government. The Court allowed the study to be disclosed on condition that the opinions related to the employees' training, personality, experience and competence were deleted.

At issue in *Dickie v. Nova Scotia (Department of Health)*[19] was whether a patient in a provincial treatment facility could access information relating to an investigation of a facility employee and the decision taken pursuant to the investigation. The patient complained that the employee had breached

[18] [1988] 3 F.C. 551 (Fed. T.D.).
[19] (1999), 1999 CarswellNS 97, [1999] N.S.J. No. 116 (N.S. C.A.).

his professional duties by engaging in an emotional and sexual relationship with her. Following the investigation, the Department of Health informed her that no disciplinary action could be taken against the employee. The patient then applied for access to information in relation to the investigation and was granted access to much of the information, including names contained in the report, the employee's work-related conduct, and information communicated in confidence by other employees, as well as their names. The Department of Health appealed the Nova Scotia Supreme Court's decision.

The Nova Scotia Court of Appeal allowed the appeal in part, ruling that while the trial judge was correct in allowing the names to be disclosed, he erred in coming to this conclusion by limiting the definition of personal information instead of interpreting the language in a clear, broad and simple manner. The trial judge also erred in ruling that the employee's work-related conduct did not relate to employment history, which constitutes personal information protected by the *Freedom of Information and Protection of Privacy Act*. Further, the Court held that the judge erred in finding that both the employee and other employees did not communicate their information in confidence. The disclosure of employees' and management's opinions and recommendations regarding the employee, and his response to the allegations were presumed to be an unreasonable invasion of his personal privacy pursuant to the Act. The information was communicated in confidence and the balance did not tip in favour of disclosure. The Court concluded that the types of information which should be disclosed were the steps followed in the investigation, the names of employees who provided statements, communications by the patient to them regarding her allegations, and the decision made in relation to the employee over the allegations.

In the *Board of School Trustees of School District No. 44 (North Vancouver)*,[20] a parent applied for access to a letter sent by a secondary school principal to a teacher and coach of a school sports team, regarding the coach's decision to dismiss the complainant's daughter from the tryouts for the team. The letter was sent to the coach following an informal investigation of the parent's allegations that the coach had unfairly and arbitrarily cut the daughter from the team tryouts, instructing the coach to reinstate the daughter on a trial basis. The school board initially refused to disclose the letter, but subsequently did so in severed form on the grounds that disclosure would unreasonably invade the coach's privacy regarding her employment history and personal evaluations, pursuant to section 22(2)(d) and (g) of the *Freedom of Information and Protection of Privacy Act*.

---

[20] Information & Privacy Commissioner for British Columbia, August 10, 2001, Order 00-38.

The withheld information in full comprised evaluations consisting of the investigators' interpretations and opinion of the coach and the facts surrounding the daughter's dismissal from the team tryouts, their conclusions of the investigation, information regarding the personnel record, and the principal's instructions to the coach. The Information Commissioner held that the information consisted of the coach's personal information within the meaning of the Act, disclosure of which would presume an unreasonable invasion of personal privacy. The Commissioner further determined that the withheld information would not provide additional insight into the school board's investigation or resolution of the complaint and was not necessary to show that the board carried out its obligations of procedural fairness.

Decisions of boards and courts with respect to conflicts arising in a unionized workplace demonstrate a somewhat different approach to the accessibility of reference information to third parties. For example, the award made in *Chilliwack School District No. 33 v. Chilliwack Teachers' Assn.*,[21] stands for the proposition that personal information of job applicants may be disclosed under the B.C. *FOIPPA* if it constitutes information "available by law to a party to a proceeding" (section 3(2)) or when "a disclosure of personal information is not an unreasonable invasion of a third party's personal privacy if . . . an enactment of British Columbia or Canada authorizes the disclosure" (section 22(4)(c)).

In *British Columbia Public School Employers' Assn. v. B.C.T.F.*,[22] the authorizing legislation was the B.C. *Labour Relations Code*, which obligates employers to do everything necessary to ensure compliance with collective agreements. The collective agreement required that upon the union's request, the employer disclose to the union information about the successful applicant's interview, as well as references for the purposes of negotiations and processing grievances. The employer appealed this decision to the British Columbia Court of Appeal, however, the Court dismissed it, stating that it lacked jurisdiction to consider the appeal.

The Court emphasized that while section 100 of the *Labour Relations Code* empowered it to deal with issues of general law, the "real substance" of the appeal in question was far beyond the general law boundaries, namely "whether, having regard to the provisions of *FOIPPA*, the *Labour Relations Code* and the Collective Agreement, the refusal by the employer to produce the requested documents constituted a breach of Article A.16 of the Collective Agreement." As such, the issue fell within the jurisdiction of the Labour Relations Board.

---

[21] (2004), 2004 CarswellBC 3470 (B.C. C.A.A.).
[22] 2005 BCCA 411, 2005 CarswellBC 1924 (B.C. C.A.).

Another similar case involved a dispute between a bus company (the employer) and a union regarding the interpretation of a provision in the collective agreement that addressed hiring, promotions, transfers and demotions and the impact that the British Columbia *Freedom of Information and Protection of Privacy Act* (*"FOIPPA"*) [23] has on that interpretation.[24] In particular, the disputed provision stated that the employer was required to provide the union, upon the union's request, with copies of applications for vacancies advertised by the employer. While the union contended that the collective agreement was not limited by *FOIPPA*, the employer's position was that it could not disclose any personal information of applicants unless they consented in writing. The union submitted its grievance under the collective agreement.

The arbitrator upheld the employer's position with respect to disclosure under the collective agreement of personal information about an identifiable individual. The union appealed this decision to the British Columbia Court of Appeal. This time, the scales tipped against the employer who was ordered to disclose the requested information to the union, albeit after having eliminated all personal identifiers. The Court of Appeal further recommended that the employer expressly notify candidates that their personal information may be disclosed to the union for the purpose of ensuring compliance with the collective agreement.

To finally clarify and resolve the question of the scope of the employer's obligation to disclose under the collective agreement, both the employer and the union agreed to submit to the British Columbia Arbitration Board. The Board identified three specific issues to be determined: (1) what documents typically generated in the job selection process are included in "copies of applications"; (2) what personal information must be disclosed to meet the union's purpose of ensuring that the employer's hiring decision complies with the collective agreement; and (3) what personal information typically collected in the job selection process is not related to the ability to perform the vacant job or to seniority?

The Board concluded that an "application" includes all of the information the applicant provides and all the information the employer requests of the applicant to assess his or her ability and seniority. More particularly, "'copies of applications' include any electronic or other form the employer requires applicants to use to make timely applications; résumés; any document voluntarily supplied by an applicant; interview questions and responses; score sheets; written tests; criteria used to evaluate candidates and

---

[23] R.S.B.C. 1996, c. 165.

[24] *C.O.P.E., Local 378 v. Coast Mountain Bus Co.* (2007), 165 L.A.C. (4th) 141, 2007 CarswellBC 3258 (B.C. Arb. Bd.).

the weight given to each; score sheets; seniority date; and overall scores achieved." References provided both in the form of letters or the names of referees leading to the collection of the referees' opinions regarding the applicant can also arguably be covered by the broad description of an "application" given by the Board.

In responding to the second question before it, the Board stated that personal information required for the union's purpose of ensuring compliance of the employer's hiring procedures with the collective agreement should include all personal information in complete "applications" of the successful candidate and union members. Two exceptions to this requirement, according to the Board, are: (1) personal information not related to an applicant's ability to perform the job or seniority; and (2) the limited class of information that qualifies as a personal identifier. A "personal identifier" was in turn interpreted by the Board to mean information that is specific to a unique individual, more specifically, names and contact information such as postal, email and other addresses and telephone numbers; passwords, social insurance number, drivers licence, care card, financial numbers and biometrics.

In its attempt to clarify what information should be considered to be unrelated to the ability to perform the job or seniority, the Board said once again that neither applications of unsuccessful candidates nor personal identifiers of all applicants should be disclosed to the union. It was also noted that there may be further information falling under this rubric which should be determined on a case-by-case basis. Once ruled out as unrelated, such information may not be used by the employer to support its decision to select a particular candidate over the others.

In another decision which drew on the conclusions in *Coast Mountain Bus Co.*, the Alberta Arbitration Board commented on the potential chilling effect caused by allowing the disclosure of reference information provided in confidence.[25] The Board stated the following:

> One particular concern expressed by the University is the chilling effect the potential disclosure of confidential references solicited from third parties might have on the frankness of future references. We accept that this is a real risk, and one that therefore calls for prudence by both parties before seeking or disclosing such references. While allegations may arise in an unusual case where disclosure would be justified by the nature of those allegations, we think this will be rare, and we urge caution by both parties in this respect. We remind the parties as well, when they are considering the potential for creating

---

[25] *University of Alberta v. University of Alberta Non-Academic Staff Assn.* (2006), 151 L.A.C. (4th) 365, 2006 CarswellAlta 1532 (Alta. Arb. Bd.).

a chilling effect, that the difference may only be between early and discreet disclosure and later and perhaps less discreet disclosure during an arbitration proceeding.

5.3 PERSONAL OPINIONS IN THE PRIVATE SECTOR

Under the purview of *PIPEDA,* personal opinions of an employee given in the course of their employment are not considered personal information about or belonging to that employee, and therefore are not protected from disclosure. Likewise, corporate opinions in relation to another individual constitute personal information about and belonging to that individual and must be disclosed to them upon an access to information request.

A complaint filed with the Privacy Commissioner against IMS Health Canada alleged that the company was selling information about the prescribing patterns of physicians without their consent. The information was gathered from Canadian pharmacies and comprised specifics such as the store number, drug identification number, drug name, form, strength, quantity, cost, doctor's first and last name, identification number, phone number, manufacturer, selling price, patient gender, and date of birth.

The Commissioner defined "personal information" as that information about an identifiable individual, not including legal persons such as corporations, partnerships or associations. The Commissioner held that a prescription in relation to an identified patient is personal health information about that patient, however, anonymized prescription information did not constitute personal information about the prescribing physician. Rather, a prescription is the outcome of professional interaction between the physician and patient and thus, is more appropriately regarded as work product. With regard to the bodies covered by *PIPEDA,* the Commissioner stated that:

> To interpret personal information so broadly as to include work products could allow for the inclusion of documents written by employees in the course of employment, reports prepared by employees for managers' use, or legal opinions, and would therefore be inconsistent with the stated purpose of *PIPEDA.*[26]

The implication of this decision is that personal opinions of employees or professionals given in the course of their employment are not viewed as personal information about or belonging to the employee as defined by the Act and therefore is afforded no legal protection.

---

[26] Privacy Commissioner of Canada, October 2, 2001, Summary #15.

A later decision by the Privacy Commission held that a corporate opinion in relation to another individual, specifically a bank customer, constituted personal information about and belonging to the customer and therefore was subject to protection under *PIPEDA*.

In this case, the individual complained over the bank's refusal to disclose her credit score to her following the denial of her application for a mortgage. The portion of the score that the bank would not release incorporated factors specific to the institution in calculating an internal credit score according to a credit scoring model developed by the bank. The bank argued that an internal credit score is not personal information coming within the ambit of *PIPEDA* as it is not collected but rather internally generated, and that an internal credit score cannot be released as it would reveal confidential commercial information, specifically the scoring model, protected under section 9(3)(b) of *PIPEDA*. Additionally, the bank submitted that it was not required to disclose an internal credit score as the score is a corporate opinion or form of commercial speech which was protected under section 2(b) of the Charter.

Stating that the Act is virtually limitless regarding what can constitute information about an identifiable individual, the Privacy Commissioner held that any information about an individual, including the customer's credit score, whether collected, internally generated, or originating with the individual was "personal information" subject to *PIPEDA*. Further, given the Act's wide ambit, its scope also includes opinions about an identifiable individual, such as corporate opinions in relation to an individual's credit worthiness.

With regard to the bank's submission that its internal credit score constituted corporate opinion protected from disclosure by the freedom of speech provisions of the Charter, the Commissioner found the argument creative but unpersuasive. He held that by generating a credit score about the customer, the bank had already broken its right not to express an opinion and must not now be allowed to invoke Charter provisions to shield it against disclosing this opinion to the customer. However, the Commissioner accepted the bank's contention that the credit scoring model qualified as confidential commercial information under *PIPEDA*, based on the bank's substantial investment in the model, its genuine regard for the model as proprietary, confidential commercial information and its efforts to protect it as such.

6

Personal Searches of Employees

6.1 Personal Searches of Employees

The majority of cases have held that while there is no common law right of employers to search employees, an employer may have an implied right to conduct searches.[1] For example, the right to conduct such a search may be found in the collective agreement, or may have effectively become a condition of employment by virtue of past practice.

In *U.A.W., Local 444 v. Chrysler Corp. of Canada*,[2] the employer asserted a right to perform a random personal search of an employee. The arbitrator expressly rejected Chrysler's assertion that there was a common law right of employers to search employees, but suggested that an implied right might be demonstrated "by reason of the size and nature of his company's operations" or because past practice had established such a right of search. It was held that this action was an invasion of the employee's privacy and without just cause. Of particular note to the arbitrator was the fact that the evidence did not disclose that theft of company property had been a major problem, nor did the company ever inform the union or employees that it claimed the right to conduct spot searches. The arbitrator also commented on the embarrassment an employee would naturally feel in being subjected to a spot check because of the suspicion of wrongdoing that might reasonably befall an employee so searched.

A search can only be justified either where the employer has a "real and substantial" suspicion of wrongdoing or pursuant to a clear provision in a collective agreement. Furthermore, where there are no express provisions permitting a search, the employer ought to be prepared to ask for

---

[1] See *Monarch Fine Foods Co. v. Milk & Bread Drivers, Dairy Employees, Caterers & Allied Employees, Local 647* (1978), 20 L.A.C. (2d) 419 (Ont. Arb. Bd.) where it was stated at 421 of the decision:

It is well established that persons do not by virtue of their status as employees lose their right to privacy and integrity of the person. An employer could not at common law assert any inherent right to search an employee or subject an employee to a physical examination without consent.

[2] (1961), 11 L.A.C. 152 (Ont. Arb. Bd.) [hereinafter *Chrysler*].

police assistance if its request to look into personal effects is denied by the employee.[3]

In *Canada Post Corp. v. C.U.P.W.*,[4] the arbitrator rejected the corporation's argument that it had a general authority as an occupier of its premises to confer wide powers of search on its security officers. The arbitrator held that an employee can assert a right of personal privacy not only over his body but also over his clothing, including outer clothing, and those accessories which constitute the immediate personal effects of the employees. Simply put, it was held that there is a basic core of privacy for each individual employee and for his or her reasonable personal effects which the collective agreement did not permit the employer to invade.

In *Amalgamated Electric Corp. (Markham) v. I.B.E.W., Local 1590*,[5] the majority of the arbitration board relied upon *Chrysler, supra*, to find that "spot checks" of purses, parcels, and lunch pails constituted an excessive invasion of privacy. As in *Chrysler,* the company had not published a rule relating to searches or the inspection of personal effects and there had been no evidence of a pilferage problem to justify the search. In balancing the right to privacy over personal effects with the company's interest in the security of its own property, the board made the following statements:

> [P]reservation of the right of privacy with respect to personal effects ought to be jealously preserved. This right of privacy should not be invaded except where there are the clearest provisions in the . . . collective agreement to the contrary, except of course where there is a real and substantial suspicion that an individual is guilty of theft. In a case where theft is suspected and where there are no expressed provisions permitting a search, the company ought to be prepared to ask for police assistance if its request to look into personal effects is denied by the employee. The suspicion of theft should be based on sufficient grounds so as to justify this action.[6]

Where a right to conduct employee searches is not found in a collective agreement, an employer must demonstrate that employee theft constitutes an immediate threat to its interests.

In *Glenbow-Alberta Institute v. C.U.P.E., Local 1645*[7] the employer instituted a policy of checking the personal effects, including purses, of employees entering certain restricted areas of the museum. The union argued

[3] *Amalgamated Electric Corp. (Markham) v. I.B.E.W., Local 1590* (1974), 6 L.A.C. (2d) 28 (Ont. Arb. Bd.) at 32 and 33.

[4] (1990), 10 L.A.C. (4th) 393 (Can Arb. Bd.).

[5] *Supra* note 3.

[6] *Ibid.* at 32 and 33.

[7] (1988), 3 L.A.C. (4th) 127 (Alta. Arb. Bd.).

that this was an invasion of the employees' privacy. The arbitrator applied the "balancing of interests" approach to determine the "reasonableness" of the search and asked whether the employer must experience serious incidents of loss, damage, injury or death before additional searches can be justified. In this instance, it was held that the employer was justified in conducting employee searches. The arbitrator noted that the museum had suffered losses for the past 10 years as a result of employee theft. The arbitrator also held that if the nature of the workplace is such that security is an unusually high concern, the employer may be able to take more intrusive search procedures than would otherwise be allowed.

Employers wishing to inspect an employee's locker also face a difficult justification test. First, the search must be based on a "real and substantial" suspicion of theft. Second, the inspection must be conducted in a fair and reasonable manner. Most importantly, with respect to the personal effects such as purses or lunch bags found in these lockers an employee has a clear right to privacy.

For example, in *University Hospital v. London & District Service Workers' Union, Local 220*[8] the issue was whether the employer had a right to inspect employees' lockers and the personal effects therein. Unlike the situation in *Chrysler* and *Amalgamated Electric Corp.*, the hospital had a significant pilferage problem which informal measures could not resolve. The search of the lockers was held to be justified on the basis of the management rights clause in the collective agreement and on the basis of an employee handbook which reserved the right to the employer to inspect lockers at any time. However, the employee was held to have a clear right to privacy with respect to his or her personal effects contained in the locker.

Any searches which are conducted should be done on a universal basis, so that all employees in a given work area are searched, or a selection process should be used which is random and does not appear to single out individual employees.[9]

Discipline may be imposed on employees for failing to comply with employer rules regarding searches. *Lumber & Sawmill Workers' Union, Local 2537 v. KVP Co.*[10] is the seminal case on the imposition of discipline for failure to adhere to these rules. This case established that the breach of

---

[8] (1981), 28 L.A.C. (2d) 294 (Ont. Arb. Bd.).

[9] See *Lornex Mining Corp. v. U.S.W.A., Local 7619* (1983), 14 L.A.C. (3d) 169 (B.C. Arb. Bd.); see also *Drug Trading Co. & Druggists Corp. v. E.C.W.U., Local 11* (1988), 32 L.A.C. (3d) 443 (Ont. Arb. Bd.). See also *Progistix-Solutions Inc. v. C.E.P., Local 26* (2000), 89 L.A.C. (4th) 1 (Ont. Arb. Bd.).

[10] (1965), 16 L.A.C. 73.

a rule imposed unilaterally by the employer without the union's assent permits just cause for discipline only if the rule meets the following criteria:

1. It is consistent with the collective agreement;

2. It is reasonable;

3. It is clear and unequivocal;

4. It was brought to the attention of the affected employee(s) before the employer attempts to act on it;

5. Where the rule is invoked to justify discharge, the employee was notified that a breach of the rule could result in discharge;

6. The employer has enforced the rule consistently since its introduction.

In addition to requiring an employer to satisfy these requirements, arbitrators will also assess the reasonableness of the rule in question. Generally, for a rule to be found reasonable the employer must establish that it promotes health and safety in the workplace or advances a legitimate business interest.

With respect to employer search policies, the decision in *Progistix-Solutions Inc. v. C.E.P., Local 26*[11] summarized the law regarding such rules in relation to the discovery of a major theft ring. Employees had been required to undergo a parcel search as they left the warehouse where they worked, to which the union had not previously objected. Following the discovery of the theft ring, the employer mandated a search of the employees' outer clothing as well. Some employees were frisked, had their clothing searched while they were still wearing it, or were asked to lift their clothing to allow for a visual inspection of their waist band area, prompting the union to file a grievance of the clothing search. Prior to the hearing, the employer extended the search to all persons using the warehouse and amended the policy to provide for random clothing and parcel searches at the exit.

In assessing the reasonableness of the employer's search policy, the arbitrator balanced the employees' right to privacy against the employers' right to control theft problems in the workplace. The arbitrator ruled that the original clothing search policy was unreasonable as it had not first exhausted less intrusive measures to deal with its security problems, however, she upheld the policy in its revised form. To meet the reasonableness test, the employer was required to prove adequate cause for implementing

---

[11] *Progistix-Solutions, supra*, note 9.

the policy by demonstrating that it had exhausted other alternatives to searches, had taken reasonable steps to notify the union and employees, and had conducted the searches in a systematic and random manner. Only outer clothing was allowed to be searched after it had been removed from the body and body searches and visual inspections were held to be impermissible without a police officer present.

6.2 Searches Conducted by Employers

Some public employees are subject to searches specifically authorized by statute. However, because of the *Charter*'s influence within the context of public employment, these searches must nonetheless strike an appropriate balance between state intrusion and an employee's reasonable expectation of privacy. In *R. v. March*,[12] the Ontario Court of Justice examined the constitutionality of section 22 and section 22(2) of Ontario Regulation 778 to the *Ministry of Correctional Services Act*, which authorized the search of employees of correctional facilities while at work. The defendant in this case had been charged with unlawful possession of marijuana after a search conducted under this statute revealed he was carrying the drug into the correctional facility. The Court held that the legislation struck "the appropriate balance between the intrusion by the state and the employee's reasonable expectation of privacy in the highly regulated environment of a correctional institution" because it explicitly states that the "Superintendent of the institution must have 'reasonable cause' [in authorizing the search], the reasonable cause must relate to the smuggling of contraband into the institution by the employee, the search is limited to the person or any property of the employee and the power to search does not extend beyond the institution or to other persons". Further the Court held that in this particular case, the search itself had been conducted in a "reasonable and respectful manner". This case also highlights how employees working in highly surveiled and secure environments have a reduced expectation of privacy which can sometimes include searches of any personal property located on the premises of the institution.

6.3 Searches Conducted by State Agents

Searches conducted by the police and other state agents in violation of the section 8 *Charter* right against unlawful search and seizure may be admitted as evidence in labour arbitration disputes. For instance, in *British*

---

[12] [2006] O.J. No. 664, 2006 ONCJ 62, 2006 CarswellOnt 1323 (Ont. C.J.).

Columbia Public Service Agency v. B.C.G.E.U. (Koprowski Grievance),[13] an employee was dismissed by the Ministry after it discovered through an anonymous letter that he had been charged with possession of marijuana for the purpose of trafficking and production of marijuana stemming from a search of the employee's home by police. A Provincial Court judge found that the search had been conducted in violation of the employee's *Charter* rights under section 8 and was therefore inadmissible within the criminal context. However, Arbitrator J.B. Hall held that despite this, any "real" evidence obtained through the illegal search was admissible at arbitration as it would not result in an unfair hearing. In determining the admissibility of the evidence, the Arbitrator relied on the B.C. *Labour Relations Code* which states that "an arbitrator may accept evidence which may not be admissible in a court of law, in order to have regard to the real substance of the matters in dispute and the respective merit of the positions of the parties". In this case, the Arbitrator found that there was no need to deter or prohibit improper conduct by the Ministry; it acted on an anonymous letter advising of the grievor's arrest for operating a marijuana grow operation.

---

[13] (2007), [2007] B.C.C.A.A.A. No. 83, 2007 CarswellBC 3333 (B.C. Arb. Bd.).

7

Monitoring and Surveillance

7.1 E-MAIL MONITORING

7.1.1 Introduction

Email has been defined as,

> [a] document created or received on an electronic mail system including brief notes, more formal or substantive narrative documents, and any attachments. . .[or] any other electronic documents, which may be transmitted. . .[1]

A 1993 study indicated that 30 per cent of 1,000 firms surveyed searched their employees' computer files, electronic mail, and voice mail, subjecting more than 20 million employees to computer monitoring. Four years later, another study revealed that monitoring had increased 33 per cent with the result that 63 per cent of mid-sized to large firms reported that they conducted some form of electronic surveillance.[2]

More recently in 2001, the American Management Association found that more than three-quarters of U.S. firms now monitor their employees' phone calls, e-mails, Internet activities and computer files. The survey also indicated that 80 per cent of U.S. companies monitor employee e-mail and Internet use, a dramatic increase from the 35 per cent of companies in 1997.[3]

The 2007 Electronic Monitoring and Surveillance Survey has considered the problem of workplace monitoring from a different angle. Now employers not only monitor various aspects of employees' actions while at work, but also use the results of their monitoring and surveillance to dismiss employees. The American Management Association and the ePolicy Insti-

---

[1] Erik C. Garcia, "E-mail and Privacy Rights" (1996) *Computers and the Law*, online: University at Buffalo Law School <http://wings.buffalo.edu/law/Complaw/CompLawPapers/garcia.html>.

[2] American Management Association, International Electronic Monitoring & Surveillance (1997 AMA Survey), online: American Management Association <http://www.amanet.org/usindes.html>.

[3] Charles Morgan, "Monitoring Employee-Electronic Mail and Internet Use: Balancing Competing Rights", *Droit du commerce électronique*, Les Éditions Thémis, 2002 [*Morgan*].

tute report that more than 25% of employers have fired workers for misusing e-mail and about 30% of employers have dismissed employees for misusing the Internet. Employers have argued that this harsh sanction is necessary to compel compliance by employees with workplace rules and policies.[4]

7.1.2   Reasons for Monitoring E-Mail

The growing use by employees of personal computers on the job, which are typically linked either to the Internet or to an internal network, has allowed employers to have easy access to employee e-mail. Access to employee e-mail in order to monitor incoming and outgoing information is important for an employer for a variety of reasons.

1. **Limiting Recreational Use**: A key preventative factor is to eliminate time wasted by employees who engage in recreational activities while at work, such as playing computer-based games or surfing the World Wide Web.

2. **Network Security**: Monitoring e-mail is a technique which protects network security. The need to monitor e-mails arises because it can be used to download infected files which can compromise the security of an employer's computer network.

3. **Misappropriation of Company Resources**: Employee recreational use of the Internet can cause significant delays in Internet connections for legitimate business use especially when the employee uses the employer's network for transmitting large image files.

4. **Security**: Surveillance techniques are useful to monitor employee behaviour. For example, monitoring e-mail messages can reveal when employees engage in contractual relationships contrary to their employer's interests, when they compromise trade secrets, and when they publicize copyright-infringing and confidential material.

5. **Corporate Reputation**: Employers may implement computer monitoring to protect the company's reputation and good will. An employer may wish to defend itself against an employee who uses company e-mail and Internet access to visit sites and/ or send external e-mail messages which could tarnish the company's image.

6. **Legal Liability**: Finally, many employers are wary of employees utilizing corporate resources for actions which may incur legal liability such as sexual

---

[4] American Management Association, 2007 Electronic Monitoring and Surveillance Survey, online: American Management Association <http://press.amanet.org/press-releases/177/2007-electronic-monitoring-surveillance-survey>.

harassment, racial discrimination, trademark/ copyright infringements, defamation, trade libel, electronic harassment and corporate espionage.[5]

7.1.3 Legality of Monitoring

Many employers consider electronic mail sent and received using company computer equipment and stored on company computer networks to be the property of the employer. From the employer's perspective this is a business resource paid for by the employer and is to be used only for business purposes. Therefore, e-mail messages and telephone conversations made on behalf of the employee in the course of business should be made available for review for legitimate business and security reasons. For these reasons, an employee acting on behalf of their employer should have no reasonable expectation of privacy.[6]

An employee's perspective, on the other hand, is that e-mail is his or her private property, similar in nature to personal handwritten letters. Many employees believe that the password requirement means that others cannot access their e-mail and that the site is secure.[7]

However, courts and legislators in the United States and Canada have come to hold that the right of privacy is a "personality right" which is held by everyone and cannot be alienated. For this reason in part, therefore, it is inappropriate to suggest that ownership rights negate or subordinate privacy rights as the two kinds of rights are different and overlapping in nature, and are not mutually exclusive.[8]

In a recent decision, the French Supreme Court ruled on workplace e-mail privacy and concluded that employers do not have the right to access their employee's e-mail or other personal files.[9]

---

[5] James Noonan, Heather Devine and Riva Richard, "Using Computer Video Surveillance to Monitor Employees: Are the benefits worth the cost?" (*Employment Law Conference Paper*, McCarthy Tétrault, November 9, 1998) [unpublished].

[6] James Noonan, et al., *supra*, note 5.

[7] "Addressing the Hazards of the New Technology Workplace", 104 *Harvard Law Review* 1909.

[8] *Supra*, note 3.

[9] See *Nikon France v. Onos*, BNA's Electronic Commerce & Law Report (2001), online: BNA <http:/ / pubs.bna.com/ ip/ BNA/ eip.nsf/ id/ a0a4u9d3a5>.

(a) American Approach

(i) Electronic Communications Privacy Act

In 1986, Congress enacted the *Electronic Communications Privacy Act ("ECPA")*. Before the enactment of the *ECPA,* federal law did not provide any guidelines for protecting electronic communications and moreover they were not protected by the constitutional right of privacy as defined by the United States Supreme Court.[10]

Pursuant to Title I, section 2511 of the *ECPA,* it is illegal for anyone to "intentionally intercept, endeavour to intercept, or procure any other person to intercept or to endeavour to intercept any . . . electronic communication".[11] While this section does not explicitly exclude the workplace from the scope of the Act, case law has substantially limited its applicability to workplace monitoring of employee e-mail. For example, in *Steve Jackson Games Inc. v. United States Secret Service,*[12] and in *Wesely College v. Pitts*[13] the Court held that there can be no interception under Title I if the acquisition of the contents of electronic communication is not contemporaneous with their transmission. Because e-mail is often in transit for only a few seconds and most often acquired only once it has been stored, Title I rarely applies to the monitoring of e-mail.[14]

Furthermore the Act provides two exceptions which effectively allow an employer, who is the provider of the e-mail service, to access stored messages and other electronic communications irrespective of the nature (personal or professional) of the message regardless of whether the employee has consented to such monitoring.[15] Section 2511(2)(d) contains a

---

[10] Erik C. Garcia, *supra,* note 1 at 1.

[11] Title I, s. 2511 of *Electronic Privacy Act* of 1986, Pub. L. 89-508 (1996). This Act amended the *Federal Wire Tap Statute, 18 U.S.C.A.*

[12] 36 F.3d 457 (5th Cir., 1994) cited in Charles Morgan, *Employer Monitoring of Employee E-Mail and Internet Use* (1999) [unpublished, archived at *McGill Law Journal*].

[13] 1974 F. Supp. 375 (D. Del., 1997) cited in Charles Morgan, *ibid.*

[14] See *Fraser v. Nationwide Mutual Ins. Co.,* Case No. 98-CV-6726 (E.D. Pa., 2001).

[15] Section 2511(2)(d) *ECPA* provides that it is not unlawful to intercept the contents of an electronic communication when the intercepting party has obtained the consent of one of the parties to the communication. Section 2511(2)(a)(i) ECPA provides a "business use exception" to the general prohibition of the interception of electronic communications. This exception applies where an officer, employee, or agent of a provider of wire or electronic wire or electronic communication services, "intercept[s], disclose[s], or use[s] that communication in the

consent exception, which provides that it is not unlawful so intercept the contents of electronic communications where the intercepting party has obtained consent from one of the parties to the communication. Section 2511(2)(a)(i) includes a business use exception, which allows an officer, employee or agent of a provider of wire, electronic wire, or electronic communication services to intercept, disclose or use that communication in the normal course of employment while engaged in any activity which is necessarily incident to rendering service or protecting the property rights of the service provider.[16]

(ii)   Common Law Tort of Invasion of Privacy

An employee may also bring an action against an employer who monitors e-mails for unreasonable intrusion into the seclusion of the employee. The key is that in order to be actionable, three elements must be present: there must be an "intrusion" which is "highly objectionable" to a "reasonable man". The U.S. courts have generally held electronic surveillance to be sufficient to establish the first element.[17] With respect to the second element, the courts examine the "degree of intrusion, the context, conduct and circumstances surrounding the intrusion, as well as the intruder's motives and objectives, the setting into which he intrudes, and the expectations of those whose privacy is invaded."[18] Lastly, the third element requires the court to find both that the employee had a subjective expectation of privacy and that the expectation was objectively reasonable. American jurisprudence suggests that an employee will have little success in bringing a claim against

---

normal course of his employment while engaged in any activity which is necessarily incident to the rendition of his service or to the protection of the rights or property of the provider of that service. Thus, the exception will apply where the employer is the provider of the e-mail service and the activity occurs in the normal course of the individual's employment. Case law has held that any monitoring done by the employer is sufficiently related to its business interests to fall within the exception — see *Briggs v. American Air Filter Co.*, 630 F.2d 414 (5th Cir., 1980); *Watkins v. L.M. Berry & Co.*, 704 F.2d 577 (11th Cir., 1993) at 582-585.

[16] Michael Geist, "Computer and E-mail Workplace Surveillance in Canada: The Shift from Reasonable Expectation of privacy to Reasonable Surveillance" (August 2003) 82 Can. Bar Rev. 151.

[17] *Billings v. Atkinson*, 489 S.W.2d 858 (Tex., 1973); *Nader v. General Motors Corp.*, 255 N.E.2d 765 (N.Y., 1970).

[18] See *Crump v. Beckley Newspapers Inc.*, 320 S.E.2d 70 (W.VA., 1983) as cited in Charles Morgan, *supra*, note 12.

an employer on the basis of this tort in the context of employer monitoring of employee e-mail.[19]

Several American cases have addressed the issue of the employer's right to review e-mail messages. In *Smyth v. Pillsbury Co.*,[20] the Court upheld the termination of an at-will employee based on a review of e-mail transmitted over the company network. The Court stated the following:

> Again, we note that by intercepting such communications, the company is not, as in the case of urinalysis or personal property searches, requiring the employee to disclose any personal information about himself or invading the employee's person or personal effects. Moreover, the company's interest in preventing inappropriate and unprofessional comments or even illegal activity over its e-mail system outweighs any privacy interest the employee may have in those comments.

A similar issue was addressed in a class action suit filed by employees of Epson American Inc. in *Flanagan v. Epson America Inc.*[21] In this case, Epson employees claimed damages based on the company's practice of reading employee e-mail. The action was dismissed as the Court found that the State (California) constitutional right to privacy did not protect employees from employer monitoring of e-mail in the workplace.

An e-mail policy was also at issue in *Bourke v. Nissan Motor Corp.*[22] The employer had read personal e-mail, including correspondence of a sexual nature, that had been sent out over the company's e-mail system. California's Second District Court of Appeal held that no privacy rights had been violated either under California's Constitution (which grants expansive privacy rights) or under common law. Critical to the court's decision was the employee's signing of a policy agreeing to restrict all use of company e-mail to company purposes. The policy also stated that by signing the policy, the employee was put on notice that e-mail would be monitored.

Likewise in *United States v. Simons*,[23] the court found no reasonable expectation of privacy where a systems manager traced visits to pornographic websites from an employee's computer and found more than a thousand pornographic files on the computer's hard drive. The court ruled that the search was not a violation of the employee's constitutional fourth amendment rights (the right of the people to be secure in their persons, houses, papers, and effects, against unreasonable searches and seizures),

---

[19] See *Smythe v. Pillsbury Co.* cited in Charles Morgan, *supra*, note 12.
[20] 914 F. Supp. 97 (U.S. Dist. Ct. E.D. Penn., 1996).
[21] (1990) SWC 112749.
[22] No. YC003979 (Cal. Sup. Ct., Los Angeles County, 1991).
[23] 29 F.Supp.2d 324 (E.D. Va., 1998).

and that the employee had no reasonable expectation of privacy since the company had an Internet policy and a business interest in preventing unauthorized use of the Internet by employees.[24]

Similar results have emerged throughout the United States as it appears the Courts are ready to accept that employees do not have expectations of privacy if the employer is clear in removing any such expectation.[25]

(b) Canadian Approach

Under current Canadian law, employee surveillance in the private sector remains virtually unregulated. In the absence of a collective agreement that provides to the contrary, an employer may use electronic monitoring systems, overtly or covertly, to supervise its employees. The propriety of monitoring depends on the nature of the monitoring, the employee's awareness of the monitoring, the classification of the monitored activity as business or private and the egregiousness of the monitoring.[26]

(i) Criminal Code

Section 184 of the *Criminal Code*[27] was enacted to protect private communications only. The protection afforded by the Code is inherently limited by its terms and does not really affect an employer's right to access business communications paid for by the employer and made in the conduct of business. Essentially, it appears that section 184 does not protect electronic communication where the communication is not private, or if consent to intercept is obtained from at least one of the parties. A communication is only private if the parties to the communication have a reasonable expectation of privacy.

Like the U.S. *EPCA*, the *Criminal Code* includes consent and business use exceptions in section 184(2)(c), though the business use exception in Canada appears to be more limited in scope to those who are in the business of providing communication services. Section 342.1(1)(b) is the *Criminal Code's* anti-hacker provision, which makes it an offence for a person to

---

[24] *Geist, supra,* note 16.

[25] See, for example, *Smyth v. Pillsbury Co.*, 914 F. Supp. 97 (U.S. Dist. Ct. E.D. Penn., 1996) and *Garrity v. John Hancock Mutual Life Insurance Co.* (U.S. Dist. Ct. (Mass.), May 7, 2002).

[26] Jeff Kray and Pamela Robertson, *Enhanced Monitoring of White Collar Employees: Should Employers Be Required to Disclose?* 15 Puget Sound L. Rev. p.144.

[27] R.S.C. 1985, C-46, as amended.

fraudulently or *without colour of right* to intercept any communication to or from a computer by means of any device. This section may cover computer surveillance in the workplace, however, employers who believe in good faith that they have a right to monitor their employees may not be subject to section 342.1(1)(b).[28]

While Canadian courts have yet to apply *Criminal Code* provisions to the context of employer monitoring of employee e-mail, in light of these provisions it is very important for an employer to have a policy concerning the use of office equipment which clearly informs employees that telephone calls, voice mail, and e-mail may be monitored for legitimate business purposes. Such a policy, combined with the fact that the employer pays for telephone and e-mail services and expects these services to be used for business purposes, may defeat any expectation of privacy that an employee might have in his or her communications. Alternatively, the employer could implement a policy which makes it a condition of employment that the employee must consent to certain types of surveillance.

(ii)   Canadian Jurisprudence

There is no definitive Canadian ruling addressing the issue of employee e-mail. Who owns the e-mail in the context of e-mail sent or received by an employee via his or her employer's computer system is a question which has yet to be addressed by the Canadian judicial system or by statute. Depending on the approach one takes to this question, different legal arguments arise.

For instance, one view is that e-mail sent or received in this context is the property of the employer, to which an employee maintains no reasonable expectation of privacy. In other words, a search of an e-mail system is really a search of an employer's property.[29] The alternative approach is to view sent or received e-mail as the property of the employee. In other words, the assignment to an employee of an e-mail address is analogous to the assignment to an employee of a company locker. Thus, this approach acknowledges that employees have an expectation of privacy in their e-mail. This approach requires the application of the same legal criteria as would apply in cases of company searches of employees.[30]

Privacy legislation, jurisprudence and doctrine suggests that the issues require a balancing of employees' privacy rights against the employer's

---

[28] *Geist, supra,* note 16.

[29] See, for example, Holly Rasky, "Can an Employer Search the Contents of Its Employee's E-Mail" (1998) 20 Advocates Q. 221 at 221.

[30] See discussion of employee searches in section 2.5.2.

legitimate business interests; however, emerging case law indicates that employee privacy rights mitigate against the position that employers have an unfettered right to monitor employees' e-mail and Internet use.[31]

In *Pacific Northwest Herb Corp. v. Thompson*,[32] a former president had used the company computer at home for both work and personal use, including correspondence with his lawyer regarding lawsuit against the company for dismissal. Before returning the computer to his employer, he attempted to have everything pertaining to him removed from the computer hard drive, however, he later discovered that some of his correspondence was still on the hard drive. The employee subsequently filed a motion for an order for production of all documents that the employer might have retrieved from the computer, as well as an injunction restraining the employer from accessing or using the communications on the basis of solicitor-client privilege and right to privacy. The employee also sought an order that the contents of the documents be kept confidential by the employer.

The court granted an interlocutory injunction restraining the employer from accessing or using communications created by or sent to his solicitors and ordered the company to keep confidential the contents of any documents that it had retrieved since the disclosure by the employee was inadvertent and he had not waived his privilege. Despite the fact that the computer system belonged to the employer, the court ruled that the employee had a reasonable expectation of privacy in relation to documents created for his own family or personal use.

The decision in *Consumers' Gas v. C.E.P.* [33] illustrates a situation in which an employer permits personal use of its e-mail system and the Internet, but very clearly draws the line between personal use and use for pornography and similar purposes by issuing a policy that prohibits the latter. This case involved an employee who was dismissed for misconduct after the employer found that she had been receiving and distributing pornographic material. While the employee argued that she had no idea about the employer's policy with respect to the e-mail system and Internet use, the arbitrator stated that common sense should have prevailed; the e-mail system and the computer's storage system is not for the grievor's own extensive use and that the transmission and storage of sexual material would not be acceptable to the business.

A very similar scenario involving an employee's abusive use of his employer's e-mail system for dissemination of offensive materials was

---

[31] *Geist, supra,* note 16.

[32] (1999), 1999 CarswellBC 2738, [1999] B.C.J. No. 2772 (B.C. S.C.).

[33] (August 5, 1999), Doc. A9801088, [1999] O.L.A.A. No. 649 (Ont. Arb. Bd.).

considered in *Telus Mobility v. T.W.U.*[34] Again, the employer's response resulted in the employee's dismissal. The union took the position that while some form of discipline was warranted, dismissal was not justified in the circumstances. However, the arbitrator followed the decision in *Consumers Gas* and held that it was "self-evident to any employee that using the employer's e-mail facilities to send seriously pornographic material to other employees or elsewhere is unacceptable conduct." The arbitrator upheld the employer's decision to dismiss the employee on the basis that the materials in issue were highly offensive and that he was a relatively short-term employee who showed very little or no remorse for his actions.

The Chair of the Ontario Crown Employees Grievance Settlement Board relied on the decision in both *Consumers Gas* and *Telus Mobility* when considering the appropriateness of the dismissal of six Ministry of Natural Resources employees who were engaged in forwarding sexually explicit materials through the Ministry's e-mail system.[35] In total, the Employer disciplined sixty-six employees for contravening the Workplace Discrimination and Harassment Prevention operating policy ("the WDHP Policy") and the Operating Procedure on Usage of I.T. Resources ("the IT Policy"). In addition to the dismissal of some of its employees, the Ministry issued letters of reprimand and suspensions of varying lengths to a maximum of 20 days.

Interestingly, drawing on the bulk of arbitration jurisprudence, the Chair stated that when fashioning an appropriate discipline for an offense, the seriousness of the offensive material involved should be determined. Referring to the two above-mentioned cases, the Chair concluded that generally, an employer should advise employees about what behaviour will result in discipline and how severe the discipline might be. This can be achieved by issuing rules and a range of penalties for violating a rule. The Chair noted, however, that notwithstanding, there is some conduct which any employee should recognize as unacceptable even without rules or some other notice from the Employer. The arbitrator found that the receiving and sending of pornographic and other offensive materials using the employer's e-mail to be one such example of conduct unacceptable to the employer.

Where an employer's right to monitor e-mail is provided for in a collective agreement, or where an employee has consented to e-mail monitoring, an absolute privilege to conduct such monitoring is created so long

---

[34] (2001), 2001 CarswellNat 3890 (Can. Arb. Bd.).
[35] *O.P.S.E.U. v. Ontario (Ministry of Natural Resources)* (2003), 2003 CarswellOnt 3343 (Ont. C.E.G.S.B.).

as the invasion of privacy does not exceed the scope of the consent.[36] The focus becomes one of reasonableness of the substance and implementation of a given workplace rule. Using this approach in relation to e-mail monitoring, the inquiry would focus on such factors as the notice given to the employee of the search policy, the clarity of the policy and/or the fairness of the administration of the policy."[37]

In *Bhamre Employment Insurance Claim Appeal*,[38] the appellant had been dismissed from his job at Imperial Oil Ltd. because of his personal use of work e-mail against company rules. The employer had access to these e-mails and stated that some of these e-mail messages could be considered sexist and racist, and were against the company's policy of a harassment-free work area. The Court found that Imperial Oil had a clear policy that its e-mail system was to be used for business purposes only and that the claimant was aware of this policy.

Even in situations where policies have not explicitly been made known to employees, it has been held that mere common sense should dictate that the promulgation of some material by email is not permitted. For example, in *Consumers Gas v. C.E.P.*[39] it was held:

> Lack of knowledge of the policy, however, in this case does not assist the grievor. Common sense should have prevailed, and suggested to the grievor that the cc mail system and the computer's storage system is not for her own extensive use and that the transmission and storage of sexual material would not be acceptable to the business. Common sense dictates that Linda Primiani's

---

[36] Where an employee has consented to e-mail monitoring, Canadian courts will examine the nature of the consent, whether express or implied, to determine whether it was validly and clearly obtained. Two Canadian cases have examined the issue of consent. In *R. v. Sanelli*, (sub nom. *R. v. Duarte*) [1990] 1 S.C.R. 30 (S.C.C.), the Supreme Court of Canada held that the fact that one party consented to monitoring does not remedy lack of consent by the second party to the communication; in *R. v. Cremascoli* (1979), (sub nom. *R. v. Goldman*) [1980] 1 S.C.R. 976 (S.C.C.) the Court held that the consent must be freely given.

[37] The approach taken by arbitrators when interpreting management's rights under a collective agreement is to contemplate various minimal restrictions to management prerogatives as summarized in *Lumber & Sawmill Workers' Union, Local 2537 v. KVP Co.* (1965), 16 L.A.C. 73 (Ont. Arb. Bd.). See Beth Wilson, "Search and Surveillance in the Workplace: An Arbitrator's Perspective" (1992) Labour Arbitration (Markam: Butterworths, 1992) at p.143. Often charter values are applied in making a determination that an employee's privacy rights have been violated. See *Doman Forest Products Ltd. v. I.W.A., Local 1-357* (1990), 13 L.A.C. (4th) 275 (B.C. Arb. Bd.).

[38] (September 23, 1998), CUB 42012A.

[39] See *Consumers Gas, supra,* note 33.

use of the computer went well beyond acceptable means. This case is similar to the *Insurance Corporation of British Columbia (supra)* case. Arbitrator Weiler found in determining what a reasonable employee would understand to be an appropriate use of the email, that the criteria would be whether the receiver or sender would want the message to be made public at the workplace. This is a basic common sense test, which in this case, the grievor did not pass.

In situations where the employer is bound to obey the Rights and Freedoms guaranteed in the Charter (e.g., a federal Department of the Government of Canada), some employees have argued that the employer's ability to monitor emails is a violation of section 8. This was the case in the Public Service Staff Relations Board case of *Briar v. Canada (Treasury Board)*.[40] In this case, several employees were disciplined after their employer, the Solicitor General of Canada–Correction Service, found emails sent and received by the employees that contained pornographic material.

The Relations Board extensively recited the various proper use policies the employer had in place as well as the various notices the employer sent to all employees. Then, while dismissing the employees' arguments that their section 8 rights were violated, the Relations Board says:

> In view of the employer's policy against the use of the email system for unacceptable purposes and a clear log-on warning that the system is monitored in accordance with such policies, it is difficult to see how, in these circumstances, the grievors can claim a privacy interest. Moreover, the employer's investigation was driven by a complaint on which it was bound to act. This is not a case of random surveillance. Nor is it comparable to urinalysis or personal property searches. These are email communications over which the grievors lost control once they pressed "Send". There are some 1,600 users on the [employer's] network.

It bears mentioning that in the Privacy Commissioner of Canada's Annual Report 2000-2001, the Privacy Commissioner expressed concern over employer policies which endorse wholesale surveillance of email or computer use, following a complaint by a Department of National Defence ("DND") employee. In this case, someone had gained access to the complainant's computer and downloaded email messages which contained personal information about the employee and derogatory comments about his colleagues. The messages were then printed and placed on the desks of several other employees, which prompted them to file a harassment complaint against the complainant. DND then hired a consultant to investigate the harassment complaints and provided him with the messages as evidence.

---

[40] 2003 PSSRB 3 (Can. P.S.S.R.B.).

The employee complained to the Privacy Commission, questioning whether his employer could use and disclose private email messages, which had been collected by improper means, in order to investigate the harassment complaints.

Because there was no evidence that managers or supervisors were responsible for accessing the employee's email, the Privacy Commissioner concluded that the employer had not contravened the *Privacy Act* and had not behaved unreasonably in the circumstances. Additionally, the employee's expectation of privacy was lost once the email messages had fallen into the hands of his colleagues, regardless of the rights or wrongs of how this occurred. However, although the Commissioner affirmed that employers must protect their employees against workplace harassment, this did not include unfettered access to employees' email:

> DND's specific policy on the Management of Electronic Mail states that there should be no expectation of privacy on the part of employees when using e-mail systems. I find this deeply troubling. The law on privacy has developed around the notion of the "reasonable expectation"; . . . But I don't agree that it follows from this that an employee's, or anyone's, privacy can be simply eradicated by telling them not to expect any. While management has the right and the responsibility to manage, it has to operate within limits, including respect for fundamental rights. It is not for management alone to determine whether an expectation of privacy is reasonable.[41]

While there may not always be a reasonable expectation of privacy if an employee is using the employer's network and if the employee has been given notice of the relevant policies, the courts have held that where the employer is not the service provider of the e-mail system (i.e. the employee is using the Internet to exchange e-mails), there is a right to privacy in e-mail. For example in *R. v. Weir*,[42] the Court found that an individual communicating on e-mail via the Internet has a reasonable expectation of privacy:

---

[41] Privacy Commissioner of Canada, "Annual Report to Parliament 2000-2001", online: Office of the Privacy Commissioner of Canada <http://www.privcom.gc.ca/information/ar/02_04_09_01_e.asp>.

[42] (1998), 59 Alta. L.R. (3d) 319 (Alta. Q.B.), affirmed (2001), 156 C.C.C. (3d) 188 (Alta. C.A.). While this case is significant, its application to workplace monitoring is limited due to the fact that in *Weir* the accused's e-mail account was a personal one purchased from an Internet provider, rather than one supplied by an employer.

In summary, I am satisfied e-mail via the Internet ought to carry a reasonable expectation of privacy. Because of the manner in which the technology is managed and repaired that degree of privacy is less than that of first class mail. Yet the vulnerability of e-mail requires legal procedures which will minimize invasion. I am satisfied that the current *Criminal Code* and *Charter of Rights* protections are adequate when applied in the e-mail environment.

However, even though a reasonable expectation of privacy has been recognized in relation to personal, internet-based e-mail accounts, the manner in which an employee uses and accesses these accounts may have an impact on how high or low decision-makers regard that reasonable expectation of privacy. For instance, in *Lethbridge College v. Lethbridge College Faculty Assn.*,[43] a professor grieving his termination for having inappropriate relations with certain students contested the admissibility of e-mail evidence obtained by his employer, the College, from his College e-mail and hotmail accounts; files from both were obtained from the computer provided to the grievor by the College. The majority of the Alberta Grievance Arbitration Board found that since the employer's property was used to send the e-mails in question and the e-mails could be retrieved from its property (although it took "some months" to obtain the hotmail e-mails due to the "technical difficulty of retrieving these emails"), these factors outweighed the privacy interests of the employee.[44]

7.1.4   E-Mail as Discovery Material

Anyone who files a lawsuit against a business can have access to all corporate e-mail if it is relevant to the litigation. Provincial and federal rules of procedure appear to include e-mail as a discoverable document, which may, therefore, be subject to subpoena.[45] E-mail messages are valuable discovery material because they are often written informally and can contain statements which would rarely be put into a written memorandum or document.

---

[43] (2007), [2007] A.G.A.A. No. 67, 2007 CarswellAlta 1839 (Alta. Arb. Bd.), affirmed (2008), 2008 CarswellAlta 911 (Alta. Q.B.).

[44] To determine this, the Board applied the test for reasonableness initially used in reaction to video surveillance evidence from *Doman Forest Products Ltd. v. I.W.A., Local 1-357* (1990), 13 L.A.C. (4th) 275 (B.C. Arb. Bd.).

[45] For example, in Ontario *Rules of Civil Procedure*, R.R.O. 1990, Reg. 194, s. 30.01(a), a "document" is defined as including a "sound recording, videotape, film, photograph, chart, graph, map, plan, survey, book of account and information recorded or stored by means of *any device*" [emphasis added].

In *Reichmann v. Toronto Life Publishing Co.*,[46] the Court ordered that the files contained on a computer disk were discoverable as documents pursuant to the *Rules of Procedure*. Similarly, in *NRS Block Brothers Realty Ltd. v. Co-operators Development Corp.*,[47] the Court ordered the production of an internal electronic memorandum despite a claim that it was privileged as it was prepared in preparation of a potential settlement position.[48]

The case of *Nesbitt Burns Inc. v. Lange*[49] involved the use of email evidence to prove that the former vice-president and other former employees had misused the company voice mail and email systems to solicit clients by emailing them confidential and proprietary information. Nesbitt Burns produced this evidence as grounds to seek an interlocutory injunction to restrain the former employees from disclosing any information regarding its clients, and to restrain them from using the client information at their new workplace. Although the Ontario Superior Court admitted the email as evidence, it upheld the motion court judge's decision that Nesbitt Burns had not shown that irreparable harm would result if the injunctive relief were not granted. The Court held that monetary damages would be sufficient compensation for any loss sustained by the broker and dismissed its application for leave to appeal the motion court ruling.

Email was also used as evidence in *Lovelock v. DuPont Canada Inc.*[50] to successfully demonstrate an employee's fraudulent activity and argue dismissal with cause. The employer alleged that the employee had forged his supervisor's signature to approve the employee's expense account for a convention. The employee denied the forgery or that he had engaged in any kind of dishonesty. The company used its email records to show that emails sent by employee to his supervisor proved that the employee's explanation of the events leading to his dismissal did not make sense, were implausible and revealed that he was being dishonest.

On December 14, 2000, the Washington Court of Appeals ruled in the case of *Tiberino v. Spokane County*[51] that personal e-mail messages could not be discovered due to privacy concerns. In this case, the employee had been terminated for sending 467 personal e-mail messages over the course

---

[46] (1988), 66 O.R. (2d) 65 (Ont. H.C.).

[47] (1994), 24 C.P.C. (3d) 132 (Sask Q.B.).

[48] See also *Merck & Co. v. Apotex Inc.*, [1996] 2 F.C. 223 (Fed. T.D.), affirmed (1996), 1996 CarswellNat 100, 1996 CarswellNat 1763 (Fed. C.A.), leave to appeal refused (1997), 1997 CarswellOnt 6337 (S.C.C.) where the Federal Court ordered the production of hard copies of electronic messages.

[49] (2000), 2000 CarswellOnt 1296, [2000] O.J. No. 335 (Ont. S.C.J.).

[50] (1998), 1998 CarswellOnt 4626, [1999] O.J. No. 4971 (Ont. Gen. Div.).

[51] No. 18830-2-III (Wash. App. Div. 3).

of 40 days, many of which contained vulgar language. After she filed a lawsuit for wrongful termination, representatives of the media sought disclosure of 3,805 pages of the e-mail messages being used by the employer to defend its decision. The Court ruled that access to the e-mails would not be granted.

7.1.5   Effect on Employees

Monitoring employee's use of e-mail may lead to employee psychological and physical health problems, increased boredom, high tension, extreme anxiety, depression, anger, severe fatigue, and musculoskeletal problems. In *United States v. White*,[52] the Court summarized other concerns with respect to the effect of monitoring on employees:

> . . . words would be measured a good deal more carefully and communication inhibited if one suspected his conversations were being transmitted and transcribed. Were third-party bugging a prevalent practice, it might well smother that spontaneity-reflected in frivolous, impetuous, sacrilegious, and defiant discourse-that liberates daily life.[53]

Additionally, others argue that as employee autonomy in the workplace is eroded by overly intrusive monitoring practices, so too may employees' inclination towards creativity and experimentation be curtailed. Unwarranted or overzealous monitoring may have a deleterious impact on working conditions:[54]

> When invasions of privacy occur, employees often feel that self-worth, morale, and the overall quality of working life are eroded. The ensuing negative impact of invasions of privacy on work quality and productivity is hidden human and real costs (for example, absenteeism and employee compensation claims), not often calculated by employers.[55]

---

[52] (1970), 401 U.S. 745, at 787-89, cited in *Duarte, supra*, note 15 at 54.

[53] See also Laura Pincus Hartman, "The Rights and Wrongs of Workplace Snooping", *DePaul University*, online: <http://wwww.depaul.edu/ethics/monitor.html>. Research conducted by Swiss economist Bruno Frey found evidence that monitoring worsened employee morale and thereby negatively affected their performance. This was primarily the result of the employees feeling like the employer had low expectations of them because the firm felt the need to monitor.

[54] *Morgan, supra*, note 3.

[55] *Ibid.*

7.1.6   Establishing an E-mail Policy

In light of the *Criminal Code* provisions and the direction provided by the small amount of judicial consideration of the issue, a company considering monitoring employee e-mail should first establish a policy in this respect. At a minimum, the policy should set out the following:

a.   Purposes for which the e-mail system may be used;

b.   Access to email on the part of third parties; and

c.   Consequences of breaches of the e-mail policy.[56]

In developing these policies, attention must be placed on the purposes for which e-mail systems are used, the nature of the information exchanged via e-mail, the business of the organization and the technical limitations of e-mail systems. By informing employees that e-mail messages are subject to monitoring, an employee's expectation of privacy can be reduced or even extinguished.

In addition, a well-established and publicized policy of e-mail monitoring may be the basis for a finding of implied consent, and exempt the employer from liability pursuant to section 184 of the *Criminal Code*. Alternatively, employers may consider requiring employees to consent to monitoring as a term of their employment. If possible, such a policy should be made part of the terms and conditions of employment at the time of hire. Otherwise, signed acknowledgements may be obtained from employees indicating they understand the policy and consent to monitoring.

7.2   VIDEO SURVEILLANCE

7.2.1   Introduction

The widespread use of video surveillance in workplaces raises fundamental questions related to the employee's right to privacy. The information and images that can be captured by video surveillance, such as a person's physical characteristics, voice, speech and mannerisms, are unique and highly personal.[57] The systematic observations of employees, regardless of

---

[56]   Tom Wright, *Privacy Protection Principles for Electronic Mail Systems* (Ontario: Information and Privacy Commissioner, February 1994) at 15, online: <http://www.ipc.on.ca>.

[57]   New South Wales Privacy Committee, "Inquiry into Video Surveillance in the Workplace," c. 3.1 online: <http://www.austlii.edu.au/au/other/privacy/video/31.html>.

any involvement in wrongdoing, is a *prima facie* invasion of privacy. The advent of private sector privacy legislation such as the federal *Personal Information Protection and Electronic Documents Act* is now a further consideration that must be examined when looking at the propriety of video surveillance.

7.2.2   Reasons Cited for Using Video Surveillance

Employers justify implementing surveillance for the following reasons:

1. To prevent theft or the general misappropriation of company resources, and as a protection mechanism against fraud.

2. To enable an employer to document employee actions over a period of time (for example in cases where employee behaviour is difficult to intercept), and also to document misconduct such as sexual harassment and aggression.[58]

3. To ensure employees conform to required health and safety standards and regulations.

4. In the financial service industry (i.e. banks, brokerages, insurance firms, realtors) employers have a special interest in monitoring activities to ensure compliance with federal and local laws.

The significance of the employer's stated objectives for using video surveillance is that the actual use and application of video evidence must match those objectives for surveillance in order for the actual use of the video not to amount to an unreasonable invasion of employee privacy.[59]

---

[58] For example, in the case of *Richardson v. Davis Wire Industries Ltd.* (1997), 28 C.C.E.L. (2d) 101 (B.C. S.C.) at 114: video surveillance was used successfully by an employer to dismiss a long-term employee who was sleeping during his night shift. Justice Kirkpatrick of the British Columbia Supreme Court held that a videotape of an employee engaged in wrongdoing was admissible as evidence in a wrongful dismissal hearing:

> In my view, if the videotape evidence is probative of a matter in issue, and is made in the context of the company's legitimate right to investigate Mr. Richardson's misconduct, then it ought to be admitted.

[59] *U.F.C.W., Local 1000A v. Janes Family Foods* (2006), 2006 CarswellOnt 7588, [2006] O.L.A.A. No. 611 (Ont. Arb. Bd.) Ontario Labour Arbitration, where the arbitrator found that although the digital footage could be useful in determining how a workplace accident occurred, it was not one of the company's central objectives and there was no evidence that the number of accidents was so sig-

7.2.3 Video Surveillance in the Workplace

The legitimacy of the use of video surveillance in the workplace depends on whether there are compelling circumstances to justify such action. An employer must be able to demonstrate a substantial interest which requires protecting through this medium. The installation of video cameras in particular areas will only be permitted if it can be shown that there is an imminent threat in that workplace area of theft or other kinds of crime.[60] It is a matter of balancing competing considerations after recognizing that any use of cameras to observe employees at work is intrinsically objectionable to the person being observed.[61] The degree of objection depends on the way the cameras are deployed and the purpose for which they are used, ranging from unacceptable in the case of constant surveillance of conduct and work performance to non-objectionable in the case of short-term individual application for training purposes.

Video cameras cannot be used to intimidate[62] nor can they be used unless there is a real and substantial suspicion of wrongdoing and they are

---

nificant that it should outweigh the employees' interest in not being under constant camera surveillance and having their images recorded.

[60] Gordon F. Luborsky and John C. O'Reilly, *Employee Surveillance: Defining the Boundaries* (Toronto: Thomson Canada Limited, 1997) at 15.

[61] In a recent case before the Ontario Superior Court of Justice, Clayton Ruby attempted to obtain an order prohibiting the use as evidence of a surveillance camera videotape catching his client allegedly stealing computer equipment from a police station anteroom. In support of his argument that people visiting this room had a reasonable expectation of privacy, Mr. Ruby used footage of a sexual encounter caught on tape by the same camera. He then posed this question to Humphrey J.: "Why would the trysting couple have chosen the room for a sexual encounter if it were not a spot everyone understood to be private?" However, see also *Fraser Surrey Docks Ltd. v. International Longshore and Warehouse Union Ship and Dock Foremen, Local 514 (Skibo Grievance)* [2007] C.L.A.D. No. 48 Canada Labour Arbitration, where preventing the theft of gasoline from the dockyards by employees assisted in justifying surveillance.

[62] See *K-Mart Canada Ltd. v. S.E.I.U., Local 183* (1981), (sub nom. *S.E.I.U., Local 183 v. K-Mart Canada Ltd.*) 81 C.L.L.C. 16,084 (Ont. L.R.B.), where it was held that:

In this case the Board must first consider the impact of the open and continuous surveillance of two employees who were the spearhead of the union organizing campaign. Spying on employees is not new to the catalogue of unfair labour practices resorted to by employers who are extreme in their determination to stop their employees from exercising their collective bargaining rights. This Board has previously found instances of covert surveillance to be unlawful interference with the rights of employees under the Act; (see, for example, used in a reasonable manner.[63] Furthermore, there must be a direct relationship between the use of the video camera and the likelihood that it will address the employer's concerns.[64]

In *Puretex Knitting Co. v. C.T.C.U.*,[65] the employer had installed cameras in work areas for the said purpose of deterring theft. The union, however, argued that the cameras were installed for the purpose of spying on employees and this constituted an abuse of management rights. While it was likely that the surveillance was within the company's management rights, the arbitrator, upon a review of American jurisprudence on this issue, ordered the cameras removed despite his statement that the surveillance was likely within the company's management rights. It was held that the use of video surveillance which would constantly monitor the work performance and conduct of employees was "seriously offensive in human terms". After analysis, only the cameras located in the parking lot, loading dock area and storage areas were allowed to remain.[66]

In *U.A.W., Local 707 v. Ford Motor Co. of Canada*[67] the union objected to the company's use of closed circuit television as part of a remote control system at certain gates of a manufacturing plant. There was no issue of surveillance in this case, rather the cameras simply upset the employees. In actuality, the cameras were installed to enable guards located at other gates to identify those employees seeking entrance through gates where guards were no longer on duty and thereby facilitate the employee's entrance. The arbitrator dismissed the grievance, finding that there had been no change in rules or regulations, rather only a change in the technique of implementing those rules. The new techniques were found not to violate the collective agreement or invade the privacy of the employees.

Tandy Electronics Ltd. v. U.S.W.A., [1979] O.L.R.B. Rep. 248 (Ont. L.R.B.), affirmed (1979), 79 C.L.L.C. 14,216 (Ont. Div. Ct.)). In its very first reported decision the National Labour Relations Board was confronted with the tactic of surveillance as a method of discouraging union activity. From that time to the present, with the endorsement of the Courts, the NLRB has consistently found surveillance or the attempt to create the impression of surveillance of union activity to be unlawful interference with the rights of union association expressly protected by law.

[63] *Labatt, infra*, note 82.

[64] *Ibid.*

[65] (1979), 23 L.A.C. (2d) 14 (Ont. Arb. Bd.).

[66] In *Lenworth Metal Products Ltd. v. U.S.W.A., Local 3950* (2000), 2000 CarswellOnt 4282 (Ont. Div. Ct.), the court decided that the arbitrator's decision to permit non-operational video cameras in the workplace during working hours for internal safety purposes was not "patently unreasonable".

[67] (1971), 23 L.A.C. 96 (Ont. Arb. Bd.).

With the coming into force of the federal *Personal Information Protection and Electronic Documents Act*,[68] we are beginning to see the Privacy Commissioner of Canada issue his findings on the propriety of employers using video surveillance in the workplace.

In one such case,[69] the Commissioner investigated the use of video cameras set up by the employer in order to reduce vandalism and theft. The employer had no intention on monitoring its employees with the camera, and, in fact, when it was discovered that the camera was pointed in a direction that picked up images of the employees, the employer changed the camera's position.

The cameras could rotate and zoom in but they did not record. Notwithstanding that there was no recording, the Commissioner went on to examine if the use of the camera violated section 5(3) of the Act. That section states that an organization may collect, use or disclose personal information only for purposes that a reasonable person would consider are appropriate in the circumstances. In determining the reasonableness of the use, the Commissioner considered the following questions:

(1) Is the measure demonstrably necessary to meet a specific need?

(2) Is it likely to be effective in meeting that need?

(3) Is the loss of privacy proportional to the benefit gained?

(4) Is there a less privacy-invasive way of achieving the same end?

In this case, the Commissioner found that the company failed to prove that the incidents of vandalism were sufficiently serious as to affirmatively answer the first question. Further, the Commissioner questioned the effectiveness of the cameras in deterring the illegal activity and, at the same time, noted that employees may get the perception that their comings and goings were being watched, even if that was not objectively the case. Finally, the Commissioner noted that there were less privacy invasive solutions available, such as installing better lighting. For all those reasons, the Commissioner found that the company's use of this type of video surveillance was in contravention of section 5(3) of the Act and recommended that the company remove the cameras.

As an additional note, the Commissioner also expressed his view that had the company used any information gained through the use of the cameras

---

[68] See Chapter 4.

[69] Reported online: Office of the Privacy Commissioner of Canada <http// www.privcom.gc.ca> as *PIPED Act Case Summary #114*.

as part of any disciplinary action against an employee, the Commissioner would have strongly interpreted such use as inappropriate.

While it is impossible to be completely certain, this matter addressed by the Commissioner appears to have been challenged in the Federal Court in *Eastmond v. Canadian Pacific Railway.*[70] The Court ultimately made several findings of fact that were different than the Commissioner (because the evidence before the Court was different than that before the Commissioner), and ultimately the Court came to a different conclusion.

Importantly, the Court noted that the issue of an employer using video surveillance is something that can give rise to the application of *PIPEDA* and thus can result in the Privacy Commissioner and, ultimately, the Federal Court in having the jurisdiction to evaluate the correctness of such use.[71]

The Court was prepared to adopt the test applied by the Commissioner (referred to above) and thus first had to determine if the use of the video surveillance was reasonable. In doing so, the Court also agreed to take into account the four-part test developed by the Commissioner when he was tasked into looking into the reasonableness of the use of the surveillance. While emphasizing that this necessarily was a very contextual and fact specific type of analysis, the Court, with the aid of established arbitral jurisprudence in the area, came to the conclusion that a reasonable person would consider the purposes of the video surveillance to be appropriate. Specifically, the Court noted the following in support of this conclusion:

> The collection of personal information is not surreptitious - warning signs are displayed. The collection of personal information is not continuous - it is brief, capturing only a person's image when that person is within the footprint of the camera. The collection is not limited to CP employees - it captures the images of contractors, visitors, suppliers and trespassers. The collection is not to measure a CP employee's work performance and while it is true a camera may occasionally capture a CP employee at work outside the shops, CP could not use those images to measure that employee's productivity because such a use of the information would be a use for a purpose other than that which prompted its collection as a security measure. More importantly, the recorded images are kept under lock and key and the recordings are only accessed by responsible managers and CP police if there is an incident reported. If there are no incidents recorded which require investigations, the recordings are destroyed within an appropriate time frame. The evidence satisfies me CP has established a legitimate need to have the cameras installed where they were

---

[70] 2004 FC 852, 2004 CarswellNat 1842 (F.C.).

[71] Contrast with *L'Ecuyer c. Aéroports de Montréal*, 2003 FCT 573, 2003 CarswellNat 1286, 2003 CarswellNat 2621 (Fed. T.D.), affirmed 2004 CarswellNat 4173, 2004 CAF 237 (F.C.A.).

and to record those persons who would pass its fixed footprints. While the cross-examination of CP deponents established, in some cases, a lack of correlation between camera location and incidents and, in other cases, between cause of loss, I am satisfied, on the whole of the evidence, CP identified numerous past incidents which justify the need to have surveillance cameras in place.[72]

Furthermore, the Court found that the use of the cameras would meet the employer's needs because the cameras were an effective deterrent and the purpose of the surveillance was to stop wrongdoing. Lastly, the Court found that the loss of privacy was minimal and said:

> Indeed, if there were no recorded incidents, it means none of the images captured by the cameras were viewed. The Privacy Commissioner was of the view a person whose images might be recorded had a low expectation of privacy because the cameras were located to capture personal information in locations which were public places. I share his assessment. Generally, such a view accords with the thrust of the cases decided by the Supreme Court of Canada in section 8 Charter cases where an analysis of a reasonable expectation of privacy is weighed.

> On this point, it must be remembered the recordings are never viewed unless an incident requiring an investigation occurs. This factor, coupled with my findings of how and what the cameras capture, lead me to conclude the loss of privacy is proportional to the benefit gained from their collection.[73]

On the last part of the test (*i.e.*, whether there was a less privacy-invasive way of achieving the desired purpose), the Court was satisfied that the employer looked at alternatives such as installing fences and hiring additional security guards and weighed them in the context of its operations.

Having found that the purposes were reasonably appropriate to warrant video surveillance, the Court then went on to consider if the PIPEDA consent requirements were met. Interestingly, the Court concludes on this point that the collection of the person's information only takes place when the employer views the recording to investigate an incident of wrongdoing. Then the Court assumes that if the recording captured a wrongdoing, asking the wrongdoer's permission would compromise the availability of the information for the purpose of the investigation. That being the case, the exception to PIPEDA's general requirement that consent be obtained was available to the employer.

---

[72] *Eastmond, supra,* note 70 at paras. 176-177.

[73] *Ibid.,* at paras. 180-181.

In a recent decision by the Assistant Privacy Commissioner of Canada, the Assistant Commissioner determined that a company's video surveillance of workstations of employees was unreasonable pursuant to the four-step test.[74] The Canadian Food Inspection Agency (CFIA) employee worked as a "Veterinarian in Charge" at a federally registered meat processing plant and complained that the company was collecting his personal information by video surveillance without his consent. The plant manager had installed the video cameras without consulting the CFIA or establishing related policies and procedures. The cameras were motion activated but did not have pan or zoom capabilities, and images were recorded onto the hard drive. The company claimed to use video surveillance to monitor hygiene and safety, and address security concerns, despite the fact that CFIA inspectors and a Veterinarian in Charge were always on site, and that the cameras were not focused on workstations at other federal facilities. Further, while the complainant was told that the cameras would not be used to observe him when they were initially installed, there were documented examples of instances where the company had disclosed the employee's personal information to his supervisor at the CFIA. However, the videotaping of employees at personal workstations had ceased after *PIPEDA* was enacted on January 1, 2001; therefore, any violation of their privacy prior to *PIPEDA* was outside the Assistant Privacy Commissioner's jurisdiction.

The Assistant Privacy Commissioner held that no evidence was provided to support that the surveillance was important for monitoring food safety, particularly when the individuals responsible for monitoring food safety worked on site. The use of video surveillance did not appear to be demonstrably necessary or useful to ensuring food safety, and the focus of the cameras on the CFIA inspectors' workstations without their consent clearly constituted an invasion of their privacy. The Assistant Privacy Commissioner recommended that the company remove the cameras from the area where the inspectors' workstations were located and warned the company that it could only use personal information that it deliberately collected without employee consent pursuant to section 7(2)(a) and (b) of *PIPEDA*, specifically, if consent could not be obtained in a timely way or if the employees' knowledge, or consent of such collection would compromise the availability or the accuracy of the information and the collection is reasonable for purposes related to investigating a breach of an agreement or contravention of a Canadian law.

In cases where *PIPEDA* does not apply and a collective agreement explicitly or implicitly permits the installation of video surveillance, its use must still satisfy the reasonableness standard, which the arbitrator in *United*

---

[74] Privacy Commissioner of Canada, January 27, 2005, Summary #290.

Food and Commercial Workers International Union, Local 1000A v. Janes Family Foods (Surveillance Grievance)[75] found to be the same whether under *PIPEDA* or within the language of the collective agreement.

Further, in certain jurisdictions, the collection, use and disclosure of personal information by private sector businesses, non-profit organizations and professional regulatory organizations is governed by privacy legislation enacted by those jurisdictions, provided that the relevant laws are deemed "substantially similar" to *PIPEDA*. This is, for example, the case in Alberta where the *Personal Information Protection Act* ("PIPA") came into force on January 1, 2004. Notably, unlike *PIPEDA*, section 1(j) of *PIPA* specifically defines "employee personal information" as "personal information reasonably required by an organization that is collected, used or disclosed solely for the purposes of establishing, managing or terminating . . . an employment relationship . . . between the organization and the individual but does not include personal information about the individual that is unrelated to that relationship."

Under sections 15, 18 and 21 of the Act, employers may collect, use and disclose employees' personal information without their consent subject to three conditions: (1) the collection, use or disclosure "is reasonable for the purposes for which the information is being collected," (2) the information "is related to the employment . . . relationship," and (3) the employer first gives the employee "reasonable notification" of the purposes for which the information is to be collected, used or disclosed.

In a related case, an employee complained to the Alberta Privacy Commissioner that he had been terminated from his job as a result of some private communication between him and another worker after his employer, an oilfields maintenance services company, installed motion-activated video surveillance cameras on the premises of the maintenance workshop.[76] The company contended that the cameras did not record and therefore could not intercept any private communications of employees. The purposes cited for the installation of the cameras were the safety and security of the workplace, detection and deterrence of theft and management of employee performance.

The Alberta *PIPA* Director conducted an investigation and determined that there was no collection of private communication, therefore, the complaint of improper collection and use of information about an identifiable individual by video cameras was not well-founded. Notwithstanding, she reviewed the reasonableness of the collection of other information about

---

[75] *Ibid.*
[76] Information and Privacy Commissioner for Alberta, Investigation Report P2005-IR-004, May 13, 2005.

identifiable individuals through the use of video surveillance, and was satisfied that the employer had used the surveillance and collected the information solely for the purpose of managing the employment relationship. However, the Director reiterated that *PIPA* stipulated that personal information being collected under the Act should be "reasonably required" by the employer and the collection and use thereof had to be reasonable for the purposes for which the information is being collected, pursuant to sections 15(2) and 18(2). Thus, in an attempt to assess the reasonableness of the collection and use of the information in question by the employer, she formulated a three-step test:

(1) whether there are legitimate issues that the organization needs to address through surveillance;

(2) whether the surveillance is likely to be effective in addressing these issues; and

(3) whether the surveillance is conducted in a reasonable manner.

Applying this test to the facts in this situation, the *PIPA* Director concluded that the company's use of surveillance met the reasonableness test for the purposes of workplace safety and security, but failed to meet it with respect to the use of the cameras to manage employee performance. While she acknowledged that the employer had an interest in ensuring that employees are fulfilling their work commitments, the Director held that this interest alone did not mean that collection and use of personal information through video surveillance is reasonably necessary to manage employees. This conclusion was based on the employer's failure to demonstrate that the employees were doing anything other than performing their job duties as expected. Moreover, in the Director's opinion, "surveillance cameras would [not] be any more effective in meeting the perceived need to monitor employee performance than a well-timed visit from a supervisor."

7.2.4   Video Surveillance outside the Workplace

Employers engage in video surveillance of employees outside of the workplace because of concerns that employee absences are not due to legitimate illnesses or injuries. Employers are also generally skeptical with respect to the medical profession's ability to diagnose the actual extent of an employee's alleged disability. These concerns, coupled with the fact that employee absences cause the employer to incur great costs in long term disability and workers compensation premiums, are the impetus behind video surveillance outside of the workplace.

Within the context of arbitration decisions there are, broadly speaking, two approaches in analyzing whether to admit video surveillance into evidence.[77] The first approach, adopted in the recent decision of *Greater Toronto Airports Authority v. P.S.A.C.*,[78] holds that arbitrators have no discretionary basis on which to exclude video or other evidence, and that the only considerations are whether it has relevance to the proceeding and is not prejudicial.[79]

In *Greater Toronto Airports Authority*, Arbitrator Bendel stated that the Supreme Court of Canada's decision in *R. v. Wray*[80] is still authoritative in situations where the *Charter* does not apply, "therefore, courts are not concerned with the manner in which evidence is obtained, nor do they have the discretion to reject relevant evidence on the ground that its admission would bring the administration of justice into disrepute." In discussing the "reasonableness" approach whereby the employer's rights are balanced with the privacy rights of employees, the arbitrator stated that these arbitral awards "proceed on the wholly mistaken assumption that there exists a discretion to exclude evidence that is tainted by an invasion of privacy. . . I am unable to detect any point in these discussions about the existence of a right to privacy." The arbitrator in this case seems to indicate that the exclusion of evidence due to a violation of privacy rights is not permitted

---

[77] The two approaches were recently discussed in *C.U.P.E., Local 27 v. Greater Essex County District School Board* (2006), [2006] O.L.A.A. No. 355, 2006 CarswellOnt 7341 (Ont. Arb. Bd.), Ontario Labour Arbitration and *I.U.E.C., Local 50 v. ThyssenKrupp Elevator (Canada) Ltd.* (2006), [2006] O.L.R.D. No. 1818, 2006 CarswellOnt 9139 (Ont. L.R.B.), Ontario Labour Relations Board.

[78] (Buehler Grievance) (2007), [2007] C.L.A.D. No. 1, 2007 CarswellNat 353 (Can. Arb. Bd.) Canada Labour Arbitration. In this case, an employer hired a private investigator to conduct covert video surveillance of an employee on extended sick leave for a sore elbow. She had overdrawn on her sick pay account, but was in frequent contact with the employer and continuously provided notes from her chiropractor as to her need to avoid work. The notes did not indicate any progress or further treatment. Her Supervisor was concerned that he had received no indication of any improvement in the Grievor's condition, new medical initiatives or date for an expected return to work. The arbitrator held that the video evidence was admissible.

[79] 2007 Can LII 21 (ON L.A.). Other decisions following this "relevance" approach are *Kimberly-Clark Inc. v. IWA-Canada, Local 1-92-4* (1996), 66 L.A.C. (4th) 266 (Ont. Arb. Bd.), (Bendel), *Toronto Transit Commission v. A.T.U., Local 113* (1999), 79 L.A.C. (4th) 85 (Ont. Arb. Bd.) (Solomatenko) and *Canadian Timken Ltd. v. U.S.W.A., Local 4906* (2001), 98 L.A.C. (4th) 129 (Ont. Arb. Bd.) (Welling).

[80] [1971] S.C.R. 272 (S.C.C.).

unless the *Charter* directly applies. In *Greater Essex County District School Board*, Arbitrator Hunter points out that this approach does not mean reasonableness is irrelevant, but should instead be considered when weighing the evidence once admitted to the proceedings.

The second "reasonableness" approach, on the other hand, holds that certain conditions must be met before an arbitrator will accept video surveillance evidence of an employee engaging in activities inconsistent with their alleged disability. In deciding whether to admit video surveillance evidence, the privacy rights of the employee must be balanced against the employer's rights to investigate potential abuses of employment benefits.

In *Alberta Wheat Pool v. Grain Workers' Union, Local 333*[81], the arbitrator held that:

> [C]onducting surveillance on an employee and videotaping his or her conduct without knowledge or consent will amount to a breach of the employee's right to privacy, unless such intrusive conduct can be demonstrably justified by the employer. The onus of establishing that justification rests with the employer.
>
> In the course of that investigation, however, before the employer goes so far as to intrude on the right to an employee's privacy, it must be able to justify that such a course is the only one open to it and the only way in which the truth can be ascertained.

In making a determination as to the admissibility of video surveillance evidence, the analysis will entail the following questions:

(i)   Was it reasonable, in all the circumstances, to request surveillance?

(ii)   Was the surveillance conducted in a reasonable manner?

(iii)   Were other alternatives open to the company to obtain the evidence it sought?[82]

---

[81] (1995), 48 L.A.C. (4th) 332 (B.C. Arb. Bd.) at 341.

[82] See *Doman Forest Products Ltd. v. I.W.A., Local 1-357* (1990), 13 L.A.C. (4th) 275 (B.C. Arb. Bd.). Note that there has been a marked difference in arbitration decisions from provinces with privacy legislation in place from those which have not enacted a *Privacy Act*. For example, in *Doman* and *Steels Industrial Products, infra*, note 90, the arbitrators took "Charter values" into account when balancing the rights of the parties. That case took place in British Columbia where legislation governing privacy rights between private litigants is enacted. Conversely, in *Labatt Ontario Breweries (Toronto Brewery) v. Brewery, General & Professional Workers Union, Local 304* (1994), 42 L.A.C. (4th) 151 (Ont. Arb. Bd.) the arbitrator found that the absence of such privacy legislation in Ontario precluded

In some cases, the arbitrators have effectively incorporated question 3 into 1.[83] In general, video surveillance will never be "reasonable" unless the circumstances demonstrate that the employee's alleged injury/ disability may not be legitimate.[84] Further, cases for admissibility will be strengthened where the employer can demonstrate that they have taken less intrusive steps to confirm such suspicions before resorting to surveillance. For example, an employer should offer modified duties,[85] confront the employee of its suspicions, or demand further medical verification of the disability[86] before resorting to the use of video surveillance.

The three part admissibility test outlined above was first implemented in *Doman Forest Products Ltd. v. I.W.A., Local 1-357*,[87] a British Columbia decision that addressed the admissibility of video tape surveillance evidence. Video surveillance was conducted by an employer who had suspicions that the employee did not legitimately suffer from injury. The union challenged the videotape's admissibility at the arbitration. The arbitrator applied the three part test outlined above, and determined that the video surveillance was inadmissible.

The same test was applied in the Ontario case, *Labatt Ontario Breweries (Toronto Brewery) v. Brewery, General & Professional Workers Un-*

---

the application of such "Charter values". Notwithstanding this distinction, all the arbitration decisions appear to point to a consensus that the three-part test (or a modified two-step version) is to be applied.

[83] See *infra*, note 90; *Labatt, ibid.*

[84] See *New Flyer Industries Ltd. v. CAW-Canada, Local 3003* (2000), (sub nom. *New Flyer Industries Ltd. v. C.A.W.-Canada, Local 3003*) 85 L.A.C. (4th) 304 (Man. Arb. Bd.). See also *Toronto Transit Commission v. A.T.U., Local 113* (1999), 95 L.A.C. (4th) 402 (Ont. Arb. Bd.) in which the Arbitrator held that the employer's decision to continue conducting surveillance of the employee's home, after successfully contacting the employee in question, was unreasonable.

[85] See *Labatt, supra*, note 82.

[86] See *Air Canada v. C.U.P.E.*, [1995] C.L.A.D. No. 114 (Can. Arb. Bd.) where an employer hired a private investigator to undertake video surveillance of a flight attendant who suffered a lower back injury while at work. The arbitrator applied the three part test set out in *Doman, supra*, note 82, and refused to admit the videotape evidence. Significant was the fact that the employer had been suspicious for a long while and yet never had its medical director or other medical staff carry out examinations of the employee. It was held that it was not reasonable in all the circumstances for the employer to conduct video surveillance of the employee without first confronting the employee of its suspicions and further informing her that it intended to pursue the matter to ascertain the state of her health.

[87] *Supra*, note 82.

ion, Local 304.[88] The employer had conducted video surveillance of an employee because of repeated absenteeism from work. This particular time, the employee had been absent from work due to an alleged car accident. The video surveillance showed the employee engaged in strenuous physical activity of a kind which did not correspond to an individual who was to be physically incapacitated. The arbitrator found that the employee's absenteeism did not justify the surveillance, given that the company appeared to treat such absenteeism as non-culpable. The arbitrator took particular account of the fact that no offer of modified work was ever made to the employee despite the company having a modified work program in place.

The arbitrator in *Walbar Canada Inc. v. U.S.A., Local 9236*,[89] applied a modified version of the three part test (*i.e.* a two question test).[90] The employer felt that the employee's injured ankle should not have prevented his return to work and terminated his employment when he failed to attend three separate pre-arranged appointments to have his ankle examined by the company doctor. The employer then conducted video surveillance of the employee so as to collect further evidence to use as additional grounds for his termination. The union held that this was an invasion of the employee's privacy.

Two points were determinative with respect to the first part of the test. First, the medical staff and the employee's own doctor diagnosed the injury as a minor one and that full recovery would take place within two to three weeks. Additionally, as the employee avoided all contact with the employer, this prevented the employer from communicating with the employee and being informed as to the extent of the injury. Second, the employer received information that the employee was working as a superintendent in an apartment building, notwithstanding his alleged total disability.

As for the second part of the test, the arbitrator found that the video surveillance was conducted in a reasonable manner since it was carried out on public property where the employee was open to public scrutiny. Consequently, the surveillance was not intrusive in the sense that it did not seek to trespass upon private places, such as the employee's apartment. Accordingly, the arbitrator held that it was reasonable for the employer to request

---

[88] *Labatt, supra,* note 82.
[89] Dated April 22, 1993, unreported.
[90] This two-part test is from *Steels Industrial Products v. Teamsters Union, Local 213* (1991), 24 L.A.C. (4th) 259 (B.C. Arb. Bd.) where the arbitrator found that the third question in the *Doman* test could be considered part of the first. See also *Greater Vancouver Regional District v. G.V.R.D.E.U.* (1996), 57 L.A.C. (4th) 113 (B.C. Arb. Bd.) where the arbitrator, upon review of the case law, applied the two-part formulation of the test for admissibility as set out in *Steels.*

the surveillance, and further, that the surveillance was conducted in a reasonable manner.

Another factor in evaluating the reasonableness of video surveillance is dishonesty. Examples of an employee's previous dishonesty will further justify an employer's choice to undertake video surveillance and may obviate the need for the steps described above. In particular, arbitrators have appreciated that it may not be realistic to confront an employee with suspicions where the employee has demonstrated dishonesty.[91]

For example, in *Canadian Pacific Ltd. v. Brotherhood of Maintenance of Way Employees*[92] an employee was terminated when video surveillance evidence undertaken by the employer showed that he was not suffering, as alleged, from a work-related back injury. The employer conducted the video surveillance for the following reasons: a supervisor observed the employee walking with no signs of discomfort four days after the alleged injury; a doctor who first examined the employee reported that he felt that the employee was "pulling a scam" and that there was nothing wrong with him; the employee had provided false information to the Workers' Compensation Board in a previous application for benefits; and the employee had a long record of absenteeism caused by on-the-job injuries. The union objected to the admissibility of the videotape stating that it was an invasion of privacy.

Upon review of the case law the arbitrator set out the test in terms of the following two-part analysis:

1. Was it reasonable, in all of the circumstances, to undertake surveillance of the employee's off-duty activity?

2. Was the surveillance conducted in a reasonable way, which is not unduly intrusive and which corresponds fairly with acquiring information pertinent to the employer's legitimate interests?

Applying the test, the arbitrator held that conducting video surveillance was justifiable in this case. The arbitrator determined that the employer did not have any other reasonable alternatives open to it given the employee's prior willingness to deceive the Workers Compensation Board, and the medical opinion that the employee was pretending to be disabled. In fact, the arbitrator stated that it would have been "naively unrealistic, and indeed counterproductive to determining the truth, for the Company to have com-

---

[91] *Canadian Pacific Ltd. v. B.M.W.E.* (1996), 59 L.A.C. (4th) 111 (Can. Arb. Bd.).
[92] *Ibid.*

municated its suspicions or concerns to the employee . . ., as it had little reason to expect a truthful answer".[93]

The actual type or nature of the supposed injury is another factor which plays into the reasonableness of surveillance. If the injury is difficult to verify medically, then a doctor's report may be deemed to be of limited usefulness. In these circumstances, surreptitious surveillance may be the only practical way to confirm suspicions.[94]

When the employer is an arm of government, the protection found in section 8 of the *Canadian Charter of Rights and Freedoms* will also be a consideration in determining if video surveillance is permissible. In *A.T.U., Local 569 v. Edmonton (City)*,[95] the Court of Queen's Bench concluded that the Charter was applicable and rejected the city's argument that the Charter was not engaged when the city was involved in private actions such as dealings with its employees. The Court reasoned, however, that it is not the nature of the act that exposes the city to Charter standards, it is the fact of the city's status as a form of government entity.

The Court continued its analysis and looked at the issue of whether or not the employees in this instance had a reasonable expectation of privacy. Relying heavily on Supreme Court jurisprudence, the Court said that if an individual has reasonable grounds to believe his communications are private in the sense that his words will only be heard by the person he is addressing, the unauthorized surreptitious electronic recording of those communications will be perceived as an intrusion on a reasonable expectation of privacy. However, the Court also expressed its opinion that, since the Charter did not create a right to privacy itself (just a right to be free from an invasion of that privacy), any violation of the section 8 Charter protection could only occur if an individual reasonably feels, wants or believes that his or her actions are or ought to remain private.

Importantly, the Court then says:

> It is generally thought that when an individual is in a public place, his or her actions are not private at all, but fully public. In those circumstances, it cannot be said that the individual has a reasonable expectation of privacy. This is not an application of the risk analysis rejected in *Duarte*, but is an acknowledge-

---

[93] The company had also offered the employee modified duties and the evidence was recorded in areas where the employee was visible to the public.

[94] See *Western Grocers v. U.F.C.W.U., Local 1400* (unreported) a Saskatchewan decision dated July 21, 1995 where it was held that is was reasonable to conduct the video surveillance since the nature of the injury was such that there were no objective tests to prove the extent of pain and there were few other alternatives open to the employer to obtain the evidence sought.

[95] 2004 ABQB 280, 2004 CarswellAlta 435 (Alta. Q.B.).

ment that the privacy that people can expect to enjoy in our society does not generally extend to their public activities.

Later, the Court acknowledged that some public action may still attract a reasonable expectation of privacy if the circumstances are right, but in this case, the surveillance undertaken by the city was of a public place and was of public activities engaged by an employee. The employee was in a place of business open to the public and there was no evidence that the employee took precautions from being observed. Therefore, he could not have a reasonable expectation of privacy.[96]

The introduction of private sector privacy legislation is now also making its way into the mix when deciding if the use of video surveillance to monitor employees outside the workforce is appropriate. In *Ross v. Rosedale Transport Ltd.*,[97] the arbitrator was faced with a claim by a laid-off employee that the employer's use of video surveillance was contrary to the *Personal Information Protection and Electronic Documents Act* and therefore could not be admitted as evidence in the grievance proceeding.

The employee had been fired because the employer believed the employee was not as injured as the employee had explained. Because of the employee's alleged injury, he had been re-assigned but the employer became suspicious that the employee's alleged back injury was not that serious when he found out that the employee was going to help family members move over the weekend. The employer surreptitiously obtained video footage of the employee over the course of the weekend and later terminated him as a result of the faked injury.

First in dealing with the jurisdictional and threshold questions raised, the arbitrator said:

> It is common ground between the parties that the Act applies to Rosedale as it is a federal work, undertaking or business and interprovincial in nature, as the trucking operations extend beyond the borders of the Province of Ontario. It was also my view and remains that the video surveillance as captured on tape contains personal information, namely, the physical movements of an identifiable individual in carrying furniture from his house to a truck parked in his driveway.

---

[96] Without explaining why, the Court then found that since the employee did not have a reasonable expectation of privacy (or any other right to privacy found in law), the video tape surveillance could be used against him in employment related matters. The Court seems to have ignored the remaining tests for admissibility of such evidence that exist notwithstanding whether or not the Charter is triggered.

[97] (2003), 2003 CarswellNat 3620, [2003] C.L.A.D. No. 237 (Can. Arb. Bd.).

Then the arbitrator examined section 7(1)(b) of the Act, which stipulates that an organization may collect personal information without the knowledge or consent of the individual only if it is reasonable to expect that the collection with the knowledge or consent of the individual would compromise the availability or the accuracy of the information and the collection is reasonable for purposes related to investigating a breach of an agreement. The arbitrator quickly conceded that there was no doubt that had the employee known about the collection, that it would have compromised the accuracy of the information collected.

However, the arbitrator continued by examining the first part of the test in section 7(1)(b), *i.e.*, whether or not the video surveillance was reasonable for purposes related to investigating a breach of his employment agreement. In the arbitrator's view, the principles emanating from previous jurisprudence[98] on the issue of video surveillance played a key role in determining this part of the question:

> In my opinion, these general principles are also apposite in the interpretation of section 7(1) of the Act given the purpose of the Act as prescribed in section 3. In my view, the question that must be answered is whether or not it was reasonable for Rosedale to conduct the video surveillance without the knowledge and consent of Ross for purposes related to the investigation of an alleged breach of the employment agreement.

In this case, there was absolutely no other reason or previous conduct that warranted suspicion. There were also a number of other means available to the employer to test the veracity of the employee's injury allegations. Quoting *Canadian Pacific Ltd. v. Brotherhood of Maintenance of Way Employees*, the arbitrator said:

> As a general rule, (the employer's interests) does not justify resort to random video surveillance in the form of an electronic web, cast like a net, to see what it might catch. Surveillance is an extraordinary step which can only be resorted to where there is, beforehand, reasonable and probable cause to justify it. What constitutes such cause is a matter to be determined on the facts of each case.

---

[98] The arbitrator quoted *Transit Windsor v. A.T.U., Local 616* (2001), 99 L.A.C. (4th) 295 (Ont. Arb. Bd.) for the proposition that the following three questions (referred to above) had to be looked at when performing the balancing act between the employee's right of privacy and the employer's right to protect its own interest: (1) Was it reasonable, in all the circumstances, to request a surveillance? (2) Was the surveillance conducted in a reasonable manner? (3) Were other alternatives open to the company to obtain the evidence it sought?

Having concluded that the use of video surveillance was not reasonable, the arbitrator found that the personal information had been collected in violation of the Act and excluded the evidence.

The analysis undertaken by the arbitrator in *Ross* seems consistent with the analysis adopted by the federal Assistant Privacy Commissioner when the issue of surreptitious videotaping was brought before her as a possible violation of the *Personal Information Protection and Electronic Documents Act*. In *PIPED Act Case Summary #269*, the Assistant Privacy Commissioner was asked to rule that an employer's hiring of a private investigator to capture video evidence of an employee performing tasks inconsistent with the employee's assertions of injury. However, in all the circumstances of that matter, the Assistant Commissioner found that the purposes of the collection of personal information by use of the video camera was reasonable in the circumstances. In coming to this conclusion, she found that the employer supplied ample evidence: to prove the organization's suspicion that the relationship of trust had been broken, that showed that it has exhausted all other means of obtaining the information that it required in less privacy-invasive ways, and that it limited the collection to the purposes to the greatest extent possible.

7.2.5   EMERGING SURVEILLANCE ISSUES

In addition to the use of video and e-mail surveillance in the workplace, new technologies are further expanding the ways in which employers can monitor employee conduct and performance at work. Modern networked systems can interrogate computers to determine which software is being run, how often, and in what manner. Audit trails provide employers with a profile of each employee and a complete view of how workers interact with their machines. Software programs allow employers to control individual computers and remotely modify or suspend programs on any machine. Employers can measure how much an employee is using their computer by the amount of time the computer is idle during the day and by calculating the number of keystrokes the employee enters into a word processing program within a specified time. Certain inexpensive programs enable employers to compile and analyze the above-mentioned information to develop performance profiles of their employees.[99]

---

[99] Marc Rotenberg & Cedric Laurant, "Privacy & Human Rights 2004: An International Survey of Privacy Laws and Developments", November 2004 at 58, 59, online: Privacy International <http://www.privacyinternational.org>.

A recent case in Alberta illustrates, however, that there are limits to employers' use of such technology.[100] The Parkland Regional Library installed keystroke logging software on the computer of an information technology employee, unbeknownst to the employee, due to the Director's concerns about the employee's work performance. When the employee discovered the software, he disabled the program and filed a complaint with Alberta's Privacy Commissioner. The Privacy Commissioner stated that despite the fact that no one other than the complainant himself read the information collected prior to the program being disabled, the material was personal information. Even if most or all of the information that was collected from the employee was work-related activity, all of it had a personal component in this case because it was used to determine how much work he did, or his style or manner of doing it, or his own choices and how to prioritize it. Additionally, the employee's banking information was collected by the software program.

The library relied on section 33(c) of the *Freedom of Information and Protection of Privacy Act*, R.S.A. 2000, c. F-25, which permits the collection of information relating directly to and necessary for an operating program or activity of a public body, to argue that the collection was necessary to manage the employee due to concerns about his productivity and his use of his time at work. However, on reviewing the evidence, the Privacy Commissioner expressed doubt that a perceived shortfall in the employee's productivity prompted the decision to install the keystroke logging software. Rather, the Director's testimony indicated that the software was installed following the employee's performance appraisal interview because she felt that he had not 'heard' her concerns that he was not a 'team player' and was too independent in his approach to problem-solving. Further, the Privacy Commissioner noted that during the interview, the Director had not raised any concern with the employee about his lack of productivity, use of his working time or his way of prioritizing tasks. Therefore, it was unclear as to what concerns prompted the Director to direct the installation of the software.

The Privacy Commissioner held that the Parkland Library did not have the authority under section 33 of the Act to collect the complainant's personal information through keystroke logging, and stated that information collected by keystroke logging software becomes "necessary" within the meaning of section 33(c) of the Act only when there is no less intrusive way of collecting sufficient information to address a particular management

---

[100] Alberta Office of Information and Privacy Commissioner, Order F2005-003, June 24, 2005.

issue. In this case, there were less-intrusive means available for the library to effectively manage its employees.

Other technologies, such as location badges and geostationary satellite-based mobile communications systems can track the geographic movements of mobile workers to ensure that they can be located at all times.[101] Some telephone surveillance systems can record and analyze all phone transactions and determine patterns of use by grouping calls into networks. Employers can also monitor or access employees' voice mail systems via default pass codes.[102]

Biometrics is also providing employers with advanced methods of enhancing workplace security. In one case, bank employees complained to the Privacy Commissioner that their employer required them to consent to the collection of biometric information, specifically their voice print, so that the employees could access the bank's business applications, which were used to document work-related information and report employee absences. The employees considered this an invasion of privacy and also objected to the system prompting them to provide a reason for their absences (though they were unaware that providing reasons was not obligatory, since this was not evident to users of the applications).

---

[101] In *PIPEDA* Case Summary #351, November 9, 2006, the employer installed GPS systems in the vehicles that were used by field employees. The employer asserted the need to manage workforce productivity, ensure safety and development and protect and manage assets as its reasons for installing the technology. To manage workforce productivity, the GPS would be used to locate, dispatch and route employees to job sites. To ensure safety and development, the GPS would be used to determine if a vehicle had remained stationary for an inordinate amount of time and could provide an indication that the employee's safety may be at risk. As well, the information gathered by GPS could identify those employees who required defensive/safe driver training or individual coaching based on speed statistics. To manage assets, the GPS on a vehicle's location would be used to retrieve it in the event that it was stolen, abandoned or scheduled for maintenance. The GPS did not contact managers if an employee was not following policy or adhering to road safety. The Assistant Privacy Commissioner applied the same test that is used to determine whether video surveillance is appropriate (see section 7.2 – *Video Surveillance*) and found that GPS, in and of itself, is not highly privacy-invasive because it only tells "part of the story." The Assistant Privacy Commissioner decided that GPS was acceptable in this instance but warned the employer about the potential to evaluate the performance of an individual based on inferences drawn from GPS data. Doing so would shift the balance significantly towards the "loss of privacy" end of the spectrum.

[102] *Supra* note 100 at 59.

The biometrics in question involved accessing a portal that used voice password technology to authenticate company employees by way of identifying the behavioural and physical characteristics of the way that an employee speaks. The bank provided the employees with documents that explained the technology, its purposes and uses, and assured them that their voice prints were secured in a tightly controlled database. Few individuals at the bank had the authority to view or remove a voice print record, and voice prints could not be altered or reverse engineered to synthesize a voice. Voice prints were to be deleted one month after an employee was no longer eligible to use the system and the technology company claimed that a voice print could only be used to identify an employee to log on to the system.

The employer claimed that the applications using voice password technology were introduced for the purposes of security, efficiency, and cost-effectiveness. The Assistant Commissioner stated that job requirements which infringe on employees' privacy must be assessed in accordance with the reasonable person test under section 5(3) of *PIPEDA*, and held that while a voice print was an invasion of privacy on the person, she did not consider that the print disclosed much information about the employee in the circumstances of this case. In balancing the employees' privacy rights against the bank's needs, a reasonable person would likely view the bank's purposes to be appropriate. The purposes for the voice print system were reasonable and had been explained to the employees, and an alternative system was not likely to provide the same level of security. However, the Assistant Commissioner held that the system component which prompted employees to disclose medical reasons for work-related absences was excessive and requested that the company change the application to exclude the requirement for such information.[103]

In *PIPEDA* Case Summary #264,[104] an employee was concerned with the employer's new security measures, which included facial recognition swipe cards. When employees swiped their cards, their pictures would appear on the computer terminal screen in the control booth at the main entrance. The security guard could then compare the picture on the card with the features of the person that he or she sees on the digital cameras posted at entry points, and refuse entry to an individual if there was a concern. The Assistant Privacy Commissioner found that the information collected achieved its purpose of implementing enhanced security measures in accordance with section 5(3) of the Act, and that facial recognition swipe cards were permitted as a reasonable means of achieving those purposes.

---

[103] Privacy Commissioner of Canada, September 3rd, 2004, Summary #281.
[104] See online: Office of the Privacy Commissioner of Canada <http://www.privcom.gc.ca>.

In *Canada Safeway Ltd. and U.F.C.W., Loc. 401 (Re)*,[105] the employer introduced a hand scanning system at three of its facilities. On entering and exiting these facilities, employees would place their hands on a scanning device which verified their identities and recorded the time of entrance or exit. The information was used for payroll and attendance purposes, replacing the time clock and punch card system that had previously been in place. The employer testified that information was stored on company servers, and computer access was restricted to management personnel on a "need to know" basis. The hardware was physically located in locked rooms. Once an employee's information was removed from the hand scanner device, the information was also removed from the main computer system. The computer system which stored the template information was backed up every day using a digital tape system and the tape was reused every ten days, erasing the stored data. The tapes were also kept in a locked room and there were no archival tapes created and kept elsewhere. In the result, the arbitrator found that the employer had justified the use of a hand scanning system and that it was not a violation of the collective agreement. However, in *IKO Industries Ltd. v. U.S.W.A., Local 8580*,[106] the arbitrator found that a finger scan system that was to be used for payroll and timekeeping purposes contravened the 'management rights' clause of the collective agreement; consequently, further use of the system was not permitted.[107]

An interesting discussion of the use of sign-in systems based on employees' biometric information is provided in a recent report issued by the Alberta Office of the Information and Privacy Commissioner.[108] In that case, the Portfolio Officer conducted the investigation of an employee's complaint, which alleged that she had been terminated following her refusal to submit her thumbprint to register on to the biometric sign-in system introduced by the employer. The employee claimed that the collection of this type of personal information was highly intrusive and that the employer had failed to inform her of the purpose for which the thumbprint was going to be used.

---

[105] *Canada Safeway Ltd. v. U.F.C.W., Local 401* (2005), 145 L.A.C. (4th) 1, (Alta. Arb. Bd.) (A. Ponak).

[106] (2005), 140 L.A.C. (4th) 393 (Ont. Arb. Bd.) (M.L. Tims).

[107] See also, *407 ETR Concession Co. v. CAW-Canada, Local 414* (2007), [2007] O.L.A.A. No. 34, 158 L.A.C. (4th) 289 (Ont. Arb. Bd.), Ontario Labour Arbitration, where employees successfully challenged their termination for refusing to submit to the employer's new biometric hand scanner system on account of their religious beliefs.

[108] Investigation Report P2008-IR-005, August 27, 2008.

In conducting her investigation, the Portfolio Officer contacted the manufacturer of the sign-in system and learned that it was a technologically improved system which in fact did not collect any personal information, but rather extracted attributes from a person's live thumbprint to create a unique number for each employee, to be used later to recognize employees when they signed in by scanning their thumbs each time thereafter. Further, the information collected and stored could not subsequently be reverse engineered or reconstructed into an image of the thumbprint.

As a result of this finding, the Officer distinguished between collection of actual biometric information used for "one-to-one identification" of a person, and collection of numeric representations of biometric attributes for one-to-one authentication of an individual.

Having confirmed that for the purposes of Alberta's *Personal Information Protection Act* "personal information" is information about an individual that makes him or her "identifiable" and not necessarily "identified", the Officer concluded that the thumbprint templates collected in this case did constitute personal information. As such, the question arose as to whether the employer had complied in collecting personal information of its employees with the relevant statutory requirements. Despite the fact that the *PIPA* recognizes personal employee information as a subset of personal information and allows its collection, use and disclosure without employees' consent, the Officer found the employer in contravention of the Act.

Having analyzed sections 15 and 18 of the Act which govern the collection and use of personal employee information, she deliberated that the sections require the employer to provide its employees with reasonable notification of what information exactly is going to be collected and used. The Officer emphasized that this requirement becomes even more important under a statutory regime, like the one in Alberta, which allows for reduced consent requirement for personal employee information. To the extent that the complaining employee had not been provided with this information, the Officer found that the employer did not comply with the Act. However, since the employee refused to provide her personal information as was required by her employer, no personal information had been collected, and therefore no contravention of the Act had occurred.

"Blogging" (web logging, or online journal entries) has emerged as a new Internet trend and appears to be on the rise with employees and contractors both in and outside the workplace, causing conflict between workers and employers over the propriety of commentary about employers on the Internet. In the U.S., employees can be terminated even if blogging takes place from home on their own time if their employer comes across the employee's blog on the Internet and is offended by the content. Most U.S. states (45 at present) offer no protection against being fired in such instances.

Only five states have enacted laws limiting an employer's right to dismiss an employee for off-duty activity that is not related to their job.[109]

Delta Air Lines, Friendster, Google, and Microsoft have all reportedly fired employees or contractors over the content of their blogs, which contained criticisms of their employer or colleagues or disclosed confidential company information. In particular, one employee with eights years experience at Delta Air Lines was suspended and subsequently fired for posting suggestive pictures of herself in uniform inside the company airplane on the Internet in connection with her blog. Even where employees create an anonymous blog that offends their employer, a company could attempt to identify the employee by filing a "John Doe" lawsuit and sending a subpoena to the blog hosting company. The increase in terminations of employees in relation to blogging suggests that although many companies have implemented policies prohibiting employee misuse of the Internet, few of the policies directly address blogging, particularly outside of the workplace.[110]

Another emerging issue that requires attention is the difficulty in reconciling how an employer ensures that its employees are consenting to the collection of their personal information. In those jurisdictions where privacy legislation exists to deal specifically with the employment relationship, there is more guidance on whether consent is required and if it is, when and how an employer meets this general obligation. In other jurisdictions, however, the overriding obligation to ensure that consent is obtained prior to any collection, use or disclosure of personal information by an employer has led to interesting decisions by the Privacy Commissioner and the Courts.[111]

---

[109] CNET News.com, "Blogging on the job" by Declan McCullagh and Alorie Gilbert, March 8, 2005, online: <http://news.com.com/2100-1030_3-5597010.html>; CNN.com, "Blog-linked firings prompt calls for better policies", March 6, 2005, online: <http://www.CNN.com/2005/TECH/internet/03/06/Firedfor-blogging.ap/index.html>.

[110] *Ibid.*

[111] See for example, the decision by the Federal Court in *Eastmond v. Canadian Pacific Railway*, 2004 FC 852, 16 Admin. L.R. (4th) 275 (F.C.), where the Court was forced to conclude that a video tape of employee activity was not a "collection" of personal information until the moment in time where the tape is viewed. Once it is viewed, the personal information will be seen as "collected" and there must either be consent to view the tape, or an exception to the need for consent present in the circumstance (i.e. it is reasonable to expect that the collection with the knowledge or consent of the individual would compromise the availability or the accuracy of the information and the collection is reasonable for purposes related to investigating a breach of an agreement or a contravention of the laws of Canada or a province.)

Of particular interest is the decision of the Federal Court of Appeal in *Turner v. Telus Communications Inc.*[112] where the Court, while having recognized that *PIPEDA* requires the employer to obtain an employee's consent to the collection, use and disclosure of his/her personal information unless one of the exceptions set out in section 7(1) of the Act is invoked, dodged ruling on the issue of whether the employer is empowered to discipline employees refusing to provide such a consent.

In that case, the appellants, employees of Telus Communications Inc., filed a complaint with the Privacy Commissioner in connection with Telus' practice of collecting their voiceprint information following the company's implementation in its operations of a new technology called "e.Speak". e.Speak uses voice recognition technology to allow Telus employees to remotely access and use the company's internal computer network by speaking commands through any telephone, including a cellular telephone.

When employees attempt to access e.Speak by phone, their identity must be verified through a computer program known as "Nuance Verifier" to protect confidential information held in the data stores of Telus' network. Nuance Verifier requires employees to initially participate in a one-time enrolment process that produces and stores a voiceprint, which is a matrix of numbers representing the employee's voice and vocal tract. Access to e.Speak then requires production of a second voice template which in turn is digitized and matched against the caller's enrolment voice template. During the Commissioner's investigation, evidence provided by Telus indicated that the enrolment voice templates are stored under tight security for as long as individuals remain in the employ of the company; the access voice template, on the other hand, is destroyed within one or two months.

Prior to collecting the voiceprints, Telus sought the consent of certain employees, three of whom refused to provide a sample and another who initially agreed, allegedly under coercion, but subsequently withdrew his consent. The four employees then filed a complaint about Telus' voiceprint practices to the Privacy Commissioner. The Commissioner's findings indicated that the purposes for which Telus had collected the personal information were appropriate in the circumstances, that the employees were properly informed of these purposes and that appropriate safeguards were in place to protect the voiceprint information. The Commissioner also found that Telus had met the consent requirements set out in *PIPEDA* for the collection of personal information.

On appeal to the Federal Court of Appeal, the Court unequivocally defined the characteristics of a person's voice as personal information, a

---

[112] 2007 FCA 21, 2007 CarswellNat 172 (F.C.A.).

determination which did not appear to be at issue with the parties before the Court. This contrasts with the Federal Court of Appeal's ruling in *Canada (Information Commissioner) v. Canadian Transportation Accident Investigation & Safety Board*,[113] which held that the voice recordings of pilots and air traffic controllers were not considered personal information under the *Privacy Act* because they did not import any notion of privacy, but instead were mere recordings of what these employees were doing at work. Interestingly, the definition of "personal information" was regarded the same under *PIPEDA* and the *Privacy Act* for purposes of addressing the issues raised in these respective cases.

Notwithstanding, the Federal Court of Appeal agreed with the lower court's assessment that voice characteristics are at the lower end of the privacy rights spectrum since a voice-print does not reveal much about an individual, particularly given that what is used by Telus is not the voice itself but the voiceprint, which is a matrix of numbers and not an audio sample. Weighing the employees' privacy rights against Telus' business interests, its security measures, the effectiveness of using voiceprints to meet its objectives and the degree of sensitivity associated with voiceprints, the Court further concurred that a reasonable person would find the use of e.Speak technology to be reasonable in the circumstances that existed at the time of the collection.

Regarding the requirement for consent, the Court emphasized that Parliament has clearly and exhaustively limited the instances in which personal information may be collected without the knowledge of consent of individual to five exceptions in subsection 7(1) of the Act, none of which could be applied in these circumstances. Specifically, subsection 7(1)(a) allows for the collection of personal information without knowledge or consent only where collection is clearly in the interest of the individual and consent *cannot* be obtained, as opposed to *is not* obtained, from the individual in a timely manner. The Court stated that in this case, consent was initially refused by three employees and given by the fourth employee, demonstrating that if consent could be refused or given here, it cannot be said that there was no opportunity to obtain consent. Moreover, the employees' refusal to consent indicated that they did not consider the collection of their voice characteristics to be clearly in their interest. Concluding that Telus had the timely opportunity and the obligation to obtain the employees' consent prior to collecting their voiceprints, the Court noted that the design of the e.Speak system in fact renders it impossible to create a voiceprint without an employee's knowledge or participation, thereby necessitating consent prior to the collection of a voiceprint.

---

[113] (2002), 2002 CarswellNat 349 (Fed. C.A.).

On the issue of disciplinary measures, the Court agreed with the employees' argument that threats of disciplinary measures will vitiate consent. However, the judge clarified that section 27.1(1)(b) of *PIPEDA* protects employees from being disciplined for refusing to comply with an employer's direction to perform job functions where this would result in a violation of *another's* privacy rights. Additionally, no evidence had been presented to indicate what the allegations of progressive discipline involved and no measure of any kind had yet been taken. Moreover, because Telus had a duty under section 27.1(1) of *PIPEDA* to inform the employees that a refusal could lead to certain consequences, the company was not making actual threats of disciplinary measures in fulfilling this requirement.

Given that the purpose of the collection was considered appropriate in the circumstances by a reasonable person, that Telus had sought the employees' consent to collect their voiceprint and that no disciplinary measures had yet been taken, the Court of Appeal concluded that the application had been properly dismissed by the Federal Court and therefore dismissed the appeal. The Court declined to address whether Telus' management rights allowed it to discipline employees who refuse to submit their personal information on the basis that Telus had not yet taken disciplinary measures, making the question hypothetical. Further, the Court held that this issue comprised a labour law dispute, which should be settled in a labour law context since such disputes did not fall within the purview of *PIPEDA*.

Arbitral jurisprudence has generally strictly enforced an employee's right to privacy where issues of physical searches of an employee or his/her personal effects have arisen. As a general principle, arbitrators and privacy commissioners require an employer to meet a high standard of reasonableness before the employee's right to privacy will be displaced. The test is what is "reasonable in the circumstances" and amongst other things, is dependent upon competing interests such as the relationship between the parties.

These emerging issues clearly signal that an employee's privacy rights are not absolute and must be considered in light of the employer's right to control workplace activity and preserve its business reputation through privacy-invasive technologies and employee monitoring.

8

Medical and Genetic Information

8.1 MEDICAL INFORMATION

8.1.1 Introduction

Personal medical records are afforded substantial privacy protection via federal and provincial privacy and health legislation, constitutional law, human rights codes, and the common law. (For further information, see section 8.2.2 – *Legislation* under *Genetic Information & Privacy*). These protections are designed to safeguard individuals from the collection, use and disclosure of medical information without their consent, however, in the context of the workplace, case law has recognized a need to balance competing interests between an employee's privacy rights with an employer's obligation to operate their business in a safe and efficient manner. Notably, there is jurisprudence indicating that personal medical information within the employment context warrants a higher level of protection as compared with other privacy information.[1]

8.1.2 Mandatory Medical Examinations

Federal and provincial occupational health and safety statutes and the common law place a duty on employers to take reasonable care and ensure that reasonable care is taken for the health, safety and welfare of all employees, as well as the public. This includes a duty to maintain a safe workplace, monitor employees' health and safety at work, and to maintain health and safety records. Likewise, the employee has a duty to ensure that he or she does not create risks to his or her own health or safety and that of others in or near the workplace.[2] Employers are also required to implement

---

[1] See *Surrey School District No. 36 v. C.U.P.E., Local 728*, (February 27, 2006), Doc. A-031/06, [2006] B.C.C.A.A.A. No. 47 (B.C. C.A.A.), British Columbia Collective Agreement Arbitration, where the arbitrator stated that the standard for medical information within the employment context requires a more rigorous analysis than that provided by the KVP standard. (For discussion of the KVP test, see section 6 – *Personal Searches of Employees*).

[2] *Canada Labour Code*, R.S.C. 1985, c. L-2, ss.125, 125(1), 126(1).

workplace surveillance programs to monitor the health and safety of employees. The Ontario *Occupational Health and Safety Act*,[3] for example, requires an employer to establish a medical surveillance program for the benefit of employees as prescribed; provide for safety-related medical examinations and tests for workers as prescribed; and where so prescribed, only permit a worker to work or be in a workplace who has undergone such medical examinations, tests or x-rays as prescribed and who is found to be physically fit to do the work in the workplace.[4]

Human rights legislation protects against discrimination in employment on the basis of disability or perceived disability, unless the employer can prove that the employee's disability prevents them from fulfilling a *bona fide* occupational requirement of the position, such as the ability to conduct work safely so as not to risk the health and safety of themselves and other employees, provided the employer has exhausted its efforts to accommodate the employee to the point of undue hardship. Human rights legislation and policies may limit the employer's scope regarding workplace safety measures by restricting the type of questions that an employer can ask of prospective and current employees regarding a disability or perceived disability. Specifically, section 7 of the *Canadian Human Rights Act*[5] states:

> It is a discriminatory practice, directly or indirectly, to refuse to employ or continue to employ any individual, or in the course of employment, to differentiate in relation to an employee, on a prohibited ground of discrimination.

The Supreme Court of Canada's decision in *Ontario Human Rights Commission v. Etobicoke (Borough)*[6] is authority for the proposition that a requirement imposed by an employer in the interest of safety must, in order to qualify as a *bona fide* occupational requirement, be reasonably necessary in order to eliminate a sufficient risk of damage. In ruling that the employer had not shown that compulsory retirement for two firefighters over the age of 60 was a *bona fide* occupational qualification and requirement for the employment concerned, the Court emphasized:

> A *bona fide* occupational qualification must be imposed honestly, in good faith, and in the sincerely held belief that it is imposed in the interests of adequate performance of the work involved with reasonable dispatch, safety and economy and not for ulterior or extraneous reasons that could defeat the Code's purpose. The qualification must be objectively related to the employ-

---

[3] *Occupation Health and Safety Act*, R.S.O. 1990, c. O.1.
[4] *Ibid.*, ss. 26, 27, 28.
[5] *Canadian Human Rights Act*, R.S.C 1985, c. H-6, s. 7 [*CHRA*].
[6] [1982] 1 S.C.R. 202 (S.C.C.).

ment concerned, ensuring its efficient economical performance without endangering the employee or others.

Under numerous occupational health and safety statutes, an employee's consent is required before an employer can include him or her in a prescribed medical surveillance program, however, certain statutes oblige employees to undergo medical examinations required by the Act and regulations. In *School District No. 39 (Vancouver) v. B.C.T.F.*,[7] the British Columbia Court of Appeal upheld an arbitrator's argument that requiring employees to undergo a medical examination on the advice of a medical officer did not violate section 7 (right to "life, liberty, and security" of the person) of the Charter. The teacher had been behaving irrationally and inappropriately towards colleagues and the school administrator and had received numerous disciplinary letters.

Concern for the health and safety of students and employees prompted the school board to order the teacher to undergo a psychiatric examination under the authority of the *School Act*, R.S.B.C. 1996, c. 412. The teacher repeatedly refused to undergo the examination and was subsequently required to take forced sick leave. The teacher's union argued that her Charter right to life, liberty and security had been violated, however, the Court ruled that sections 7 and 8 (right to be free from "unreasonable search or seizure") of the Charter did not encompass protection against intrusions affecting only economic or employment rights. The right to liberty did not include the right to choose not to undergo medical exams under the Act and continue in employment in defiance of it.

A recent decision of the Federal Court in *Grover v. National Research Council of Canada*[8] once again emphasizes that mandatory medical examinations of employees are only possible under a statute or contractual term. The absence of any reasonable grounds for an employer to believe that an employee presents any safety risk to him/herself or others only further tips the scales against the employer. In this case, the National Research Council of Canada ("NRC") suspended an employee without pay who was frequently absent on stress leave because he would not undergo a medical examination by a physician chosen by the employer. The NRC demanded the examination because it was suspicious of the information that the employee was providing from his own physician and asserted that he posed a safety threat until examined. The Public Service Labour Relations Board

---

[7] (2003), 224 D.L.R. (4th) 63 (B.C. C.A.), leave to appeal refused (2003), 109 C.R.R. (2d) 188 (note) (S.C.C.).

[8] (2007), [2007] F.C.J. No. 58, 2007 CarswellNat 169 (F.C.), affirmed 2008 FCA 97 (F.C.A.).

adjudicator ruled that the NRC did not have sufficient grounds to make such a request and allowed the employee's grievance.

In upholding the adjudicator's decision, Shore J. held that since "employees have a strong right to privacy with respect to their bodily integrity and a medical practitioner, the employer cannot order an employee to submit to a medical examination by a doctor chosen by the employer unless there exists some express contractual obligation or statutory authority." Also, "the 'mere possibility' that an employee may be ill or otherwise presents a safety risk does not amount to 'reasonable and probable grounds' for so believing". Most significantly, the NRC did not specify any particular grounds for believing that the grievor posed a safety risk and ignored the employee's offer to attend a doctor mutually agreed upon by the parties, and provided no rational explanation as to why it refused this option. This decision was subsequently upheld by the Federal Court of Appeal.

In the absence of specific authority under statute or collective agreements, an employer does not have inherent power to submit an individual to a medical examination. However, case law suggests that employers may be permitted to refuse to put an employee back to work without adequate information about the employee's fitness to perform their duties. In *Re Shell Canada Products Ltd. v. Canadian Association of Industrial, Mechanical & Allied Workers, Local 112*,[9] the arbitrator did not allow the employer to demand that an employee, who had pulled a muscle in his arm, undergo a physical examination by a company doctor or compel the employee to divulge confidential information regarding his medical condition. Nor could the employee be punished for insubordination for refusing to consent to a medical exam. However, the arbitrator ruled that where an employer has reasonable cause to believe that the employee is unsafe or unfit to work, the employer may refuse to permit the employee to return to work or dismiss the employee by virtue of incapacity to perform the work.

The decision in *Re NAV Canada v. C.A.T.C.A.*[10] established that although an employer is not entitled to sensitive medical information about an employee, an employer may request an employee to consent to the release of medical information to a physician retained by the employer and to undergo a medical examination by that physician where the position involves risks to public safety. The Arbitrator concluded that if, in the all circumstances, the request is reasonable and the employer can only be reasonably satisfied by the disclosure of evidence to its own medical advisors or by its own physician or one agreed to between the parties, "the employee may have to choose between suffering the continued administra-

---

[9] (1990), 14 L.A.C. (4th) 75 (B.C. Arb. Bd.).
[10] (1998), 74 L.A.C. (4th) 163 (Can. Arb. Bd.).

tive consequences, or consenting to the release [of medical information] or the examination".

This dispute involved a grievance filed by the Canadian Air Traffic Controllers' Association against NAV Canada over whether NAV Canada had the authority to require an employee to consent to the release of his or her medical information to the employer's physician and whether the employer could require an employee to submit to a medical examination by that physician, failing which, sanctions such as discipline, withholding sick leave benefits, or refusal to allow the employee to work could be imposed. The arbitrator ruled that the employer is not entitled to sensitive medical information and has no independent right to require disclosure of medical information or third party medical examination which can be enforced by disciplinary action. However, an employer is entitled to know whether an employee is fit or not, and any limitations which may have to be accommodated. In this case, the collective agreement was broad enough to justify administrative action to withhold sick leave benefits or refuse to allow an employee to return or continue to work.

Employees and applicants may refuse to undergo medical examinations, or alternatively, provide misleading or incomplete medical information for fear that positive results will invite social stigma and prove detrimental to their current employment status or to future career opportunities. Employers, on the other hand, are required by law to provide a safe and healthy work environment. Occupational health and safety statutes, human rights legislation and other laws attempt to balance these competing interests by imposing duties on both employers and employees to ensure a safe workplace, while preventing employers from obtaining information about employees' health or disabilities that is not strongly related to the duties required of the position.

8.1.3 Medical Certificates

Legislation and case law have established that the employer has a right and an obligation to ensure an employee's fitness to perform the tasks required of their position in a manner that ensure the health and safety of others in the workplace. However, an employer must have reasonable and probable grounds for questioning an employee's capacity to do the work before demanding medical certification of fitness or better certification than that provided by the employee.

In *Masterfeeds and U.F.C.W., Local 1518*[11], the arbitrator determined that the employer had reasonable grounds to question the employee's as-

---

[11] (2000), 92 L.A.C. (4th) 341 (B.C. Arb. Bd.).

sertion that he was fit to return to work following a medical leave of absence due to substance abuse, since the information provided by the employee's physician indicated that he continued to have difficulty with substance abuse. The employee, who occupied a safety-sensitive position as a tractor-trailer driver, agreed to submit to an independent medical examination but revoked his authorization to release the report to his employer after learning that the results indicated that he was not fit to resume his duties. The employer subsequently dismissed the employee, asserting that the revocation gave rise to just cause.

The arbitrator ruled that where an employee seeks to return to work after illness or injury, an employer can refuse to permit the employee from resuming his or her duties where the employer is not satisfied that the employee can capably fulfill their work duties. However, an employer does not have the right to discipline an employee for failing to provide additional information, or for refusing to be examined by a doctor chosen by the employer. The employee was reinstated, though his return to active duty was conditional on providing proper medical certification.

At issue in *Ontario Nurses' Association v. St. Joseph's Hospital*[12] was the type of information that an employer can require in a medical certificate. In this case, the arbitrator ruled that in fulfilling its duty to assure that employees are fit to return to work without compromising the safety of themselves and others, an employer does not require a specific diagnosis of the employee's condition provided that the medical certificate supports a safe return to work. In this case, a nurse who had been on sick leave informed the hospital that she needed time off for surgery. The hospital requested that she complete its short-term disability form, authorizing her physician to release specific medical information, including a diagnosis of her present condition.

The nurse refused to complete the form due to concern about the hospital's ability to keep the information confidential. In his decision, the arbitrator stated that the hospital was required to show some flexibility in ensuring an employee's safe return to work, and must restrict the types of questions on the medical certificate to those of a more general nature, such as confirmations that the employee was physically and mentally capable of returning to work, that her judgment was not impaired for any reason, and that she had been totally incapacitated from performing her duties during her absence.[13]

---

[12] [2002] O.L.A.A. No. 869.

[13] See also *Ontario Nurses' Association v. St. Joseph's Health Centre*, 76 O.R. (3d) 22, 2005 CarswellOnt 2981, where the majority of the Ontario Superior Court of

An arbitrator ruled similarly in *B.C. Teacher's Federation v. B.C. Public School Employers' Association*,[14] regarding how much information an employer can require in a certificate for extended and partial medical leave. Here, the arbitrator determined that a school board could unilaterally introduce a policy requiring that teachers submit detailed medical certificates with applications for medical leave where the policy was reasonable and the collective agreement was silent on the matter. However, the employer was not entitled to request a specific diagnosis of an employee's health problem, inquire as to when the employee first saw the physician, or elicit information regarding the teacher's ability to perform partial duties where the teacher had requested an extended medical leave.

The decision in *Peace Country Health v. U.N.A.*[15] illustrates what can be viewed as an unreasonable policy with respect to provision by employees of their health or medical information to their employer. In this case, the employer instituted a new blanket system of obtaining medical information from employees for them to qualify for sick leave benefits for any sick leave beyond 14 days, which involved a "medical management approach." This approach included among its objectives: "Providing employees with the best available medical care through a team of professionals monitoring progress and treatment, liaising with the employees' health care providers and facilitating access to "the best medical care." Notably, the employee's medical information was to pass from their physician directly to the employer and was to include information on such matters as diagnosis and treatment. The arbitrator found the policy unreasonable as demonstrating an intention to actively monitor, guide and assist in the employee's health care, and also held that it was not authorized by the collective agreement.

Further, the arbitrator concluded that since the medical management approach was a cornerstone of the policy, and the use of consent to secure direct access to healthcare providers so infused the entire policy, this was

---

Justice stated:

> The weight of the arbitral cases is that employers are entitled to seek medical information to ensure that a returning employee is able to return to work safely and poses no hazard to others. The employee's initial obligation is to present some brief information from the doctor declaring the employee is fit to return to work. If the employer has reasonable grounds on which to believe that the employee's medical condition presents a danger to herself and others, the employer may ask for additional information to allay the specific fears which exist. The request must be related to the reasons for absence; no broad inquiry as to health is allowed.

[14] [2002] L.C.C. No. 4454.

[15] (April 16, 2007), Doc. 2007-015, [2007] A.G.A.A. No. 17 (Alta. Arb. Bd.), Alberta Grievance Arbitration.

not a case where he could simply "cull out the offending sections, allowing other aspects of the policy to stand."

Another recent decision supports the reasoning that in requesting employee medical information via prescribed forms, a significant factor to consider in the reasonableness analysis is whether the employer is seeking information on diagnosis and treatment.[16] In this case, the Canadian Merchant Service Guild challenged a questionnaire sent to the physicians of its members on sick leave to obtain information on their condition, treatment and anticipated dates of return to work. The arbitrator found that the questionnaire, in its overall objective and in not seeking a diagnosis, was reasonable, with the exception of offering a contact number to discuss an employee's medical state directly with the employer's medical staff. The requirement of a contact number was viewed as unnecessary and unreasonable.

The Privacy Commissioner of Canada has, on a number of occasions, forwarded the Office's position with respect to inclusion of diagnoses and other sensitive information in employees' medical certificates required by their employers. In one case, the employer insisted on the provision of a medical diagnosis by employees who worked in high-risk, safety-sensitive positions and who were on a sick leave that exceeded the five days of annual uncertified leave.[17] According to the employer, the reasons for this requirement included the safety-sensitive nature of the complainants' positions and the fact that usually an employee's physician is not aware of the type of work performed by the employee. As a result, the company argued that its own medical personnel was in a better position to assess whether the employee is fit for work based on his/her specific diagnosis and treatment received. Another reason cited by the employer for requiring medical diagnoses was "suspicious absences."

The Commissioner based its findings on Principle 4.4 of *PIPEDA*, which states that the collection of personal information must be limited to that which is necessary for the purposes identified by the organization. Acknowledging that the Office of the Privacy Commissioner has always recognized that an employer has both the right to satisfy itself that an employee's absence from work is justified, and the obligation to determine whether an employee returning to work after sick leave is fit to resume assigned duties or must be otherwise accommodated, the Commissioner determined that the word of the employees' physicians should have been

---

[16] *Canadian Merchant Service Guild v. Seaspan International Ltd. (Carlson Grievance)* (February 27, 2006), C. Taylor, Arbitrator, [2007] C.L.A.D. No. 57, (Can. Arb. Bd.).

[17] Privacy Commissioner of Canada, Fall 2003, Summary # 257.

sufficient for both stated purposes. Interestingly, the Commissioner added that diagnostic information may in some circumstances be necessary to fulfill the purpose of determining an employee's fitness for work. However, in the circumstances of this case, it was both unnecessary and inappropriate for the organization to have demanded such information.

An employee of a telecommunications company filed a complaint with the Office of the Privacy Commissioner of Canada alleging that her employer required her to provide it with sensitive personal medical information necessary for administering her long-term disability claim.[18] Normally, the information in question is submitted directly to an insurance company that manages the respective long-term disability plan. In this case, the submission guide of the insurance company specified that employees might submit the requisite documents either directly to the insurance company or through their employer. The employer contended that their role was that of an intermediary and they simply intended to assist its employees in the application process.

However, the employer had not allowed the complainant to choose between the above two options. Rather, the employer used the word "must" in its standard letter sent to the employee. Further, the employee was concerned with the lack of security measures her employer had in place to protect the sensitive personal information of its employees. Further, Human Resources personnel were involved to a large degree in administering the short-term disability plan of the employer and had direct access to all documents necessary for this purpose, which were faxed by respective employees as per request of the company.

In coming to a final conclusion, the Assistant Privacy Commissioner again considered Principle 4.4 of *PIPEDA*, Principle 4.7, which states that personal information shall be protected by security safeguards appropriate to the sensitivity of the information, and section 5.3 which allows an organization to collect, use or disclose personal information only for purposes that a reasonable person would consider appropriate in the circumstances. The Assistant Commissioner deliberated that because the collection of the information was not necessary for the purposes identified by the company since it did not simply offer its assistance to their employees in the application process but rather left them with no alternatives, the company was in contravention of Principle 4.4 and section 5(3) of the Act. The security safeguards were also found to be unsatisfactory and in contravention of Principle 4.7.

The Assistant Privacy Commissioner stressed that the Office is strongly of the view that any organization that collects medical diagnoses about

---

[18] Privacy Commissioner of Canada, October 31, 2003, Summary # 226.

employees for any purpose must only do so with strict safeguards in place; that is, such information must be shared among qualified medical practitioners only.

Yet another Principle of *PIPEDA* came into play when dealing with the issue of the collection, use or disclosure of medical information of employees, namely Principle 4.3. Principle 4.3, which requires the knowledge and consent of the individual for the collection, use, or disclosure of his/her personal information, except where inappropriate, was relied upon by the Assistant Privacy Commissioner in determining whether or not an employer may contact an employee's physician in order to verify the medical information submitted by the employee. An individual complained that without authorization, a member of his employer's medical personnel had telephoned the hospital that had issued him the medical certificate he used to request sick leave. His employer subsequently denied him sick leave because the length of time of the leave request exceeded the length of time recommended by the physician following his medical examination at the hospital.

The Assistant Commissioner determined that the telephone call to the hospital by the employer's occupational health and safety advisor contravened Principle 4.3 of *PIPEDA* due to lack of authorization from the employee.

In a case involving a private sector employer, an employee of a telecommunications company who was on extended sick leave complained to the Privacy Commissioner of Canada that his employer was collecting more medical information than was necessary, and was disclosing it to company managers without his consent.[19] The company's policy required employees on extended sick leave to sign a consent form authorizing his or her physician to release medical information regarding the employee's medical condition, treatment, and prognosis to the company's occupational health professionals.

The Commissioner determined that the company's occupational health staff, doctors, and nurses were bound by their respective codes of ethics to provide managers only with information pertaining to the abilities and limitations of the employee, and that the company had policies and procedures in place to safeguard employee medical information. The Commissioner could find no evidence supporting the employee's claims that health care employees had disclosed his medical information to managers without his consent. Therefore, the Commissioner found that the company's purposes for collecting the employee's medical information was legitimate and it had met all of its obligations under the *PIPEDA*.

---

[19]   Privacy Commissioner of Canada, February 17, 2003, Summary #118.

When a situation necessitates an employee to take emergency sick leave from work, the employer may subsequently require the employee to produce evidence that is reasonable in the circumstance to confirm that the employee is entitled to the leave, pursuant to section 50(7) of the *Employment Standards Act, 2000*, S.O. 2000, c. 41. In *Tillbury Assembly Ltd and United Auto Workers, Local 251*[20], an employee was given a one-day suspension for failing to follow company policy requiring that she produce a doctor's note after leaving her shift early with a severe headache causing blurry vision and one of her eyes to swell almost fully closed. The employee had experienced similar headaches prior to this incident and had an absenteeism problem, thus, she had been told on previous occasions that the company required a doctor's note for medical absences.

The arbitrator concluded that as the employee's supervisors did not testify that they did not believe that she was suffering form a severe headache in this instance, the supervisors merely applied the company policy requiring the doctor's note without considering the situation. The arbitrator ruled that requiring the employee to obtain a doctor's note was not reasonable in the circumstances and expunged the suspension from her record.

8.1.4 Medical Records

Case law emphasizes that although an individual does not own his or her medical records, the individual has an inherent right to access their own medical information, subject to such access being in their best interests. The Supreme Court of Canada decision in *McInerney v. MacDonald*[21] affirmed:

> Information about oneself revealed to a doctor acting in a professional capacity remains, in a fundamental sense, one's own. . . . The confiding of the information to the physician for medical purposes gives rise to an expectation that the patient's interest in and control of the information will continue. . . . Disclosure serves to reinforce the patient's faith in her treatment and to enhance the trust inherent in the doctor-patient relationship. As well, the duty of confidentiality that arises from the doctor-patient relationship is meant to encourage disclosure of information and communication between doctor and patient.

The case of *Ontario Human Rights Commission v. Dofasco Inc.*[22] defines an employer's right to access an employee's medical records when the employee makes a complaint of discrimination against the employer on the basis of handicap. The Dofasco employee went on disability leave for

---

[20] (2004), 124 L.A.C. (4th) 375 (Ont. Arb. Bd.).
[21] [1992] S.C.R. 138 (S.C.C.).
[22] (2001), [2001] L.C.C. No. 406, 208 D.L.R. (4th) 276 (Ont. C.A.).

four years following a number of injuries sustained in her job as a crane operator. In the fourth year of her leave, the employer offered her a position as a switchboard operator. The employee requested time to speak with the specialist who was treating her, however, her employer demanded that she attend at Dofasco Medical Services and report to work two weeks later. The employee attended Dofasco Medical services as ordered, but did not report to work on the date set by her employer. Dofasco then terminated her, alleging just cause.

The employee filed a complaint with the Ontario Human Rights Commission, claiming that Dofasco had discriminated against her because of physical handicap, and the Commission referred her complaint to a Board of Inquiry. Dofasco submitted before the Board that the employee had failed to submit any documentation that she could perform even light duties, and brought a motion requesting that a number of documents be produced, including the employee's medical records, a list of all medical practitioners who had examined or treated her, and the details of those visits. The Board granted the motion in part, requiring the employee to provide Dofasco with a list of the medical practitioners who had treated her during her four-year medical leave, the doctor's areas of expertise, the dates of the visits, and the conditions for which she was treated.

The Human Rights Commission brought an application before the Ontario Divisional Court for judicial review of the Board's decision, arguing that the Board had exercised its discretion unreasonably in requiring the employee to disclose privileged medical information that was not related to her condition. The Divisional Court dismissed the Commission's application and the Commission appealed the decision to the Ontario Court of Appeal. The Court of Appeal allowed the appeal in part. Weighing the need to protect privileged or irrelevant information against Dofasco's right to full disclosure, the Court of Appeal ruled that the employee's right to privacy would be irreparably violated if all of the information requested were fully disclosed. Where a complainant's right to privacy would be jeopardized by such disclosure, the complainant's privacy interests will prevail.

Case law is clear that an employer cannot refuse an employee's written request to access to their medical files or release their file to an authorized agency. In *Ontario Nurses' Association v. North York General Hospital*,[23] a nurse was seeking to return to work after an extended medical leave due to an injury at work, however, the employer would not allow her to return. On consulting her union, the union instructed her to authorize the employer's Occupational Health Department to release a copy of her health file to the union, in accordance with the employer's "Confidentiality of Employee

---

[23] (2004), [2004] O.L.A.A. No. 109, 2004 CarswellOnt 1723 (Ont. Arb. Bd.).

Information" policy which allowed for such release to authorized agencies on written consent of the employee.

In anticipation that the union might file a grievance against the hospital, the hospital directed the Occupation Health Department not to release the health file to the union unless the employee also consented to provide a copy to the hospital's Human Resources Department. Though her employer did not preclude the employee from viewing her health file in the presence of an employee in the Occupation Health Department, the employer would not allow her to make copies of her file. The union then filed grievances on behalf of the employee, alleging that the employer's actions were improper and seeking a declaration that the employer had violated the collective agreement and certain statutes. The union also filed a grievance protesting the employer's refusal to return the employee to work, which was settled, leaving the former to be resolved.

The arbitrator ruled that the employer, by imposing the condition that the nurse consent to providing management with a copy of her health file as well, had breached the article of the collective agreement that prohibited the employer from discrimination or interference with respect to any nurse by reason of her exercising her rights under the collective agreement. The union was the employee's representative and in that capacity could be privy to information about the employee which the employer could not expect to access simply because the union did. Additionally, the employer's access to the employee's health file was unwarranted, since the union was merely conducting an investigation as opposed to filing a grievance when it requested the files.

An employee may be required to disclose their medical records at an arbitration hearing, pursuant to labour relations statutes and case law. In determining the appropriateness of such a disclosure, the arbitrator in *West Park Hospital and ONA*[24] established a five-step test relating to relevance to the issues in dispute and some analysis of prejudice. In this case, a nurse had been discharged for incompetence and the employer's request for pre-hearing disclosure of her medical records was denied. The five elements required to determine relevance and prejudice are:

1.   Information requested must be arguably relevant

2.   The information must be particularized so that there is no dispute as to what is being requested

3.   The board should be satisfied that the information is not being requested as a fishing expedition

---

[24]   (1993), 37 L.A.C. (4th) 160 (Ont. Arb. Bd.).

4. There must be a nexus between the information requested and the positions in dispute at the hearing

5. The board should be satisfied that disclosure will not cause undue prejudice to the employee

The arbitrator in *Re Becker Milk Co. and Milk & Bread Drivers, Dairy Employees, Caterers & Allied Employees, Local 647*[25] adopted this five-step test to ensure a fair hearing, in determining whether the employee's union should be ordered to produce all information relevant to the employee's medical condition before the employer is require to proceed with its case. The employee was dismissed after writing numerous threatening letters to the company's vice-president for which he was charged under the *Criminal Code*. The employee was subsequently diagnosed with bipolar disorder and it was determined that at the time of his dismissal, he was in fact suffering from delusions and psychotic breaks. The arbitrator stated that some medical information such as that relating to mental disorders tend to stigmatize individuals, and in such cases, a higher onus must be put on the requesting party to satisfy the arbitrator as to why this information is essential. However, the arbitrator ruled given the nature of the employee's letters, the doctor's reports, and the company's concerns over the employee's conduct, the pre-hearing production of pertinent medical records and a medical examination of the employee by a doctor of the employer's choice was necessary to ensure a fair hearing.

8.1.5   Monitoring & Surveillance/Surveillance as Evidence

(See Chapter 7 - *Video Surveillance outside the Workplace*)

8.2   GENETIC INFORMATION & PRIVACY

8.2.1   Introduction

Genetic information includes DNA sequence information revealed by a genetic test, and inferences that can be made from knowledge of the sequence. Genetic information may also be revealed by studying entire chromosomes, RNA, proteins, substances in blood or tissues, and medical imaging techniques; diagnosing a genetic disorder by clinical examination; or studying a person's family medical history. While rare, inherited monogenic diseases, such as Huntington's disease, involve a mutation in a single

---

[25] (1996), 53 L.A.C. (4th) 420 (Ont. Arb. Bd.).

gene and can indicate a certainty of acquiring the disease. However, most genetic diseases, such as heart disease, cancer and Alzheimer's, involve many genes and often also involve environmental components, making it highly difficult to predict with certainty through genetic testing.[26]

The information generated by DNA testing can be very precise in indicating that a particular mutation is or is not present, though such precision is not especially helpful in predicting future health conditions. Thus, genetic information tends to contemplate possibilities rather than certainties, since most genetic tests reveal risk factors without necessarily addressing an individual's current physical or mental health status.[27] The use of such potentially imprecise information has disquieting implications in employment, as the information could be incorporated into decision-making by employers and insurance companies, allowing them to draw conclusions about the health status of employees and adversely affect the employability, insurability and career prospects of individuals.

DNA can uniquely identify an individual and their physical and behavioural characteristics. The amount of information that can be extracted and inferred from a single DNA sample is potentially staggering, and if stored in genetic data banks or "biobanks", the sample has the potential to reveal information about an individual far into the future and beyond the purposes for which the individual first provided the sample.[28] "As more and more genetic links are uncovered, the holder of one blood sample may have access to a tremendous reservoir of deeply private, deeply personal, information about an individual."[29]

In fact, research into the development of DNA chip and micro-array technology is already in progress and soon will likely allow for the scanning of entire genes to detect a variety of mutations. Genetic tools will become faster, more efficient, and cheaper.[30] Therefore, the volume of information

---

[26] Eugene Oscapella, "Genetics, Privacy and Discrimination: A Survey Prepared for the Canadian Biotechnology Advisory Committee" [unpublished], October 2000, online: BioPortal Canada <http://www.cbac-cccb.ca> or request copies by mail [*Oscapella*].

[27] Australian Health Ethics Committee, *Protection of Human Genetic Information*, Issues Paper 26, October 2001 at 86, 87 [*AHEC*].

[28] Trudo Lemmens & Lisa Austin, "Of Volume, Depth and Speed: The Challenges of Genetic Information" (Ottawa: Republication of the original discussion paper for the Canadian Biotechnology Advisory Committee, February 2001) online: BioPortal Canada <http://www.cbac-cccb.ca> or request copies by mail [*Lemmens*].

[29] Mark Sabourin, *OHS Canada Magazine*, "Bad Blood", March, 1999, online: <www.ohscanada.com/virtual-issue/artucle/badblood.html>.

[30] *Ibid.*, at 1.

that can be extracted from one sample, the rapid speed of testing, and the link between genetics and computer technology underscore the need to assess the effectiveness of current regulatory schemes in Canada *vis-à-vis* their ability to protect individual privacy.

8.2.2 Legislation

At present, Canada has not enacted any legislation relating specifically to genetic information and privacy, apart from criminal legislation regarding the use of DNA in criminal investigations. Nor is there any specific prohibition against genetic testing in employment. Most of the laws which affect genetic privacy are more general in their application, and do not identify genetic privacy as requiring explicit legal protection.[31] However, these laws do provide a basic legal framework for dealing with genetic information and privacy. Such legislation includes constitutional law (i.e., the *Canadian Charter of Rights and Freedoms*), quasi-constitutional law (i.e., Quebec's *Charter of Human Rights and Freedoms*), federal and provincial human rights codes, federal and provincial data protection/privacy statutes, provincial health information protection legislation, laws governing professional confidentiality, statutory privacy torts in some provinces the emerging common law tort of invasion of privacy, and the criminal law (i.e., protections against physical intrusion).

In 1992, the Privacy Commissioner of Canada issued a report entitled *Genetic Testing and Privacy*, which made 22 recommendations regarding the need to protect the privacy and confidentiality of personal genetic information.[32] Since then, many technological advances have occurred that could have significant implications with respect to genetic privacy. Notably, the Privacy Commissioner's *Annual Report* (1999-2000) stated:

> In 1992, we recommended the government adopt legislation to ensure that genetic material was collected within a legal framework, that no one was forced to give up genetic material, that genetic testing would not be a condition of employment, and that no one would suffer discrimination for refusing to be tested. We also proposed amending the definition of personal information

---

[31] B.M. Knoppers & C. Schriver (eds.), *Genomics, Health and Society: Emerging Issues for Public Policy* (Ottawa: Policy Research Initiative, Canada, 2003) at 160.

[32] Privacy Commissioner of Canada, "Genetic Testing and Privacy" (Ottawa: Minister of Supply and Services Canada, 1995) online: Office of the Privacy Commissioner of Canada <http://www.privcom.gc.ca/information/02_05_11_e.pdf>.

in the *Privacy Act* to ensure that it included both genetic samples and the information derived from their analysis.

Virtually all the recommendations have fallen on deaf ears. With the costs of genetic tests falling, a lengthening list of conditions that tests can identify, and pressure building to develop comprehensive linked health information banks on Canadians, we still have no legal framework for this intrusive technology. We do not even know how and how much employers are using genetic testing.[33]

As indicated by the Privacy Commissioner, there is concern and reservation over the extent to which these laws are designed to protect against privacy threats posed by new biotechnologies and computer technologies. Consequently, the Commissioner along with many other experts in the field of genetic information and privacy are calling for significant reforms and amendments to current Canadian law to address and anticipate threats to genetic privacy in the future. Moreover, despite having a basic legal framework in place in Canada, it is clear that all of the present laws include exceptions to an individual's right to privacy, emphasizing that no privacy rights are absolute. In each circumstance, the competing interests of an individual employee must be weighed against societal interests and values, such as public health and safety.[34]

8.2.3   Screening, Monitoring and Discrimination: Implications on Hiring, Job Retention and Promotion

In the employment context, genetic information can be used by employers to assess suitability for employment, job performance and promotion, and the genetic consequences of exposure to hazardous workplace materials or environmental contaminants. As of 1990, there were no reports of systematic collection or use of genetic information in the employment setting in Canada, though it is possible that such information may already be part of employees' health files.[35]

It is unclear at present how human rights legislation and case law would extend to protect a pre-symptomatic employee with the likelihood

---

[33] Privacy Commissioner of Canada, "Annual Report to Parliament 1999-2000" Minister of Public Works and Government Services Canada, 2000, online: Office of the Privacy Commissioner of Canada <http://www.privcom.gc.ca/information/ar/02_04_08_e.asp>.

[34] *Lemmens, supra*, note 28 at 22; Derek Jones, "Selected Legal Issues in Genetic Testing: Guidance from Human Rights" (Ottawa: Minister of Public Works and Government services, 2001) at 22 [*Jones*].

[35] *Ibid.* at 10, 21.

of developing a disabling disease, or an asymptomatic employee with a genetic predisposition with the potential to acquire a future disability.[36] However, the decision in *Quebec (Commission des droits de la personne et des droits de la jeunesse) v. Montreal (City)*; *Quebec (Commission des droits de la personne et des droits de la jeunesse) v. Boisbriand (City)*[37] may provide useful insight.

In this case, the Supreme Court of Canada confirmed that the term "disability" extends to include perceived disability, even though human rights codes and Canada's *Charter of Rights and Freedoms* do not specifically enumerate perceived disability as a prohibited ground. The City of Montreal had refused to hire one individual as a horticulturalist because the pre-employment medical exam revealed an anomaly of the spinal column. The City of Boisbriand dismissed another individual from his position as a police officer because he had Crohn's disease. The medical evidence in each case indicated that the individuals could perform the duties of the position and that they had no functional limitations, thus they filed complaints with the Commission alleging discrimination on the basis of handicap.

The Tribunal held that the individuals had no remedy under the Quebec *Charter of Human Rights and Freedoms* because they did not meet the definition of handicap, as their conditions did not result in functional limitations. The Quebec Court of Appeal reversed the Tribunal's decision and the cities of Montreal and Boisbriand appealed the ruling. The Supreme Court of Canada affirmed the Court of Appeal's ruling, concluding that a handicap may be real or perceived, and may exist without proof of physical limitations or other ailments other than those created by prejudice and stereotypes. The emphasis must be on the distinction, exclusion, or preference rather than the precise cause or origin of the biomedical condition.

This case illustrates that the law in Canada has broadly interpreted the notion of "handicap", suggesting that a pre-symptomatic or asymptomatic employee with a genetic trait that does not result in a present disability would likely be protected against discrimination based on a predisposition or a perceived predisposition to develop a disability in the future. Pursuant to human rights law, occupational health and safety legislation and case law, there is little evidence that medical testing, which includes genetic testing, can be justified unless an employer can show that such testing is required to fulfill its duty to ensure or enhance workplace safety and take reasonable care for the health and safety of its workers and the public. The extent to which an employer owes a duty of care to employees with genetic

---

[36] *Oscapella, supra,* note 26 at 23; *AHEC, supra,* note 27 at 275.
[37] [2000] 1 S.C.R. 665 (S.C.C.).

susceptibilities to workplace injuries or hazardous substances has yet to be considered.

It is plausible that in the near future, genetic testing providers, like drug testing providers, may attempt to persuade employers that testing is necessary to ensure a safe and productive workplace, despite the current uncertainty and unreliability of most genetic tests. As technology advances, however, employers may eventually be able to use inexpensive, commercially available genetic tests similar to home pregnancy test kits to expedite the testing process or perhaps surreptitiously test their employees through saliva or hair roots for genetic conditions or susceptibilities, thereby enabling possible discrimination against employees without their knowledge.[38] The availability of these private test kits may make it far more feasible and less costly for an employer to test employees for genetic predispositions or conditions than to remove workplace hazards.

Case law provides a basis from which the courts might formulate a ruling in cases involving surreptitious testing by an employer. Though the seminal case *R. v. Dyment*[39] pertained to a criminal matter and involved the unreasonable search and seizure by the police of an unconscious patient's blood sample, the decision signals a particular distaste by the courts of surreptitious testing by an institution to advance its purposes, seriously violating the personal autonomy of the individual. The ruling established the following:

> The use of a person's body without his consent to obtain information about him invades an area of privacy essential to the maintenance of his human dignity. . . . A violation of a person's body is much more serious than a violation of his office or even his home. The sense of privacy transcends the physical. The dignity of the human being is equally seriously violated when the use is made of bodily substances taken by others for medical purposes in a manner that does not respect that limitation.

This case, along with the decisions mentioned in section 8.1 – *Medical Information*, emphasize the requirement of an individual's consent to undergo medical and genetic testing in employment, unless otherwise required by statute, contractual obligation or court order.

If the burden of health care costs shifts to the private sector in Canada as it has in the United States, Canadian employers will develop a much greater interest in acquiring genetic information about job applicants and current employees to ensure that their organization screens for "genetically

---

[38] *Oscapella, supra*, note 26 at 22, 27.
[39] [1988] 2 S.C.R. 417 (S.C.C.).

superior" employees and carefully monitors their health during the course of their employment.[40] In other words, employers would have a larger stake in screening against and monitoring employees who may put themselves and others at risk in the workplace, have an increased susceptibility to occupational disease, or are likely to be absent from work for long periods of time as a result of their genetic conditions, so that the employer can minimize economic loss and increase productivity. Further, employees with the most promising genetic traits may be privy to better job opportunities or promotions, leaving asymptomatic or pre-symptomatic "genetic undesirables" to settle for less attractive positions or no employment opportunities at all.[41]

Workers compensation schemes, which have generally replaced common law claims by compensating sick or injured employees on a no-fault basis, are usually funded by compulsory insurance or self-insurance. Since employers cannot contract out of workers compensation, an employer could be motivated to seek to access an employee's or applicant's genetic information and screen out individuals who are more genetically predisposed to injuries or diseases caused by workplace conditions, as a means of minimizing employer premiums. Alternatively, employers could attempt to obtain waivers from employees who exhibit predispositions to avoid liability altogether for workplace injury or illness. Given the power imbalance inherent in employment relationships, there may be an element of coercion in workplace testing. Individuals may feel pressured to undergo testing or sign waivers as a condition of obtaining or maintaining employment and protecting career prospects.[42]

Conversely, an employer is entitled to the information, which could include medical and genetic test results, that is reasonably necessary to maintain a safe and healthy workplace and to operate a business, particularly where the employer has substantially invested in senior employees and

---

[40] The prevalence of genetic testing by U.S. employers prompted former President Bill Clinton to sign an Executive Order in February 2000 which prohibits federal departments and agencies from using genetic information in hiring or employment actions. By the end of 2000, 23 American States had also enacted legislation regarding the use of genetic information in employment, indicating a clear trend by federal and state governments to provide more comprehensive protection against discrimination in employment on the basis of genetic information or status.

[41] *Ibid.*, at 287, 291, 300.

[42] *AHEC, supra,* note 27, at 284, 285, 299; Ontario Workplace Safety Insurance Board, "Injured at Work? We're Here to Help", online: <http://www.wsib.on.ca/wsib/wsibsite.nsf/LookupFiles/DownloadableFileWSISGuide/$File/3576AWSIS.pdf>.

employee training.[43] Further, an employer could argue that genetic testing, surveillance, and monitoring may be their best defense against liability resulting from an individual's false, inaccurate or incomplete disclosure of medical information.

8.2.4 Impact on Eligibility for Health Benefits, Long Term Disability Insurance, Life Insurance

Insurance companies, especially life insurers, have collected and used medical information, including family medical histories for over a century.[44] An individual seeking to be insured has a legal obligation to disclose all information that is deemed relevant for calculating premiums and underwriting the insurance policy, such as age, gender, occupation, health status, lifestyle, tobacco and alcohol use, and family history.[45] While federal and provincial human rights legislation prohibits discrimination in employment, it exempts some areas like pensions and insurance plans from its ambit.[46] This implies that insurers could lawfully exclude an employee from insurance coverage or charge higher premiums on the basis of genetic status, with no legal recourse available to the applicant, thereby creating a genetic underclass.[47] On the other hand, healthy applicants might wish to undergo genetic testing and voluntarily disclose their test results in order to take advantage of cheaper premiums. Further, employees who know that they are at high risk for disease or injury for instance,[48] could exploit insurance companies by shopping around for companies with the best benefits or by purchasing substantial amounts of life insurance.

The argument in support of genetic testing arises in particular as a result of attempts by prospective policy holders to conceal unfavourable information or incorrectly disclose information in the underwriting process (an act termed as "adverse selection"), thereby allowing higher risk policyholders to pay lower premiums or apply for extended coverage while the

---

[43] See generally, CCH Canadian Limited, *Canada Labour Law Reports*, (2001) para. 6426; Béatrice Godard et al., "Genetic Information and Testing in Insurance and Employment: Technical, Social, and Ethical Issues" (2003) 11 European Journal of Human Genetics, Suppl 2 at S127 [*Godard*].

[44] *AHEC, supra,* note 27 at 305.

[45] Bartha M. Knoppers et al., "Genetics and Life Insurance in Canada: Points to Consider" (April 2004) 170 Canadian Medical Association Journal (9) at 1 [*Knoppers*].

[46] *CHRA, supra,* note 5, ss. 20-22.

[47] *AHEC, supra,* note 27 at 346.

[48] *Godard, supra,* note 43 at S124.

insurer pays out more claims and the general cost of insurance increases. In turn, higher insurance premiums for the entire pool of insurance might provide a disincentive for low risk applicants to obtain insurance.[49] Further, since family history is already used as a basic form of predictive genetic information, insurers view genetic testing as a natural extension of the risk information that could be used in the underwriting process.[50] Opponents of genetic testing argue that genetic tests, other than those which test for and diagnose dominant single-gene disorders, are not yet accurate, reliable or currently available on the market and therefore can rarely be used effectively in risk assessment.[51] There is also concern that permitting insurers to collect and use genetic test information may deter employees from undergoing tests which might enable early detection and treatment of disease, or from participating in genetic research, fearing that insurance companies may reject their applications for insurance.[52]

The Supreme Court of Canada has ruled that restricting disability insurance benefits is discriminatory. In *Battlefords & District Co-operative Ltd. v. Gibbs*,[53] the insurance company terminated the benefits of an employee receiving disability payments due to mental illness. The policy required benefits to cease after two years if the employee was not institutionalized, even if the employee was permanently unable to work. However, employees suffering physical disabilities continued to receive benefits until age 65. The Court determined that the mental and physical disability schemes were designed for the same purpose, thus, limiting the employee's entitlement to benefits because of her type of disability was discriminatory and contravened the human rights code. This decision suggests that in the context of genetic predispositions or disease, a disability insurer would likely be prohibited from discriminating against an employee currently enrolled in a disability plan on the basis of genetic status. How the Court would rule in a case where the employee was not yet a holder of such a policy is less clear, however, human rights legislation clearly indicates that discrimination in relation to insurance plans is not prohibited under its purview.

In the United States, at least 44 States have enacted specific legislation that regulates the use of genetic information by insurance companies and generally prohibits insurers from excluding applicants from coverage or raising premiums on the basis of genetic abnormalities. In 1996, the federal

---

[49] *AHEC, supra,* note 27 at 338.
[50] *Ibid.,* at 334.
[51] *Supra,* note 31 at 2.
[52] *Godard, supra,* note 43 at S124, S130.
[53] [1996] 3 S.C.R. 566 (S.C.C.).

government introduced the *Health Insurance Portability and Accountability Act of 1996*, which includes protection against excluding an individual from group insurance because of genetic information, charging a higher premium to one individual than to others in group insurance, exclusions in a group health plan for a pre-existing condition to 12 months, as well as exclusions if the individual has been previously covered for that condition for 12 months or more. The Act also provides explicit provisions stating that genetic information in the absence of a current diagnosis of illness shall not be considered a pre-existing condition.[54]

8.2.5   The Tension between the Potential Benefits and Harms of Genetic Testing

Genetic technology shows great potential for the prediction, diagnosis, treatment and prevention of diseases, however, the foregoing discussion indicates that threats to genetic privacy and risk of discrimination in employment and insurance could inhibit an employee from undergoing tests and treatment, and could seriously undermine scientific progress and the potential to improve health and health care.[55]

Another salient issue involves balancing respect for individual autonomy and an employee's right *not* to know about a potential or pending disease, particularly where there is no cure or effective medical treatment, against an employer's right or duty to know the results of a genetic test. The matter is further complicated by the question as to whether a duty exists to inform biological relatives of the employee's test results, even though the employee may not want this information to be disclosed to his or her family members. However, one employee's test results could inadvertently affect the employability and insurability of a wide range of family members.[56]

Thus, Canada's laws are challenged to reconcile the potential conflict between individual privacy rights and public interests, including those of a family member, institutions, researchers, and perhaps the right of citizens to receive the health benefits from genetic testing.[57]

---

[54] *AHEC, supra*, note 27 at 353, 354.
[55] *Oscapella, supra*, note 26 at 21, 29.
[56] *Ibid.*, at 22, 23.
[57] *Jones, supra*, note 34 at 16, 24.

9

Drug Testing & Privacy

9.1 DRUG TESTING

9.1.1 Introduction

Workplace alcohol and drug programs, in various forms, have been in place in Canada for over 25 years. Some have consisted solely of employee assistance programs, while others have been more comprehensive and have included the implementation of drug and alcohol testing policies.[1]

The implementation of drug testing policies by employers is felt to be justified due to the prevalence of drug use in the workplace and the serious consequences associated with such use, such as: accidents resulting in serious personal and property damage; excessive absenteeism giving rise to sick-leave benefits, insurance and compensation claims; loss of overall productivity and human potential; lower quality products and services; and increased corporate liability attributable to employee negligence and wrongdoing.[2] However, the implementation of such company policies have been heavily criticized by those who maintain that drug testing is an unwarranted intrusion into the employee's privacy. Consequently, there continue to be legal challenges to an employer's right to request these tests.[3]

---

[1] Roger K. MacDougall, *Canadian Workplace Privacy Rights–Alcohol and Drug Policy and Testing Issues: Development, Implementation and Legal Overview* (Ottawa: Canadian Bar Association-Continuing Legal Education Seminar, 1999) at 10. Since 1986, the number of Canadian companies which have instituted mandatory drug and alcohol testing has significantly increased both in the private and public sectors. Air Canada, Imperial Oil, the Ontario Racing Commission, the Toronto-Dominion Bank, Canadian National Railway, Canadian Pacific, and American Motors (Canada), are some of the employers who have introduced testing programs in their respective workplaces.

[2] B. Butler, *Alcohol and Drugs in the Workplace* (Markham: Butterworths, 1993) at 27.

[3] Roger K. MacDougall, *supra* note 1 at 10.

9.1.2   Is Drug Testing an Invasion of Privacy?

Policies of drug and alcohol testing are personally invasive in three distinct manners. First, routine drug tests are intrusive. The tests are often set up so that another person must accompany the employee so as to ensure there is no specimen tampering. Similarly, the requirement to remove one's outer garments and to urinate in a bathroom is degrading.

Second, the laboratory procedure itself is an invasion of an employee's privacy. Urinalysis reveals not only the presence of illegal drugs, but also the existence of many other physical and medical conditions, including pregnancy and/ or the genetic predisposition to disease.[4]

Third, the potential for false positive results due to human error in the labotatory is present. Frequently drug tests fail to distinguish between legal and illegal substances. For example, Depronil, a prescription drug used to treat Parkinson's disease, has shown up as an amphetamine on standard drug tests. Over-the-counter anti-inflammatory drugs like Ibuprofen have shown up positive on marihuana tests. Even the poppy seeds found in baked goods can produce a positive result for heroin.[5]

9.1.3   The American Approach

While presently there is no Canadian legislation providing for man-datory drug testing of employees, companies doing business in the U.S., may be obliged to respect U.S. legislation and policy and perform drug tests on their employees. For example, the Federal Highway Administration (FHWA) which regulates the motor carrier industry, has in place regulations requiring drug and alcohol testing of commercial motor vehicle drivers.[6] As of July 1, 1996, these regulations were extended to Canadian trucking

---

[4] For example, in 1988, the Washington, D.C. Police Department admitted it used urine samples collected for drug tests to screen female employees for pregnancy without their knowledge or consent (See American Civil Liberties Union, News Release, "Privacy in America: Workplace Drug Testing," (1999), online: American Civil Liberties Union <http://www.aclu.org/library/pbr5.html>.

[5] *Ibid.*

[6] *Federal Motor Carrier Safety Regulations, Title 49 Code of Federal Regulations, Parts 40 and 382*, U.S. Department of Transportation, Federal Highway Administration. The workplace drug and alcohol policy and program is to consist of pre-employment drug testing as well as random drug and alcohol testing at a minimum annual rate of 25 per cent of the driver pool for alcohol and 50 per cent for drugs. Employers are responsible for complying with the regulations, including the testing requirements, and can not use a driver in cross-border work who is un-qualified or in violation of these rules.

companies. Previously, there had been an exemption for Canadian carriers and drivers. This foreign carrier exemption was lifted when the Government of Canada announced in December 1994 that it would not be proceeding with similar legislation.[7]

An Interim Report issued in January 1999 by the Special Senate Committee on Transportation Safety and Security, recommended that Transport Canada reconsider its position and that the Canadian government should proceed to permit mandatory, random drug and alcohol testing in the transportation industry similar to United States legislation.[8] It remains to be seen if the government will act on this recommendation.

There have been cases in the United States which have ruled that mandatory urine testing of public sector employees is a violation of the constitution. Many state and federal courts have ruled that testing programs in public sector workplaces are unconstitutional if they are not based on reasonably based suspicion. Throughout the country, courts have struck down programs that randomly tested police officers, fire-fighters, teachers, civilian army employees, prison guards and employees of many federal agencies.[9]

In 1989, the United States Supreme Court ruled on the constitutionality of drug testing public sector employees. The court held that while urine tests are searches, a public sector employer may have the right to search an employee who is not a suspected drug user so long as an employee's Fourth Amendment right to privacy is outweighed by the government's interest in maintaining a drug-free workplace.[10]

With respect to United States private sector employees, it remains to be seen whether or not drug testing programs will be uniformly sanctioned by the courts. In most states, private sector employees have virtually no protection against drug testing's intrusion on their privacy unless they belong to a union that has negotiated the prohibition or restriction of workplace testing. One exception is California, in which the state constitution specifies a right to privacy that applies, not only to government action, but to actions by private business as well.[11]

---

[7] Nancy Holmes, *Drug Testing: Legal Implications*, (Research Branch: Law and Government Division, Library of Parliament, 1996) at 6.

[8] Recommendation 3 of the Interim Report issued on January 1999.

[9] *Department of Public Education – American Civil Liberties Union*, *Briefing Paper Number 5*, "Drug Testing in the Workplace," (23 Nov. 1992) online: <http://www.eff.org/pub/Privacy/Workplace/acludrugtestingworkplace.faq>.

[10] *Skinner v. Railway Labour Executives' Assn.*, 489 U.S. 602 (U.S. Cal., 1989).

[11] In addition to California, only a handful of other states have enacted protective legislation that restricts drug testing in the private workplace and gives employees

9.1.4   The Canadian Approach

There is no Canadian legislation dealing specifically with drug testing - either mandating it, or prohibiting it. There has been no decision from the Supreme Court of Canada addressing the question and cases from lower courts and administrative tribunals have varied considerably. As a result, there remains some level of uncertainty in the Canadian legal environment concerning company drug testing programs.

(a)   The Charter of Rights and Freedoms

If a government institution has instituted a program requiring the mandatory testing of employees, any challenges to such a policy would likely be brought under sections 7 and 8 of the Charter.[12] Such challenges could also be based on section 15 which holds that every individual is equal before and under the law and has the right to the equal protection and equal benefit of the law without discrimination on the basis of race, national or ethnic origin, colour, religion, sex, age or *mental or physical disability*.[13]

---

some measure of protection from unfair and unreliable testing. The states of Montana, Iowa, Vermont and Rhode Island have banned all random or blanket drug testing of employees (i.e., testing without probable cause or reasonable suspicion), and Minnesota, Maine and Connecticut permit random testing only of employees in "safety-sensitive" positions. The laws in these states also mandate confirmatory testing, use of certified laboratories, confidentiality of test results and other procedural protections. These laws place significant limits on employers' otherwise unfettered authority to test and give employees the power to resist unwarranted invasions of privacy. Only in California, Massachusetts and New Jersey have the highest courts ruled out some forms of drug testing on state constitutional or statutory grounds. [See Department of Public Education — American Civil Liberties Union, Briefing Paper Number 5, "Drug Testing in the Workplace," (23 Nov. 1992) online: <http://www.eff.org/pub/Privacy/Workplace/acludrugtestingworkplace.faq>].

[12] The constitutionality of mandatory drug and/ or alcohol testing has been considered in *R. v. Chatham* (1985), 23 C.R.R. 344 (B.C. S.C.); *Jackson v. Joyceville Penitentiary*, [1990] 3 F.C. 55 (Fed. T.D.) in the context of drug testing regulations in penitentiaries and in impaired driving cases, where it was held under section 7 that the non-consensual taking of an individual's bodily fluids infringes the security of the person. The taking of bodily samples has been held to constitute a seizure within the meaning of section 8 in *R. v. Dyment*, [1988] 2 S.C.R. 417 (S.C.C.).

[13] The same type of argument as used under the *Canadian Human Rights Act* (i.e., discrimination on the basis of "disability").

(b) *Canadian Human Rights Act*[14]

The *Canadian Human Rights Act* applies to all federal government departments, agencies, Crown corporations, and to businesses which fall under federal jurisdiction such as banks, airlines and railway companies. A 2002 policy statement issued by the Canadian Human Rights Commission states that under the Act, employee drug testing might be considered to be a discriminatory practice on the ground of disability. Furthermore, in the tribunal decision discussed below, it was held that as a blanket policy, mandatory urinalysis represents a major invasion of privacy in the employment field.[15]

Disability is defined in the Act as including any previous or existing dependence on alcohol or drugs.[16] Sections 7, 8 and 10 of the *Canadian Human Rights Act*, allow a federal employee who has been disciplined for testing positive in a drug test to file a complaint with the Commission alleging discrimination on the basis of disability.

Under the Act, an employer has a defence to a charge of discriminatory practice if they can show that the practice is justified as a "bona fide occupational requirement". In drug testing cases, the employer would have to demonstrate objectively that a "positive" test result indicated decreased ability to perform the job safely, efficiently and reliably, and, wherever possible, that assessments of capacity to perform were individualized.

In *Canadian Civil Liberties Assn. v. Toronto Dominion Bank*[17] the Toronto-Dominion Bank implemented a drug testing program which re-

---

[14] *Canadian Human Rights Act*, R.S.C. 1985, c. H-6.
[15] See *Canadian Civil Liberties Assn. v. Toronto Dominion Bank, infra* note 17.
[16] See section 25.
[17] (1994), 22 C.H.R.R. D/301 (Can. Human Rights Trib.), reversed (1996), (*sub nom. Canadian Human Rights Commission v. Toronto Dominion Bank*) 112 F.T.R. 127, 25 C.H.R.R. D/373 (Fed. T.D.), reversed (1998), 163 D.L.R. (4th) 193, 32 C.H.R.R. D/261 (Fed. C.A.). The test screened for cannabis (marihuana and hashish), cocaine and opiates (codeine, morphine and heroin). Where the first test is positive for an opiate and the employee has provided a credible medical explanation for taking prescription medications, the matter is reviewed with the Medical Director and the employee is usually given the benefit of the doubt. In the case of a finding of cocaine use, the employee's file is immediately transferred to a rehabilitation nurse for follow-up with that employee. In the case of a finding of cannabis, the employee is notified and advised that a second test will be necessary. If the second test is positive for cannabis, then the employee is referred to a rehabilitation nurse and to an assessment centre. If the third test is positive, steps are taken to terminate the employment regardless of whether the employee's medical assessment indicates drug dependence or persistent casual use.

quired newly hired employees to undergo urine tests within 48 hours of being accepted for employment. This program was challenged by the Canadian Civil Liberties Association who argued that the program was discriminatory on the basis of disability under section 10 of the *Canadian Human Rights Act*.

The Canadian Human Rights Tribunal found that the drug testing policy of the TD bank did not discriminate against drug dependent persons pursuant to the *Canadian Human Rights Act*.[18] Relevant to the Tribunal's decision was the fact that the Bank's testing requirement was not a prerequisite for employment but rather came into effect only after a candidate had been hired. Since all prospective employees were notified of the requirement to submit to the drug test as a condition of employment, a failure to comply constituted a breach of a condition of employment, rather than discrimination. Moreover, the Bank's ultimate dismissal of an employee who failed to pass all three of the company's drug testing stages was based on a finding of persistent use of an illegal substance. Lastly, the Board held that any finding of drug dependency is one of diagnosis and not of perceived disability as contemplated under the *Canadian Human Rights Act*.

The Federal Court of Canada (Trial Division)[19] overturned this decision and found that the drug testing policy of the Bank did amount to discrimination under the Act. The Court held that the policy was indirectly discriminating in that while neutral on its face, it had a negative impact on drug-dependent persons, a subgroup protected by the human rights legislation. However, it was held that an employer may implement a drug testing policy if able to show that it is rationally connected to the employment and that reasonable steps have been taken to accommodate the complainant, short of undue hardship to the employer. In summary, the Trial Division held that where an employee has consented to a drug test and it is clear that the employer has implemented its policy as a condition of employment, it would be difficult to establish discrimination under section 10 of the *CHRA*.

The Bank appealed this decision to the Federal Court of Appeal.[20] In a 2:1 decision, the Court of Appeal held that the Bank could not justify testing in the circumstances. While the majority decision differed on whether the discrimination was direct or indirect, some of the key factors relevant to their determination were: the Bank had failed to make out the *bona fide* occupational defence; there was no evidence of a drug problem in the workforce; the employer could not show that mandatory testing was the least intrusive reasonable method to assess job performance; and the

---

[18] *Toronto Dominion Bank, ibid.*
[19] *Canadian Civil Liberties Assn. v. Toronto Dominion Bank, supra,* note 17.
[20] *Ibid.*

Bank failed to prove that employee work performance was affected by drugs. Interestingly, two of the three justices likely would have upheld testing in the appropriate circumstances in safety sensitive industries.

This case placed importance on the distinction between adverse impact and direct discrimination as well as the meaning of reasonable accommodation to the point of undue hardship within the context of the *bona fide* occupational requirement exception.[21] However, *Bill S-5* in 1998 has since removed the word "reasonable" and restricted the meaning of "undue hardship" to considerations of health, safety and cost.[22] Furthermore, a recent Supreme Court of Canada judgment eliminated the adverse impact/direct impact dichotomy.[23]

The general principles which emerge from decisions under the Human Rights regime are that an employer has a right to ensure that its business operations are conducted safely, and a corresponding right to assess whether employees are incapable of performing their essential duties. This right generally outweighs an employee's privacy right in cases where an employee is hired to work in a safety sensitive position. For example, in *Entrop v. Imperial Oil Ltd.*[24] the employer's (Imperial Oil) drug testing program was alleged to discriminate on the basis of "handicap" under the *Ontario Human Rights Code*.[25] Imperial Oil's Alcohol and Drug Policy subjected all job applicants to a urinalysis test for drugs as a condition of employment. Any employees wishing to work in safety sensitive positions were also required to undergo drug testing in order to be certified for such work.

---

[21] For further information on the issue of what is reasonable accommodation to the point of undue hardship, see: *O'Malley v. Simpsons-Sears Ltd.*, (sub nom. *Ontario Human Rights Commission v. Simpsons-Sears Ltd.*), [1985] 2 S.C.R. 536 (S.C.C.); *Renaud v. Central Okanagan School District No. 23*, (sub nom. *Central Okanagan School District No. 23 v. Renaud*), [1992] 2 S.C.R. 970 (S.C.C.); *Chambly (Commission scolaire régionale) c. Bergevin*, (sub nom. *Commission scolaire régionale de Chambly v. Bergevin*), [1994] 2 S.C.R. 525(S.C.C.); *Central Alberta Dairy Pool v. Alberta (Human Rights Commission)*, [1990] 2 S.C.R. 489 (S.C.C.).

[22] See *CHRA* section 15(2).

[23] See *British Columbia (Public Service Employee Relations Commission) v. B.C.G.E.U.* (1999), [1999] S.C.J. No. 46, 1999 CarswellBC 1907 (S.C.C.).

[24] There were a series of human rights adjudication decisions on this matter culminating in *Entrop v. Imperial Oil Ltd.* (1996), 24 C.C.E.L. (2d) 122 (Ont. Bd. of Inquiry), affirmed (1998), 35 C.C.E.L. (2d) 56 (Ont. Div. Ct.), leave to appeal allowed (1998), 1998 CarswellOnt 1955 (Ont. C.A.), reversed (2000), 189 D.L.R. (4th) 14 (Ont. C.A.). This was the first decision in Ontario in the area of substance abuse testing.

[25] R.S.O. 1990, c. H.19.

Furthermore, as a condition of employment, employees could be subjected to random drug and alcohol testing. In addition to being tested, prospective and current employees in safety-sensitive positions were placed under a continuing obligation to disclose to management whether they have, or have ever had, a substance abuse problem or have received treatment or counselling for such a problem.

The Ontario Human Rights Board held that Imperial Oil has a right to ensure that its business operations are conducted safely, and a corresponding right to assess whether employees are incapable of performing their essential duties. For safety sensitive positions, Imperial Oil was also found to have the right to assess whether its employees are free from impairment on the job, whether by alcohol, drug abuse, or otherwise. However, while freedom from impairment of drugs and alcohol is a *bona fide* occupational requirement, it was held that Imperial Oil's Policy overreached this legitimate goal. It was further held that drug testing for cause, post-incident, certification into safety sensitive positions or post-reinstatement reasons may be upheld if testing is only one component of the overall assessment of abuse.[26]

The decision of the Board of Inquiry was upheld on appeal to the Ontario Divisional Court, but on further appeal to the Ontario Court of Appeal, the Board's decision was reversed in part. The appeal dealt with the issue of whether the Board of Inquiry had jurisdiction to expand the scope of its inquiry to include a determination as to whether Imperial's drug testing policy violated the *Ontario Human Rights Code*. The Court of Appeal ruled that the Board should not have expanded its inquiry to include an analysis of whether drug testing as well as alcohol testing, breaches the *Human Rights Code*. Despite this ruling, however, Laskin J.A. did examine the issue of whether Imperial's drug testing policy violated the Code.

Laskin J.A. applied the new three-step test developed by the Supreme Court of Canada in *British Columbia (Public Service Employee Relations Commission) v. B.C.G.S.E.U.* (1999), 176 D.L.R (4th) 1 (S.C.C.), (referred to by Laskin J.A. and herein as "*Meiorin*"). The test adopted by the Supreme Court was designed to eliminate the necessity for an inquiry into whether a particular type of discrimination is "direct" or "adverse effect" discrimination. This line of inquiry was seen by courts as being increasingly prob-

---

[26] *Entrop v. Imperial Oil Ltd.* (1998), 35 C.C.E.L. (2d) 56 (Ont. Div. Ct.), leave to appeal allowed (1998), 1998 CarswellOnt 1955 (Ont. C.A.), reversed (2000), 189 D.L.R. (4th) 14 (Ont. C.A.). This case was appealed by Imperial Oil to the Ontario Divisional Court where the Court decided that it would not interfere with the adjudicator's rulings. Leave to appeal this decision was granted by the Ontario Court of Appeal (May 12, 1998), Doc. CA M22074 (Ont. C.A.).

lematic and given to inconsistent and arbitrary remedies, depending upon the characterization of the discrimination.

In *Meiorin*, McLachlin J. proposed the following test, which can be used by an employer to justify an impugned employment standard as being a *bona fide* occupational requirement ("BFOR"). By establishing, on the balance of probabilities, that:

(1)　The employer adopted the standard for a purpose rationally connected to the performance of the job;

(2)　The employer adopted the standard in an honest and good faith belief that it was necessary to the fulfilment of that legitimate work-related purpose; and

(3)　The standard is reasonably necessary to the accomplishment of that legitimate work-related purpose. To show that the standard is reasonably necessary, it must be demonstrated that it is impossible to accommodate individual employees sharing the characteristics of the claimant without imposing undue hardship upon the employer,[27]

the employer can justify the impugned employment standard as a BFOR. Applying this analysis to Imperial Oil, Laskin J.A. held that the company's alcohol testing policy was a BFOR. However, its drug testing policy did not pass the test set out in *Meiorin*.

Laskin J.A. held that substance abusers are handicapped within the meaning of the *Ontario Human Rights Code* and are therefore entitled to freedom from discrimination in their workplace based on their handicap. Since perceived as well as actual substance abuse is included in the definition of "handicap" under the Code, anyone testing positive under the alcohol and drug testing provisions of Imperial Oil's policy is entitled to the protection of section 5. The sanctions imposed by the company applied to any person testing positive in an alcohol or drug test and were *prima facie* discriminatory. As a result, Imperial Oil bore the onus of proving that the testing and the sanctions imposed for testing positive are BFORs.

The Court of Appeal held that Imperial Oil had adopted a drug and alcohol testing policy for a purpose rationally connected to the job, and that Imperial Oil did, in fact, have an honest and good faith belief that its policy was necessary to accomplish the company's purpose. Therefore Imperial Oil met the first two steps of the *Meiorin* test. However, with respect to the third stage of the test, whether the means used to accomplish the purpose

---

[27] *British Columbia (Public Service Employee Relations Commission) v. B.C.G.E.U.* (1999), (sub nom. *British Columbia (Public Service Employee Relations Commission) v. B.C.G.S.E.U.*) 176 D.L.R. (4th) 1 (S.C.C.), at 24-25.

were reasonably necessary, Laskin J.A. found Imperial Oil's policy deficient.

Dealing first with the issue of drug testing, Laskin J.A. held that the drugs listed in Imperial Oil's policy have the capacity to impair job performance and that urinalysis is a reliable method of showing the presence of drugs or drug metabolites in a person's body. However, he held that:

> ... drug testing suffers from one fundamental flaw. It cannot measure present impairment. A positive drug test shows only past drug use. It cannot show how much was used or when it was used. Thus, the Board found that a positive drug test provides no evidence of impairment or likely impairment on the job. It does not demonstrate that a person is incapable of performing the essential duties of the position. The Board also found on the evidence that no tests currently exist to accurately assess the effect of drug use on job performance and that drug testing programs have not been shown to be effective in reducing drug use, work accidents or work performance problems. On these findings, random drug testing for employees in safety-sensitive positions cannot be justified as reasonably necessary to accomplish Imperial Oil's legitimate goal of a safe workplace free of impairment.

Laskin J.A. also found that the sanction provisions of Imperial Oil's drug testing policy were too severe, as they mandated automatic termination for all employees after a single positive test. Imperial Oil had failed to demonstrate why it could not tailor its sanctions to accommodate individual capabilities without incurring undue hardship.

Laskin J.A. found that the provisions for random alcohol testing stand on a different footing. Breathalyzer tests can show present impairment. Expert evidence before the Board confirmed the reliability and utility of breathalyzers to measure alcohol impairment. The Board relied on evidence to the effect that increased supervision of employees by properly trained personnel would be more likely to detect impairment on the job. However, random alcohol testing will not pass the third step of the *Meiorin* test unless the employer meets its duty to accommodate the needs of those who test positive. As a result, Laskin J.A. set aside the Board's conclusion that random alcohol testing for employees breached the Code, and held instead that this type of testing is a BFOR, provided that the sanctions imposed for an employee testing positive are tailored to the employee's circumstances.

Laskin J.A. also held that requiring an employee to disclose a past substance abuse problem, no matter how far in the past, is an unreasonable requirement. The Board found, on evidence before it, that a point can be reached by former substance abusers when the risk of relapse or recurrence is small. The Board found the cut-off point to be five to six years of successful remission. In applying its policy of relocation and reassignment of individuals identifying themselves as former substance abusers, without consideration of the length of time the individual had been drug or alcohol free, Imperial Oil's treatment of the employee was unjustified. In conclusion, Laskin J.A. ruled that random alcohol testing for employees in safety sensitive positions is a BFOR, provided that the sanctions for an employee testing positive are tailored to the employee's circumstances.

As a result of the Court of Appeal ruling in *Entrop*, and, in particular Laskin J.A.'s *obiter* comments respecting the efficacy of random drug testing, the status of drug testing in the workplace under Ontario human rights legislation remains somewhat unclear.

A recent arbitration decision reinforces the differing approach to mandatory workplace drug and alcohol testing in Canada as opposed to the United States.[28] While federal legislation requires certain types of United States employees to undergo that kind of testing, the Canadian approach involves a case-by-case balancing of the employer's interest in implementing such a regime against the intrusion into the employees' privacy that is inherent in the testing process itself.

The company, Bulk Systems, was acquired by Trimac in 1990. Trimac is a publicly-traded Canadian company, headquartered in Calgary, Alberta, with operations throughout North America. Bulk Systems, as with the other Trimac companies, utilized Trimac equipment, policies, insurance, operating authorities, accounting, human resource, pension and training system. Safety rules and safety training were structured on a company-wide basis. Given the homogeneity of the Trimac organization it is not surprising that there is a single drug and alcohol policy company-wide in Canada and a parallel policy in the United States. This policy was amended in 1996 to incorporate mandatory random drug and alcohol testing for its drivers to reflect the statutory regime in the United States (where mandatory drug and alcohol testing of transport drivers is required by federal law and where the parent company has sizeable operations). No such regime exists in Canada.

The Transport and Communications union challenged the application of the mandatory random drug testing policy to Bulk Systems' drivers whose work was confined to Canada. The union argued that there was no clear provision for drug and alcohol testing in the collective agreements covering those drivers, nor was there a legal requirement that they be tested. Even if the company could impose a drug and alcohol testing policy without clear contractual or statutory authority, the union argued that a "balancing of interests" test applied.

---

[28] *Trimac Transportation Services - Bulk Systems v. T.C.U.* (1999), 88 L.A.C. (4th) 237 (Can. Arb. Bd.).

The arbitrator found that the company's mandatory random drug and alcohol testing program was unenforceable under the collective agreement. Although the grievance was decided by the arbitrator within the parameters of the collective agreement, the issue of compliance with human rights legislation, raised by the parties, was also addressed in the arbitrator's reasons. The company attempted to distinguish its case from that of *Entrop*, on the basis that the policy under attack in that case targeted persons with a handicap, while Bulk Systems' policy was aimed at all its drivers and had the legitimate business purpose of preventing drivers who have drugs or alcohol in their systems from reporting to work. The company argued that this type of "adverse effect" discrimination on individuals with a drug or alcohol addiction was accommodated by the company to the point of undue hardship. However, the arbitrator held that the company failed to discharge the onus upon it of establishing that its policy was rationally connected to its legitimate business interest and that it had also failed to establish any pre-existing experience or incidents within the particular bargaining unit which would support the necessity for mandatory random drug testing. Following the line of reasoning in *Entrop*, the arbitrator held that the urinalysis mechanism used to detect drug use does not establish whether an employee is under the influence at work.

Two other arbitration decisions have further clarified when employers are justified in using drug and alcohol tests to ensure safe workplaces. In *J.D. Irving Ltd. v. C.E.P., Locals 104 & 1309*,[29] an arbitration board held that the company's policy on alcohol and drug use, which provided, among other things, for mandatory drug and alcohol testing, is acceptable when the testing is employed for "reasonable cause". Examples of reasonable cause include a grounded suspicion of alcohol or drug use by employees; for instance, after an incident causing serious bodily injury or significant damage to company property, or following a "near miss" that may have resulted in serious damages to property or injury. The board further ruled that this policy might only apply to employees in safety-sensitive positions.

A similar outcome was reached in *Canadian National Railway v. CAW-Canada*.[30] An arbitrator held that an employer who has reasonable grounds to be concerned about the impairment of an employee in a safety-sensitive position may subject the employee to drug and alcohol testing. As a positive drug test may not confirm actual impairment, but rather indicates consumption at some point in time, the test cannot be used as the grounds for dismissal. However, the board concluded that the employer should not be

---

[29] (2002), 111 L.A.C. (4th) 328 (N.B. Arb. Bd.) (M.G. Picher).
[30] (2000), 95 L.A.C. (4th) 341, 2000 CarswellNat 2285 (Can. Arb. Bd.) (M. Picher).

precluded from considering the results of the test as one of the factors in favour of discipline or discharge.

The 2002 Federal Human Rights Commission, after public consultation and a review of the jurisprudence, released a comprehensive policy indicating the types of testing that will be considered permissible. The Policy states:

> Because they cannot be established as bona fide occupational requirements, the following types of testing are not acceptable:
>
> - Pre-employment drug testing
>
> - Pre-employment alcohol testing
>
> - Random drug testing
>
> - Random alcohol testing of employees in non-safety-sensitive positions.

The following types of testing may be included in a workplace drug- and alcohol-testing program, but only if an employer can demonstrate that they are *bona fide* occupational requirements:

> - Random alcohol testing of employees in safety sensitive positions. Alcohol testing has been found to be a reasonable requirement because alcohol testing can indicate actual impairment of ability to perform or fulfill the essential duties or requirements of the job. Random drug testing is prohibited because, given its technical limitations, drug testing can only detect the presence of drugs and not if or when an employee may have been impaired by drug use.
>
> - Drug or alcohol testing for "reasonable cause" or "post-accident," e.g. where there are reasonable grounds to believe there is an underlying problem of substance abuse or where an accident has occurred due to impairment from drugs or alcohol, provided that testing is a part of a broader program of medical assessment, monitoring and support.
>
> - Periodic or random testing following disclosure of a current drug or alcohol dependency or abuse problem may be acceptable if tailored to individual circumstances and as part of a broader program of monitoring and support. Usually, a designated rehabilitation provider will determine whether follow-up testing is necessary for a particular individual.
>
> - Mandatory disclosure of present or past drug or alcohol dependency or abuse may be permissible for employees holding safety-sensitive positions, within certain limits, and in concert with accommodation measures. Generally, employees not in safety-sensitive positions should not be required to disclose past alcohol or drug problems.

In the limited circumstances where testing is justified, employees who test positive must be accommodated to the point of undue hardship. The *Canadian Human Rights Act* requires individualized or personalized accommodation

163

measures. Policies that result in the employee's automatic loss of employment, reassignment, or that impose inflexible reinstatement conditions without regard for personal circumstances are unlikely to meet this requirement. Accommodation should include the necessary support to permit the employee to undergo treatment or a rehabilitation program, and consideration of sanctions less severe than dismissal.

The policy continues by explaining in what circumstances an employer would be relieved of the duty to accommodate.

The question of protection under a human rights code for employees not suffering from drug or alcohol addiction emerges in the case of *Milazzo v. Autocar Connaisseur Inc.*[31] At issue was whether a recreational user of marijuana could invoke protection under section 7 of the *Canadian Human Rights Act*, which makes it a discriminatory practice to refuse to continue to employ someone due to his/her disability. Disability is defined in section 25 of the Act as a "previous or existing dependence on alcohol or a drug."

The complainant, a bus driver with five years of seniority, tested positive for cannabis metabolites and was dismissed in accordance with his employer's "zero tolerance" drug policy. The same policy provided for rehabilitation opportunities for those employees who admitted drug problems voluntarily. The bus company, Autocar Connaisseur, operated both in Canada and in the United States. As all Canadian bus drivers who have "the reasonable potential for crossing the border" are subject to the U.S. Federal Department of Transportation's Alcohol and Drug Testing Regulations, Autocar Connaisseur was running the risk of losing its American operating licence if any of its drivers were caught driving in the U.S. while impaired.

When confronted with the results of the test, the employee explained that he had smoked marijuana several weeks earlier. However, the level of cannabis metabolites in his urine indicated recent consumption or long-term use. Nonetheless, the complainant did not claim that he had any drug dependence problem and was therefore disabled. Rather, he contended that the employer discriminated against him on the basis of perceived disability. In the opinion of the Canadian Human Rights Tribunal, however, the evidence adduced did not corroborate this submission. The company had no concerns with the employee's performance and had never suspected that he had been using drugs until he tested positive, which triggered his immediate dismissal. The Tribunal confirmed that the Act prohibits discrimination on the basis of both disability and perceived disability. However, as the complainant had not claimed to suffer a disability and had failed to prove that

---

[31] (2003), 47 C.H.R.R. D/468, 2003 CarswellNat 4798 (Can. Human Rights Trib.).

the employer perceived him to be disabled, he failed to successfully establish a *prima facie* case of discrimination before the Tribunal.

Turning to the issue of whether the random alcohol and drug testing policy was reasonable, the Tribunal applied the *Meiorin* test and concluded that in a workplace where drivers spend considerable time on the road totally unsupervised, "urine testing for the presence of cannabis metabolites does assist in identifying drivers who are at an elevated risk of accident." This fact, coupled with the requirements for drivers established by the U.S. testing legislation, allowed the Tribunal to rule that the policy in question was reasonably necessary. The only factor that the Tribunal took issue with was the policy's "zero tolerance" component, which the Tribunal found discriminatory against drug-addicted employees who tested positive for drugs as it did not provide for any form of accommodation. On the evidence, accommodation was in fact possible given that the company was willing to assist employees who came forward voluntarily with substance abuse problems. In the result, the Tribunal ordered Autocar Connaisseur to redraft its testing policy to include accommodation for employees who test positively for drug use.

In *Chiasson v. Kellogg Brown & Root (Canada) Co.*,[32] an employee who failed a pre-employment drug test filed a human rights complaint under the Alberta *Human Rights, Citizenship and Multiculturalism Act*. The complainant was offered a position as a receiving inspector at an oil sands upgrader project, subject to a clear pre-employment medical and drug test. When the employer learned that the complainant had tested positive for marijuana, the complainant's employment was terminated. The Alberta Human Rights and Citizenship Commission represented the dismissed employee and argued that he was discriminated against on the basis of perceived disability, as the test could not measure actual impairment and thus treated him as an addict. Further, the Commission stated the employer could have accommodated the grievor without incurring undue hardship.

The human rights panel dismissed the complaint. The panel Chair held that the complainant had failed to provide evidence proving that the employer perceived him to be a drug addict. Further, as the complainant had not claimed that he was an addict, he could not establish a *prima facie* case of discrimination on a prohibited ground. However, the panel acknowledged that pre-employment drug testing is *prima facie* discriminatory against drug-

---

[32] (2005), 56 C.H.R.R. D/466, 2005 CarswellAlta 2325 (Alta. H.R. & Cit. Comm.), reversed (2006), 2006 CarswellAlta 621 (Alta. Q.B.), reversed (2007), 2007 CarswellAlta 1833 (Alta. C.A.), leave to appeal refused (2008), 2008 CarswellAlta 704 (S.C.C.).

dependent persons. Therefore, the employer's drug testing policy would have to meet the three-step test established in *Meiorin*.

The first two branches of the test did not pose any difficulty for the employer. Focusing on the third requirement, the Chair noted that the complainant's job was to operate a company vehicle in "an extremely congested, inherently dangerous, heavy equipment environment". He further observed that despite the inability of urinalysis to detect actual drug impairment, substance abuse does impair an individual's work performance to some extent, whether measurable or not, and concluded that "the pre-employment drug test was a reasonable requirement for ensuring the complainant's personal safety and the safety of others, as well as protecting persons from the potential for personnel and environmental disaster from damaged or defective pressure vessels and other material.

Further, the Chair rejected the argument that the employer was required to accommodate the grievor to the point of undue hardship, finding that had the complainant provided evidence of a real or perceived disability, the withdrawal of his employment offer would have been discriminatory and the third element of the *Meiorin* test would not be totally met. However, as the complainant failed to make out a *prima facie* case of discrimination, no accommodation on the part of the employer was required.

The complainant appealed the panel's decision and the trial judge agreed with the dismissed employee that his employer had discriminated against him as the company policy treated recreational drug users as addicts. However, the Alberta Court of Appeal restored the panel's ruling. The Court relied on expert evidence confirming that effects of cannabis consumption linger for several days after the drug use. Thus, the Court agreed with the panel that the company policy, aimed at ensuring a safe working environment at their safety challenged workplace, and precluding impaired employees from operating heavy machinery, was reasonable. The application for 'leave to appeal' from the judgment of the Court of Appeal was dismissed.[33]

(c) Arbitration

If there is no collective agreement which addresses the issue of employee drug testing, management may identify the establishment of a policy as a matter for collective bargaining or may attempt to unilaterally impose the policy.[34] Arbitration cases typically centre on the ability of the employer

---

[33] *Chiasson v. Kellogg Brown & Root (Canada) Co.* (2008), 2008 CarswellAlta 704 (S.C.C.).

[34] *B. Butler, supra* note 2 at 115.

to unilaterally impose a management rule dealing with drug testing of employees. A drug testing policy will only be enforceable if it satisfies the following conditions: it must be clear, unequivocal and consistently enforced by the company from the time it is introduced; it must not be unreasonable or inconsistent with the collective agreement; and the policy must be brought to the attention of the employees with clear explanation as to the consequences of a breach of the rule.[35]

While each of these factors can be expected to be looked at in an arbitration case, the primary focus is the "reasonableness" of the rule. In considering the reasonableness of implementing a mandatory drug testing policy, the "balance of interest" test, developed in *KVP*[36] is applied (i.e., balancing the right of an employee to privacy against the right of and responsibility of an employer to ensure that his or her employees are safe and unimpaired and the public is safe). The test is a function of risk assessment. For instance, the higher the workplace risk the more reasonable it is to justify an invasion of the employee's privacy by demanding drug and alcohol testing, even on a random basis. Similarly, where the workplace risk is low, fewer forms of testing will be justifiable or none at all where there is insufficient evidence of a problem.

For example, in *Provincial-American Truck Transporters v. Teamsters Union, Local 880*[37] the collective agreement specifically gave the company the right to request medical examinations. Citing *Canadian Pacific Ltd. v. U.T.U.*,[38] the arbitrator analogized drug testing to employee searches and broadly interpreted the provision relating to medical examination to encompass drug and alcohol testing. The "balancing of interests" test was applied as follows:

> . . . If there is a reason to demand a test, then a test can be demanded. That is, if a particular employee gives the company reasonable grounds for believing that his/ her fitness to perform the job safely is impaired by use of alcohol or drugs, then the company should be able to test as part of its rights under art. 13. If mandatory universal testing is to be justified, absent a specific term allowing it, then there should at least be evidence of a drug and/or alcohol problem in the work-place which cannot be combated in some less invasive way. In this case we have no such evidence.[39]

---

[35] *Lumber & Sawmill Workers' Union, Local 2537 v. KVP Co.* (1965), 16 L.A.C. 73 (Ont. Arb. Bd.).
[36] *Ibid.*
[37] (1991), 18 L.A.C. (4th) 412 (Ont. Arb. Bd.).
[38] (1987), 31 L.A.C. (3d) 179 (Can. Arb. Bd.).
[39] *Ibid.* at 425.

Upon application of the above test, the arbitrator ruled that the employer's policy was unreasonable within the meaning of the *KVP* test. The company had not produced any evidence demonstrating any adverse impact on the company's operations by reason of substance abuse among employees, nor was there any evidence of problems regarding impaired drivers which were not being adequately addressed by the existing rules and regime of physical examinations.[40]

Drug and alcohol testing of employees has generally been upheld in the context of safety-sensitive jobs, post-accident investigations, reasonable cause, certification into safety sensitive positions and return to duty after time away from work. In order to successfully implement such a policy, the employer must have a sufficient rational. The employer must show that drug and alcohol use in the workplace is a significant issue and/or the conduct of an employee is such as to give reasonable grounds that the employee is impaired. Finally, any policy must be tailored to the individual workplace; the problems therein and the collective bargaining regime in place.[41]

In *Canadian Pacific Ltd. v. U.T.U.*[42] an employee had been charged with cultivation and possession of marihuana plants. The employee, a conductor, when asked by CP to submit to a drug test, refused and was dismissed. It was held that an employer has a right to require an employee to undergo a fitness examination, including a drug test, when the employer is a public carrier, the employee's duties are inherently safety sensitive and the employer has reasonable grounds to believe that the employee may be impaired while on duty or subject to duty. The arbitrator found that the condition must be seen as implicit in the contract of employment, absent any express provisions to the contrary.

In *Esso Petroleum Canada v. C.E.P., Local 614*,[43] like the *Entrop* case above, involved Imperial Oil's alcohol and drug employee policy which required random alcohol and drug testing, mandatory medical examinations, obligatory self-disclosure of present and past substance abuse problems and listed medications, and searches of employees working in jobs determined to be safety sensitive. The policy also provided for drug and alcohol testing of all employees for reasonable cause and after a significant accident. The union filed a policy grievance contesting the implementation of this policy at the Ioco refinery near Vancouver.

---

[40] *Ibid.*
[41] *Roger K. MacDougall, supra* note 1 at 19.
[42] *Supra,* note 38.
[43] (1994), 56 L.A.C. (4th) 440 (B.C. Arb. Bd.).

The arbitrator stated that "neither the managerial rights of the employer nor the rights of privacy of the employee are absolute". In examining the reasonableness of implementing the drug testing policy, the Board determined that the company should have first implemented alternative measures to combat the problem such as enacting rules of conduct for the workplace, supervision, and evaluation measures or employee performance testing.[44] Upon balancing the interests of the employee's right to privacy and the employer's right to a safe working environment, it was determined that the policy could not be upheld as there was no evidence of a problem specific to that workplace to justify such action.[45]

The Board did find, however, that the implementation of the following rules was reasonable: prohibitions against use, possession, distribution, offering or sale of illicit drugs or alcohol while on company premises, prohibition against intentional misuse of prescribed medications while on company premises, prohibition against being unfit for scheduled work because of use of alcohol or illicit drugs, prohibition for employees in safety sensitive positions from consuming any alcoholic or illicit drugs during working hours, whether on or off company premises (including mealtimes, breaks, paid or unpaid) and requiring them to notify management if they have a current substance abuse problem. Furthermore, it was determined that mandatory testing of all employees on the basis of reasonable and probable cause and after a significant work accident, or near miss was acceptable.[46]

In *Sarnia Cranes*[47] a contractor to Imperial Oil had implemented an alcohol and drug testing policy. The Board held all forms of testing to be unjustified. No evidence was shown of problems with drug or alcohol use in the workplace. Furthermore, the company failed the *KVP* test since the risk of discipline/ discharge was unclear and was not communicated to employees[48] and the contractor did not first consider less intrusive methods of problem detection.[49] Interestingly, the Board held that the testing itself was unreasonable under the *KVP* test since a drug test cannot measure

---

[44] *Ibid.* at 448.

[45] *Ibid.* at 441.

[46] See *National Automobile, Aerospace, Transportation and General Workers Union of Canada v. Canadian National Railway Company*, Labour Arbitration News, September/ October, 2000 (M. Picher).

[47] *I.U.O.E, Local 793 v. Sarnia Cranes Ltd.*, [1999] O.L.R.B. Rep. 479 (Ont. L.R.B.).

[48] *Ibid.* at para 179.

[49] *Ibid.* at para 213.

impairment and there had been no evidence of drug or alcohol problems in the workplace.[50]

In contrast, the Alberta Board in *Procor*[51] ruled that the testing of an employee who was convicted of possession of marihuana was reasonable, despite the fact that the company had no formal testing policy and had never previously tested any employee. The Board held that the employer was justified in requiring testing since the employee was in a safety sensitive position and had been in the possession of a substantial amount of marihuana.

In *IWA-Canada v. Weyerhaeuser Co.*[52], forestry giant *Weyerhaeuser Co.* launched a drug and alcohol testing policy entitled the *Weyerhaeuser Health and Safety Standard – Substance Impairment (Canada)*, which established five scenarios wherein all employees were required to submit to alcohol or drug testing. These situations included: (1) when applying for, or transferring into, a "safety sensitive" position; (2) for cause; (3) after a workplace accident or incident; (4) as part of the conditions attached to a "return to duty" agreement; and (5) as part of "follow up conditions" after accommodation for substance abuse problems. The Standard did not provide for any random tests.

The Industrial, Wood and Allied Workers of Canada ("IWA-Canada") filed a national policy grievance claiming that the newly introduced policy constituted an unreasonable exercise of managerial rights and discriminated against company employees in violation of the collective agreement. The union questioned the reasonableness of the testing policy based on their view that the forestry industry did not belong to safety challenged industries, and on the lack of evidence of a pre-existing substance abuse problem in the workplace.

Conversely, *Weyerhaeuser Co.* contended that the forestry industry is an inherently safety-sensitive industry, thereby justifying the employer's use of various measures, including the introduction of the disputed drug and alcohol testing policy, which are required to maintain safety in a high-risk working environment.

The arbitrator agreed with the company's characterization of the forestry industry as an inherently safety-sensitive one. Therefore, the employer was not required to prove any prior substance abuse problems in the workplace. To substantiate his position, the arbitrator referred to statistics, ac-

---

[50] *Ibid.* at para. 56.
[51] *Procor Sulphur Services v. C.E.P., Local 57* (1998), 79 L.A.C. (4th) 341 (Alta. Arb. Bd.).
[52] *IWA-Canada v. Weyerhaeuser Co.* (2004), 127 L.A.C. (4th) 73, 2004 CarswellBC 2039 (B.C. Arb. Bd.).

cording to which the forestry sector has the highest death rate of all British Columbia industries and a disturbing injury rate six times higher than all other safety challenged industries in the province. He further cited a number of cases where similar policies were upheld in the absence of any proof of a substance abuse problem because the industries involved, specifically, a chemical industry[53] and a pit mine operation,[54] were considered to be safety-sensitive industries.

Attempting to provide some guidance in determining whether an industry can be regarded as inherently safety-sensitive, the arbitrator said the following:

> The authorities do not limit the right of employers to enact testing policies to nuclear reactors, railways, mines and chemical plants. . . There is a continuum on which there are degrees of safety sensitiveness and the facts of each case will determine where a particular industry fits on the continuum. There does not need to be the potential for a catastrophe before an employer is justified in adopting a testing policy as a preventative safety measure, particularly when the policy is but one part of a comprehensive approach to safety, treatment and accommodation and does not include random testing.

A form of compromise has been reached when a line of arbitration decisions[55] served as a foundation for the development of certain rules and principles with respect to alcohol and drug testing in safety-sensitive workplaces governed by a regime of collective bargaining. These rules and principles may be summarized as follows:

- No employee can be subjected to random, unannounced alcohol or drug testing, save as part of an agreed rehabilitative program.

- An employer may require alcohol or drug testing of an individual where the facts give the employer reasonable cause to do so.

- It is within the prerogatives of management's rights under a col-

---

[53] *Dupont Canada Inc. v. C.E.P., Local 28-0* (2002), [2002] C.L.A.D. No. 146, 2002 CarswellOnt 1739 (Ont. Arb. Bd.).

[54] *Fording Coal Ltd. v. U.S.W.A., Local 7884* (January 8, 2002), Doc. X-33/00(a), [2002] B.C.C.A.A.A. No. 9 (B.C. Arb. Bd.).

[55] See for example *Trimac Transportation Services - Bulk Systems v. T.C.U.* (1999), 88 L.A.C. (4th) 237 (Can. Arb. Bd.) (Burkett); *Canadian National Railway v. CAW-Canada* (2000), 95 L.A.C. (4th) 341 (Can. Arb. Bd.) (M. Picher); *Dupont Canada Inc. v. C.E.P., Local 28-0* (2002), 105 L.A.C. (4th) 399 (Ont. Arb. Bd.) (P.C. Picher); *J.D. Irving Ltd. v. C.E.P., Locals 104 & 1309* (2002), 111 L.A.C. (4th) 328 (N.B. Arb. Bd.) (M.G. Picher).

lective agreement to also require alcohol or drug testing following a significant incident, accident or near miss, where it may be important to identify the root cause of what occurred.

- Drug and alcohol testing is a legitimate part of continuing contracts of employment for individuals found to have a problem of alcohol or drug use. As part of an employee's program of rehabilitation, such agreements or policies may properly involve random, unannounced alcohol or drug testing generally for a limited period of time, most commonly for two years. In a unionized workplace, the union must be involved in the agreement which establishes the terms of a recovering employee's ongoing employment, including random, unannounced testing. This is the only exceptional circumstance in which the otherwise protected employee interest in privacy and dignity of the person must yield to the interests of safety and rehabilitation, to allow for random and unannounced alcohol or drug testing.

- The cases generally recognize that an employee's refusal or failure to undergo an alcohol or drug test in the three circumstances described above may properly be viewed as a serious violation of the employer's drug and alcohol policy, and may itself be grounds for serious discipline. The failure or refusal to take an alcohol or drug test, however, like the registering of a positive test, does not necessarily justify automatic termination. The appropriate disciplinary sanction in such a case remains subject to the general 'just cause' provisions of the collective agreement and is an issue to be determined on a case-by-case basis, having regard to all of the relevant facts.[56]

Canadian safety-sensitive industries have approved and widely accepted the above principles. Indeed, the rules and limitations as set out above have been "codified" as the "Canadian Model" which is adopted in the Alberta construction industry.[57] The bottom line of these developed principles is that any attempts on the part of the employer to exceed the set limits should be viewed as an unwarranted encroachment on the dignity and privacy of the employees. As a result, any such measures contemplated by

---

[56] *Imperial Oil Ltd. v. C.E.P., Local 900* (2006), 2006 CarswellOnt 8621 (Ont. Arb. Bd.) at para. 100.

[57] See *Construction Labour Relations Assn. (Alberta) v. I.U.O.E., Local 955* (2004), 129 L.A.C. (4th) 1 (Alta. Arb. Bd.) (Beattie).

the employer must be subject to negotiations between the employer and the union.

However, new disputes have been rekindled by differing interpretations of the ruling in *Entrop*, a case wherein Imperial Oil learned about a new saliva test which allegedly measures actual drug impairment, and established a policy requiring all employees to submit to random drug testing.[58] The union was quick to file a grievance challenging the company's use of random and post-incident drug and alcohol tests. The company took the position that the grievance was time-barred and was nothing more than an attempt to re-litigate issues already decided. The company based this argument on its interpretation of the decision in *Entrop* as legitimizing drug and alcohol testing as long as the test can determine actual impairment. Further, the employer stated that the union's acquiescence of the use of random breathalyzer tests, which had been in place before its first collective agreement was negotiated with the company in 1996, precluded the union from protesting against it now. The union responded that the *Entrop* board was concerned with the human rights complaint of an individual employee and not a grievance under the collective agreement. Therefore, no time limitations applied and no abuse of process argument made by the employer could stand.

The Ontario Arbitration Board agreed with the employer's argument that the union had lost its right to challenge the use of random breathalyzer tests as it had tolerated the tests for about seven years. However, the union's challenge of the newly introduced oral fluid tests for drug detection was allowed to proceed. The Board accepted the union's argument that since the board in *Entrop* dealt with a complaint filed under Ontario's *Human Rights Code* rather than under the collective agreement, its decision may not be viewed as "having resolved in any conclusive way the issue of whether randomness in drug testing, even assuming that such a test can detect impairment, has been effectively ruled upon for the purposes of the collective agreement."

In considering the grievance on its merits, the Board made numerous references to the aforementioned Canadian Model and to arbitral jurisprudence that has emerged in Canada regarding alcohol and drug testing in safety-sensitive workplaces, noting in particular that arbitrators have overwhelmingly rejected mandatory, random drug testing for all employees in safety-sensitive workplaces as being an implied management right under the terms of a collective agreement. The Board further emphasized that given the publicity the issue has received recently and the volume of arbitral

---

[58] *Imperial Oil Ltd. v. C.E.P., Local 900* (2006), 157 L.A.C. (4th) 225, 2006 CarswellOnt 8621 (Ont. Arb. Bd.).

jurisprudence in this respect, Canadian legislatures are well aware of the principles developed by the arbitrators. The fact that Canadian lawmakers have not adopted similar drug and alcohol testing legislation enacted in the United States, which vests U.S. employers with much broader rights with respect to subjecting employees to the respective tests, indicates that currently, the scope of testing authority available to Canadian employers is considered sufficient to ensure safe workplaces.

In the Board's view, another aspect revealed by the arbitral jurisprudence on the issue in question is that the Canadian Model has gained broad acceptance among employers in safety-sensitive industries. The lack of serious incidents or accidents related to drug use in the reported cases provided grounds for the majority of the Board to conclude that the limitations on the use of alcohol and drug testing fashioned by the arbitrators allow them to strike the right balance between the interest of the employers to ensure safety at work and the interest of the employees to safeguard their privacy and dignity.

Having outlined the main trends stemming from arbitral jurisprudence, the Board closely examined the decision in *Entrop*. Again, the Board confirmed that one of the features distinguishing the case at hand from *Entrop* is that this time, the Board was concerned with the interpretation of the collective agreement, while the focus of the board in *Entrop* was to consider the narrow application of the [*Human Rights*] *Code* to the employer's drug and alcohol policy. Considering the thrust of the dispute, namely, whether the *Entrop* decision gives the green light to random drug and alcohol tests as long as these tests can detect actual impairment, the majority of the Board disagreed with the employer. First, the Board rejected the employer's argument that the breathalyzer test is analogous to the saliva test in that both conclusively determine impairment, reasoning that the result of the cheek swab test is revealed several days after it has been administered because the swab is sent to a laboratory where the necessary analysis is conducted. More importantly, however, the Board emphasized that subjecting all employees to random drug or alcohol testing would fly in the face of the well established Canadian arbitral jurisprudence which holds that in a safety-sensitive working environment, drug and alcohol testing can be required of an employee only where the employer has reasonable and probable cause, or where there has been an accident or incident justifying such a measure.

The majority of the Board expressed their skepticism about efforts to interpret the *Entrop* decision as making the ability of a test to detect impairment crucial for the test's legitimacy by stating: "It would . . . be fallacious to believe that arbitrators have ruled against random drug testing merely because the predominant form of testing, urinalysis, could not prove impairment." They suggested that the issue was more complex and endorsed the more cautious approach taken by a majority of arbitration boards towards administration by the employers of drug and alcohol testing, as this matter bears on the dignity and privacy of the employees:

> The dignity, integrity and privacy of the individual person is among the most highly prized values in Canadian society. Employment is a large part of the human experience, normally spanning the better part of an adult life. The place of a person in his or her profession, trade or employment is therefore a significant part of his or her humanity and sense of self. That reality is deeply reflected in the law of employment and labour relations in Canada. It is therefore not surprising that, as contrasted with developments in other countries, the federal and provincial governments in Canada have not rushed to enact legislation or regulations authorizing employers to alcohol or drug test their employees. Nor is it surprising that boards of arbitration have been careful to seek a balance which protects the privacy and dignity of employees in this area.

The majority of the Board reminded the parties that strict limitations and rules are imposed in other areas of law, for example Criminal Law, which are also concerned with administering bodily fluids tests. Comparing privacy rights in criminal law with the right to privacy in employment, the Board did not consider it acceptable or logical that where a police officer requires a search warrant to search an individual's person or property, an employer needs no justification for using testing methods which are considered to be highly intrusive. Relying on the above-mentioned reasons, the Board ruled that to the extent that the company's alcohol and drug policy mandated random drug testing, it violated the collective agreement.

Conversely, one of the Board members, Arbitrator Filion, wrote a vigorous dissent. He argued that the random drug testing regime introduced by the employer is reasonable, given that safety at the company's refinery is the 'number one' priority. He further stressed that violations of workplace safety are strict liability offences giving rise to serious penalties. Arbitrator Filion also relied on expert evidence detailing the disturbing effects of cannabis consumption on "many functions critical to the safe performance of work-related tasks." His criticism pointed to a number of factors which in his opinion favoured the company's policy, one of them being that the random drug testing would pass the test formulated in *Entrop* and, as a result, would comply with the Ontario *Human Rights Code*.

Arbitrator Filion expressed surprise by the view that a testing regime which satisfies the *Code*, specifically designed to protect an individual's dignity, can violate the "respect and dignity" clause in the collective agreement. He further stated that in light of the random alcohol testing regime used by the employer and upheld by this very Board, it was hard to argue that randomness of testing was an issue.

Unsatisfied with the Board's decision , the employer applied to the Ontario Superior Court of Justice for judicial review of this arbitration award.[59] The company advanced two main arguments. First, it claimed that the Board altered the collective agreement by imposing on the employer the Canadian Model, which was not part of the collective agreement negotiated between the employer and the union. Since the random alcohol testing was upheld by the Board as not violating the collective agreement, the company argued there was nothing in the same agreement to limit the testing authority of the employer with respect to drugs. Second, the company took the position that the random drug testing complied with the *Entrop* decision and as such, it complied with the *Human Rights Code* as well; bearing in mind that the *Code* is a quasi-constitutional document that aims to protect the dignity of individuals, the decision that the drug testing regime violates the 'respect and dignity' clause of the collective agreement was unreasonable. The Court rejected both arguments. Responding to the company's first contention , the Court said that the Board had not imposed on the company any rules not negotiated between it and the union. Rather the majority of the arbitrators considered the language of the collective agreement in light of the well-established arbitral jurisprudence in Canada - the 'Canadian Model' - and applied the 'balancing of interest' approach from that jurisprudence.

Considering the company's second argument, the Court stressed that the task of the Arbitration Board was to interpret the collective agreement and its provisions, the wording of which had no ties with the grounds of discrimination under the *Human Rights Code*. The Court pointed out that the *Code* provides only a minimum standard of protection and that parties covered by it are free to negotiate with the employer a regime which guarantees better safeguards for their rights.

Given the strong commitment by decision-makers to the "reasonable grounds" requirement for the administration of alcohol or drug testing as evidenced by the preponderance of arbitral jurisprudence in this area, the question arises with respect to what constitutes "reasonable grounds". In one case, the employer dismissed three construction workers after a guard reported that he had smelled marihuana in their truck when they stopped at a security checkpoint while returning to the worksite from lunch.[60] The guard radioed his colleague at the next checkpoint and asked her to check

---

[59] *Imperial Oil Ltd. v. C.E.P., Local 900* (2008), 169 L.A.C. (4th) 257, 2008 CarswellOnt 669 (Ont. Div. Ct.).

[60] *Trace Canada Co. v. H.F.I.A., Local 110* (October 26, 2004), Doc. 2004-069, [2004] A.G.A.A. No. 68 (Alta. Arb. Bd.).

the truck for the smell. However, her report stated that she simply "smelled something." When asked for an explanation of the suspicious odour, one of the workers said that he had burned the lining of his jacket with a cigarette. Nonetheless, the supervisor instructed the workers to submit to a drug test as per Rule 4.4.1 of the Alberta Construction Owners Association's *Canadian Model for Providing a Safe Workplace – Alcohol and Drug Guidelines and Work Rule* (the Canadian Model). The rule reads: "A supervisor or manager of an employee must request an employee to submit to an alcohol or drug test . . . if the supervisor or manager and the next level of management present at the company workplace, if any, have reasonable grounds to believe that an employee is or may be unable to work in a safe manner because of the use of alcohol and drugs." The tradesmen's refusal to undergo the test resulted in their immediate dismissal.

The employer and the union disputed whether the company had reasonable grounds to require a drug test from the grievors. Rule 6(1)(p) of the Canadian Model defines "reasonable grounds" as "information established by the direct observation of the employee's conduct or other indicators, such as the physical appearance of the employee, his or her attendance record, circumstances surrounding an accident, near miss or potentially dangerous incident and the presence of alcohol, drugs or drug paraphernalia in the vicinity of the employee of the area where the employee worked." The union took the position that the grievors were dismissed based on the words of a person who was "barely old enough to be on the job" and was not trained to detect the smell of marihuana, and on an inconclusive report of another guard.

The Board sided with the union and held that the employer did not have reasonable grounds to submit the workers to a drug test. While the arbitrators acknowledged that a 'red flag' raised by a guard's suspicions gave the company legitimate reason for concern, they reproached the employer for failing to respect due process. The Chair of the Board clarified that while a full investigation is not necessary before requiring a drug test, the following steps should have been taken by the employer given the need for timely action: interviewing both security guards, asking the second guard for her written statement, questioning the fact the grievors were not removed from their jobs immediately as required by company policy, searching the vehicle, interviewing the grievor's foreman, listening to the grievors' explanation, and considering the grievors' clear disciplinary and safety records as well as the fact that they were never seen or presumed to be under the influence of drugs or alcohol. In the result, the Board reinstated the grievors stating that "the rights of individuals to resist an invasive procedure, which is not based on reasonable grounds, must be protected."

The same principles hold true for post-incident drug testing, as illustrated by the ruling of an arbitration board in a case where a crane operator refused to undergo a drug test after his crane had smashed into a live lightning fixture, nearly killing three people.[61] As a result of his refusal to submit to a drug test, with which the two other co-workers of the grievor involved in the incident took no issue, the grievor was terminated.

The employer based its decision to terminate the crane operator on the company drug testing policy, which was designed to follow the Canadian Model. Specifically, the company relied on Rule 4.5.1 which states: "A supervisor or manager of an employee *must* request an employee to submit to an alcohol or drug test . . . if the supervisor or manager and the next level of management present at the company workplace, if any, have reasonable grounds to believe that an employee was involved in an accident." [emphasis added]. The employer argued that since human error was the only explanation for the incident and the use of alcohol or drugs could not be completely ruled out, it had the required grounds to demand the employees involved to submit to a drug test.

The board of arbitration disagreed. It stated that had the employer conducted a thorough investigation, it would not have been necessary to subject the grievor to such an invasive procedure. In particular, the employer should have interviewed the crane operator, enabling it to determine that he had not used alcohol or drugs for many years. Further, the Board concluded that the employer failed to consider whether there were reasonable grounds to believe that the use of alcohol and drugs *did not* cause the accident within the meaning of Rule 4.5.4, which states that drugs and alcohol could be ruled out in situations where the individual could not have avoided the incident. The Board held that in this case, even a cursory investigation should have revealed that the grievor could not have avoided the accident. Consequently, the Board ruled that the employer did not have reasonable grounds to demand a drug test.

In *Weyerhaeuser Co. v. C.E.P., Local 447*,[62] the arbitrator considered if and when it is appropriate for an employer to demand that an employee submit to drug and alcohol testing following a workplace incident, and what method is appropriate to use in conducting such tests. This case involved grievances filed by two employees who were subjected to drug testing under a new "Substance" section introduced into the employer's Health and Safety Standards. In each instance, the testing requirement followed an incident at work. Neither test proved positive so neither employee was subjected to

---

[61] *Construction Labour Relations Assn. (Alberta) v. I.U.O.E., Local 955* (2004), 129 L.A.C. (4th) 1, 2004 CarswellAlta 1522 (Alta. Arb. Bd.).

[62] (2006), 154 L.A.C. (4th) 3, 2006 CarswellAlta 1859 (Alta. Arb. Bd.).

any direct consequence under the policy as a result of being tested. However, the alleged failure on the part of the employer to introduce the testing policy in accordance with the *KVP* principles and the manner in which the employer administered the tests gave the union and its members serious concerns regarding the implementation of the policy.

In both incidents, each employee was taken to a local, inexpensive motel almost immediately following each incident to undergo testing by an agent hired by the employer. No employee had any chance to explain the incident or refuse the testing.

Discussing the issue of whether the decision to test the employees was reasonable, the arbitrator observed that any policy purporting to meet the reasonableness component of the *KVP* test "must mandate a real investigation and a real exercise of judgment by the responsible manager. It must be written in such a way as to make it clear to the responsible person that they are balancing rights and not simply checking off a list." Even when an employer has a reasonable cause to demand that an employee submit to a test, the arbitrator continued, the test must be carried out in a reasonable manner.

In the cases before him, the arbitrator found that the policy treated any refusal by an employee to undergo a drug or alcohol test in the same way as a positive test, making no provision to allow employees to challenge the validity of the employer's decision to test an employee, or any step in the test process that is either unreasonable or fails to comply with the employer's own policy. If the employees refused to participate, they were immediately suspended from work and forced to submit to an assessment by a Substance Abuse Professional. The arbitrator held that this "may be appropriate where the refusal is indicative of avoiding a drug test, but it is, itself, an invasion of privacy and . . . unjustified where a valid objection is based on an unreasonable demand, or on a non-compliant or unreasonable testing procedure." Therefore, several sections of the policy were found to be an unacceptable invasion of an employee's privacy rights where their refusal to undergo testing is not an effort to hide their own drug use but rather a protest against the employer's own unreasonable conduct.

A contrasting approach towards what can constitute reasonable grounds for subjecting employees to a drug test is demonstrated by the ruling of the British Columbia Grievance Arbitration Board in *Elk Valley Coal Corp. v. I.U.O.E., Local 115*.[63] In this case, an employee was involved in a fender-bender while driving a company truck, causing minor damage to the vehicle, and did not report the incident. The employer learned about the accident from the report of the driver of the other vehicle and required

---

[63] (2004), 2004 CarswellBC 3748 (B.C. C.A.A.).

the employee to submit to a drug test several days later in accordance with the company's drug testing policy. Initially, the grievor refused the drug test but subsequently provided a urine sample. After marijuana metabolites were found in the sample, the employee admitted that he had been casually smoking marijuana for 21 years. The company offered to continue his employment subject to the employee's consent to an assessment by an independent addictions specialist and his willingness to complete any recommmended treatment and submit to random drug testing for a two-year period. When the grievor rejected the offer, the employer terminated his employment.

The union grieved the termination and, among other arguments, contended that the company did not have reasonable cause to require drug testing. However, the arbitrator dismissed the grievance ruling that the grievor's "evasive, uncooperative and at times . . . deliberately misleading" answers during the interview preceding the drug test were sufficient to justify the employer's request to submit to a drug test. The arbitrator was also of the opinion that the company's testing policy explicitly provided for testing "where an act or omission by an employee . . . causes or contributes to a significant event", specifically, "an incident or accident involving . . . damage to property of the company."

The statistical evidence on the extent of alcohol and drug use and abuse in a number of hazardous industries has prompted employers operating in these areas to consider further risk management options.[64] In many safety challenged workplaces, employers have adopted pre-access testing, a process that requires alcohol and drug testing as a condition of access to a work site, as an effective tool for reducing substance abuse at work. Pre-access testing encourages employees to access assistance programs and improves

---

[64] See also *Greater Toronto Airports Authority v. P.S.A.C., Local 0004* (2007), 2007 CarswellOnt 4531 (Ont. Arb. Bd.). The arbitrator considered a sizeable grievance filed by the union, which contested the implementation of a drug and alcohol policy by the Greater Toronto Airports Authority. One of the disputed provisions of the policy was random alcohol testing. Having familiarized himself with the evidence adduced as to the extent of alcohol use and abuse by airport employees, the arbitrator stated: "In the result, having carefully considered the matter, in the particular circumstances of this case, I cannot conclude that the implementation of random alcohol testing of employees in safety-sensitive positions was unreasonable. As noted previously, such testing involves the use of a calibrated breathalyzer, which can accurately detect impairment. Moreover, although the Union pointed to a number of awards in which random testing was rejected, those cases are distinguishable as the Arbitrators found no evidence of an alcohol problem in the workplace which would justify that form of testing.

safety in the working environment. In the result, a new version of the Canadian Model was adopted in 2005 which added Section 4.7. This section prescribes that "When an owner directly or by contract requires site access testing, an employer may require alcohol and drug testing under [section] 4.8 of any employee as a condition of access to the owner's property".

Some unions have taken issue with this form of testing. In *U.A., Local 488 v. Bantrel Constructors Co.*,[65] a group of unions challenged the validity of the requirement of all employees assigned to complete a project for Petro Canada, including those already working on the site, to undergo pre-access testing. The contract agreement between the employee and Petro Canada stipulated that the "Contractor's Alcohol and Drug Use Policy shall meet or exceed the requirements of the Owner's Alcohol and Drug Use Policy."

The union argued that labour relations were governed by the collective agreement negotiated based on the 2001 version of the Canadian Model which, in its opinion, did not endorse pre-access testing. Further, the union claimed that this form of testing was tantamount to random testing explicitly prohibited by the Canadian Model. The Alberta Arbitration Board reasoned that the Canadian Model was not a complete and restricted code, and this reasoning was later approved and upheld by the Alberta Court of Queen's Bench. Specifically, the Introduction to the Canadian Model reads: ". . . the model strives to establish a minimum industry standard for a safe workplace and recognizes that some companies may require even higher or alternate standards based on the specific nature of the operations."

Both the Board and the Court also rejected the analogies drawn by the union between random and pre-access testing. The adjudicators acknowledged that the Canadian Model prohibited random testing in the form of unannounced testing without cause of any employee present on site. Pre-access testing, on the other hand, was deemed as "mandatory universal testing to every person who wishes to gain access to the site." What is more, all employees were notified of this requirement two months in advance, which the Board considered to be sufficient time to eliminate alcohol and drugs from their systems.

As is evident from the foregoing cases, much uncertainty and tension associated with the administration of alcohol and drug testing in the work environment continue to exist. On numerous occasions, individual employees, unions and employers have crossed swords with varying success. Adjudicators have been asked to rule on substance testing-related issues based on various premises. Most commonly disputed matters are presented either within the framework of an existing collective agreement, a *Human Rights Code*, or both. Either venue has its limitations. Arbitral jurisprudence only

---

[65] 2007 ABQB 721, 2007 CarswellAlta 1621 (Alta. Q.B.).

applies to unionized workplaces and cannot protect employees not represented by bargaining units (except in the federal jurisdiction where both
represented and unrepresented employees can file grievances and potentially proceed to adjudication). On the other hand, cases like *Milazzo v.
Autocar Connaisseur Inc.*[66] and *Chiasson v. Kellogg, Brown & Root (Canada) Co.*[67] demonstrate the inadequacies of protection afforded by human
rights legislation.

Consideration of alcohol and drug testing disputes under privacy legislation would allow complainants to overcome the identified hurdles and
would guarantee universal protection to all employees affected by testing
policies. As a result, adjudicators would be able to focus on the real interests
at stake, namely, the privacy and dignity of all working people.[68] The
imperfection of techniques currently used for detecting drug and alcohol in
an employee's system, their intrusive nature both in terms of the collection
of samples and the ability to discover information unconnected with legitimate work-related purposes (DNA mapping, pregnancy, etc.), as well as
potential for false positives, only highlight the real interests to be safe-
guarded from unwarranted intrusion. Therefore, it appears logical and ad-
visable to assess alcohol and drug testing policies using tools developed
within the privacy protection framework. As a general rule, employers are
considered justified in introducing such policies or requirements if:

---

[66] *Supra*, note 31.

[67] *Supra*, note 32.

[68] Arbitral cases decided to date acknowledge that privacy concerns go to the heart
of testing-related disputes. See, for example, *Trimac Transportation Services -
Bulk Systems v. T.C.U.* (1999), 88 L.A.C. (4th) 237 (Can. Arb. Bd.), where
arbitrator Kevin Burkett said: "The right to one's privacy is the right to protection
from the unwarranted intrusion of others into one's life. The underlying premise
is that in a democratic society, an individual is free to live as he/she pleases
without interference or monitoring, so long as there is no adverse impact upon
another nor breach of the law . . . The recognition of employee privacy as a core
workplace value, albeit one that is not absolute, has been recognized by arbitrators
in awards dealing with searches, surveillance, medical examination and, more
recently, drug testing. The ultimate determinations in these awards rest on their
individual facts. However, in all cases, the ultimate determination is arrived at
on a balancing of the aforementioned competing impacts, with the onus upon the
employer to establish that its business interest outweighs the employee's privacy
interest. In respect of drug and alcohol testing of employees, the balance has
been struck in favour of protecting individual privacy rights except where reasonable and probable grounds exist to suspect the drug and alcohol impairment
or addiction of an employee in the workplace and except where there is no less
intrusive means of confirming the suspicion."

- it is demonstrably necessary to meet a specific need;

- it is likely to meet that need;

- the loss of privacy is seen to be proportional to the benefit gained;

- it is shown, to the satisfaction of the adjudicator, that there are no less invasive ways of achieving the desired result.[69]

The comparison between the privacy test established pursuant to privacy legislation and the *bona fide occupational requirement* ("BFOR") test developed under human rights legislation reveals that the former is better suited to protect the privacy interests of employees. While the BFOR test requires a rule introduced by an employer to be rationally connected to the job and to be subjectively and objectively necessary to fulfill the work-related purpose, the privacy test goes further and ensures that privacy concerns of affected employees are considered and weighed against the interests of and benefits gained by the employer.[70]

---

[69] This is an extrapolation from other privacy cases where the commissioners and judges have looked at the issue of whether or not the implementation of a program is reasonable under the "privacy lens". For example, *Eastmond v. Canadian Pacific Railway*, 2004 FC 852, 2004 CarswellNat 1842 (F.C.), *PIPEDA Case Summary #351, Re* (2006), 2006 CarswellNat 5577 (Can. Privacy Commr.).

[70] It is necessary to note that currently in the provinces that have not passed privacy legislation "substantially similar" to *PIPEDA*, there is a gaping hole in the protection afforded under the "privacy lens". In these provinces, protection is guaranteed only to the employees of a federal work, undertaking or business or to the employees of every organization which collects, uses and discloses personal information in the course of any commercial activity. To date, only Quebec, British Columbia and Alberta have been determined to be substantially similar in privacy legislation in the private sector. Also, the Ontario *Personal Health Information Protection Act*, 2004 which applies to health information custodians has been declared to meet the criteria for recognition as being substantially similar to *PIPEDA*.

10

Disclosure of Employee Information

10.1 DISCLOSURE TO UNIONS

Privacy in the workplace also imposes an obligation on employers to keep employee information confidential. In fact, certain employers have begun refusing to communicate employee related information. Sometimes, however, the employer's obligations to safeguard its employees' information may be tempered.

For example, in *H.R.E.U., Local 448 v. Millcroft Inn Ltd.*[1] the union brought an application to the Ontario Labour Relations Board for consent to prosecute the employer on the basis that the employer's refusal to provide the addresses and telephone numbers of its employees was a flagrant violation of the *Labour Relations Act, 1995*, S.O. 1995, c. 1. Arbitrator Christopher J. Albertyn upheld his decision of August 25, 2000 and ordered the employer to provide the union with the names, addresses and telephone numbers of the employees in the bargaining unit represented by the union. However, the application for consent to prosecute the employer was dismissed.

The *Millcroft* decision was followed in *O.S.S.T.F., District 25 v. Ottawa-Carleton District School Board*.[2] In this case, the employer was governed, not only by the provisions of the *Labour Relations Act*, but also by the *Municipal Freedom to Information and Protection of Privacy Act*. Interestingly, an earlier decision by the Ontario Information and Privacy Commissioner upheld the employer's decision to refuse to disclose personal information (the home addresses and telephone numbers) of its employees to the union who had requested the information. The Information and Privacy Commissioner ruled that the union's status as the collective bargaining agent was an irrelevant consideration in deciding whether or not the release of the information would be an unreasonable invasion of privacy under the privacy legislation. However, the arbitrator in *O.S.S.T.F., District 25 v. Ottawa-Carleton District School Board* (who was the same arbitrator who heard the *Millcroft* matter) determined that the request by the union for the

---

[1] (2000), [2000] O.L.R.D. No. 2581, 2000 CarswellOnt 3073 (Ont. L.R.B.) 7 online QL (LRBD).

[2] (2001), [2001] O.L.R.D. No. 4575, 2001 CarswellOnt 4902 (Ont. L.R.B.).

employees' home addresses and telephone numbers had to be obeyed by the employer in order to comply with section 70 of the *Labour Relations Act*. Section 70 states:

> No employer or employers' organization and no person acting on behalf of an employer or an employers' organization shall participate in or interfere with the formation, selection or administration of a trade union or the representation of employees by a trade union or contribute financial or other support to a trade union, but nothing in this section shall be deemed to deprive an employer of the employer's freedom to express views so long as the employer does not use coercion, intimidation, threats, promises or undue influence.

In trying to reconcile his decision to the earlier decision of the Information and Privacy Commissioner, the arbitrator determined that the Commissioner erred by failing to appreciate the significance of the union's statutory role as agent and representative of the employees in a bargaining unit.[3]

The decision of the British Columbia Labour Relations Board in *Hudson's Bay Co. v. U.F.C.W., Local 1518*[4] continues the line of arbitral jurisprudence supporting the proposition that the employer is obligated to disclose its employees' personal information to bargaining units if required to do so by law. In this case, the relevant law was B.C.'s *Labour Relations Code* under which unions have a duty to represent employees' interests fairly. To fulfill its duty of fair representation, the union argued that it needed to obtain the current phone numbers and addresses of employees from the employer. The employer refused to provide this information, re-

---

[3] A similar case with a similar result, but involving the interplay between the federal *Public Service Staff Relations Act* and the federal *Privacy Act* is *P.S.A.C. v. Canada (Treasury Board)* (April 26, 1996), Doc. 161-2-791, 169-2-584, [1996] C.P.S.S.R.B. No. 30 (Can. P.S.S.R.B.). In this case, the Canada Public Service Staff Relations Board held that the release of the home addresses and telephone numbers to the union would be an allowable disclosure of personal information under the *Privacy Act* because the Board determined that the information would be used for a consistent purpose (section 8(2)(a)) to that purpose for which it was collected in the first place. See also *Société canadienne des postes c. S.P.C.* (January 31, 1995), Bergeron Arb. (Can. Arb. Bd.) and *Union of Canadian Correctional Officers c. Conseil du Trésor*, 2002 PSSRB 58 (Can. P.S.S.R.B.). The same result is found in the Alberta case of *U.F.C.W., Local 401 v. Economic Development Edmonton* (2002), [2002] A.L.R.B.R. No. 41, 2002 CarswellAlta 1031 (Alta. L.R.B.), application for stay denied (2002), [2002] A.J. No. 800, 2002 CarswellAlta 799 (Alta. Q.B.). See also *Northwest Territories v. Union of Northern Workers* (2001), [2001] N.W.T.J. No. 24, 2001 CarswellNWT 29 (N.W.T. S.C.).

[4] (2004), 108 C.L.R.B.R. (2d) 259, 2004 CarswellBC 3300 (B.C. L.R.B.).

lying on section 6 of the British Columbia *Personal Information Protection Act* ("PIPA"), which prohibits the collection, use or disclosure of employee personal information, subject to limited exceptions. In response, the union took the position that the employer had breached its duty to bargain in good faith with the union, thereby violating sections 11 and 47 of the *Labour Relations Code*, and filed an 'unfair labour practice' complaint against the employer with the British Columbia Labour Relations Board.

The Board held that the employer could disclose the personal information of its employees without violating *PIPA* if the disclosure was "required or authorized by law." The Board determined that the facts before it supported the union's position as the *Code* imposed a duty on the employer to bargain in good faith, which included the disclosure of information necessary to ensure "rational, informed discussion" during negotiations between the employer and the union. The Board ruled that the contact and salary information of bargaining unit members must be disclosed as part of the employer's duty.

In *General Teamsters, Local 362 v. Monarch Transport Inc.*, the Canada Industrial Relations Board confirmed that unions have the right to employees' contact information both for collective bargaining and fair representation purposes.[5] The bargaining agent representing the interests of all dependent contractors and drivers of dependent contractors filed an unfair labour practice complaint against the employer following the employer's refusal to provide the union with a list of all drivers, along with their addresses and phone numbers, who were members of the bargaining unit. The employer cited the provision of the *PIPEDA* prohibiting the release of employees' personal information without their prior consent as the grounds for the refusal. The union argued that disclosure would not violate the *PIPEDA* as the information requested was essential to maintaining good labour relations and the proper representation of employees within the employment relationship, thereby rendering its disclosure consistent with the purposes for which it was collected. Further, the union contended that the employer's refusal to co-operate constituted interference with the union's representation rights.

Relying on the jurisprudence, the Board formulated two principles for the disclosure of employee personal information to unions: (1) The union's interest in obtaining requested information must be related to legitimate labour relations interest; and (2) the employer's refusal to give the information to the union must amount to interference with the union's capacity to represent employees of the bargaining unit. In this case, the Board con-

---

[5] *General Teamsters, Local 362 v. Monarch Transport Inc.*, [2003] C.I.R.B. No. 249, 2003 CarswellNat 4213 (C.I.R.B.).

cluded that the information sought by the union was related to its representational capacity and therefore should be provided by the employer. In determining when employee personal information may be necessary for a union to fulfill its legitimate goals, the Board stated:

> During the collective bargaining process the union has the need to communicate with employees in order to formulate a bargaining position, to confer with them during the course of bargaining, to participate in a ratification or strike vote, as well as to obtain their endorsement of positions taken during bargaining. To be able to communicate expeditiously and effectively with employees, the union needs up to date information about the employees it represents. Outside of the bargaining process, the union requires such information, for example, to explore with employees the merits of pursuing a grievance, to conduct an investigation or to contact and interview witnesses, to inquire into employee concerns, all of which are part of the union's duty of fair representation. To adequately fulfill that duty, the union must have the means of communicating directly with each employee it represents.

In *Society of Professional Engineers & Associates v. Atomic Energy of Canada Ltd.*,[6] the Society of Professional Engineers and Associates brought an application to the Canada Industrial Relations Board seeking an order that Atomic Energy of Canada Limited provide requested information regarding salary increases and promotions which had been given to certain employees in July 1999. The Board granted the application and ordered the employer to provide the union with the names of all relevant bargaining unit members, together with their level and salary.

A decision by the Privacy Commissioner of Canada emphasizes that an employer's disclosure of an employee's personal information to his or her union requires the consent or implied consent of the employee prior to disclosure. In one case, an airport authority employee complained that her employer had disclosed her personal information to three third parties without her consent. The complainant had initially requested access to certain information from her employer but was subsequently denied access. The employer then sent copies of her request to two union representatives and the coordinator of employee relations at the airport without her consent. The Commissioner determined that had the employee informed the union of the request for information from her employer, the forwarding of the request would have been valid on the basis of implied consent. However, as the employee had the right to act without union intervention, the disclo-

---

[6] [2001] C.I.R.B.D. No. 7, [2001] C.I.R.B. No. 110, 2001 CarswellNat 3651 (C.I.R.B.).

sure of her personal information to the union without her consent was not acceptable.[7]

Recently, the Manitoba Labour Board followed the *Millcroft* decision in *Buhler Manufacturing (Re)*,[8] and determined that the employer had committed an unfair labour practice by refusing to provide the home addresses and telephone numbers of all of the employees in the bargaining unit, contrary to section 6 of the Manitoba *Labour Relations Act*. Uniquely in this case, the Board ruled in favour of the union despite the request by six employees to the employer that it not release their personal information to the union. Following the ruling in *Millcroft*, the Board found that a request by an employer to acquire express consents from employees to release information was inconsistent with the union's exclusive bargaining agency.

10.2   DISCLOSURE TO BOARDS/TRIBUNALS/COURTS

In *Simons v. Prince Edward Island (Workers' Compensation Board)*[9] the Prince Edward Island Court of Appeal ruled that the Worker's Compensation Board did not violate worker's privacy rights when it sent workers' medical information to consultants for assessment. The records were sent without the workers' consent or knowledge. To this end, the Court of Appeal cautioned that informing the workers should be discouraged because "a person who applies for benefits necessarily lowers his or her expectation of privacy in respect of his or her medical records . . .". In the Court's opinion, a worker's privacy interests had to give way to the Board's mandate of investigating and examining the legitimacy of one's entitlement.

In a similar complaint to the Privacy Commissioner of Canada, an employee alleged that a telecommunications company had inappropriately disclosed personal medical information about her to the Worker's Compensation Board without her consent and had then initiated a claim for compensation on behalf of the complainant. The company claimed that the disclosure was required pursuant to provincial workers' compensation legislation and that in accordance with the privacy legislation, the information had not been disclosed for purposes other than those for which it had been collected. The Commissioner held that although the employer had released the complainant's information to the Board without her consent, it had done so in compliance with provincial statute, thereby exempting the employer from the requirement to seek her consent prior to the disclosures. The Commissioner did determine, however, that the company did not have in

---

[7] Privacy Commissioner of Canada, November 5 2001, Summary #20.

[8] (February 2, 2007), Doc. 107/06/LRA, [2007] M.L.B.D. No. 10 (Man. L.R.B.).

[9] (2000), 2000 CarswellPEI 47 (P.E.I. C.A.).

place any policies or staff training materials pertaining to the handling of employee information and recommended that the company take steps to implement the necessary policies and materials.[10]

The Privacy Commissioner of Canada has determined that under the *Canada Labour Code* and section 7(3)(c) of *PIPEDA*, arbitrators have the jurisdiction to compel the production of information at arbitration hearings. An employee of a company that produces nuclear technology filed a complaint against her employer for allegedly disclosing her personal information when she appeared as a witness for a grievor in an arbitration hearing between another employee and the company. The complainant claimed that two of her performance appraisals were tendered as evidence as a means to discredit her as a witness, and that her personal information had been released inappropriately. The company argued that under *PIPEDA*, the arbitrator had jurisdiction to allow for the introduction of the performance appraisals and that the appraisals were used solely within the context of an arbitration hearing. Moreover, the appraisals were disclosed only to the arbitrator, the complainant, and the lawyer who represented the grievor's union. The Commissioner held that under the *Canada Labour Code*, arbitrators have the jurisdiction to compel the production of information and that the disclosure of the appraisals was permissible according to section 7(3)(c) of *PIPEDA*, as it was made pursuant to an "order made by a person with jurisdiction to compel the production of information". The arbitrator's allowance of the appraisals as an exhibit qualified as an order as per section 7(3)(c).[11]

Pursuant to the rules of court in Quebec, the Privacy Commissioner of Canada has confirmed that if a plaintiff introduces evidence that the defendant intends to question at trial, the issue must be raised in discovery. Following a trial in a Quebec Court involving a class action lawsuit by a consumer group, a former employee of a telecommunications company who had offered to testify complained that his former employer had disclosed the reasons for his dismissal to a third party. The employer conceded that it had disclosed this information in discovery and contended that it had the right to do so since the disclosure pertained to litigation in a court proceeding in which the company was defending its interests. In this case, the Commissioner held that because the employer did intend to question the consumer group's material that was based on the complainant's statements, the employer was required to produce the proper evidence. In producing the affidavit regarding the appraisals, the employer was acting in accordance with the section 7(3)(c) exception in *PIPEDA* which allows for disclosure

---

[10] Privacy Commissioner of Canada, July 11 2003, Summary #191.
[11] Privacy Commissioner of Canada, August 1 2003, Summary #198.

without an individuals' knowledge or consent where the disclosure is required to comply with the rules of court relating to the production of records.[12]

Certain provincial labour statutes also grant arbitrators the express power to order pre-hearing disclosure of documents containing the personal information of employees.[13] In *Toronto District School Board and C.U.P.E., Local 4400*,[14] the arbitrator held that at the pre-hearing stage, all documents in the parties' possession which have a semblance of relevance ought to be disclosed or at least identified where privilege applies. In this case, the employer filed grievances against the union claiming that the union had violated the collective agreement and workplace policy by distributing a partisan political message using the employer's email system. At the hearing, the employer made a preliminary motion to compel the union to produce certain documents prior to the hearing. The arbitrator ruled that all documents which are arguably or seemingly relevant, or have a semblance of relevance must be disclosed prior to the hearing at the request of the opposing party, and that once a general request for production is made, all documents relating to any matter in issue that is or has been in the possession, control or power of the opposing party must be disclosed, including documents for which privilege is claimed. In circumstances involving sensitive information such as medical records, an arbitrator has ruled that strict rules of confidentiality and relevance apply in order to protect a grievor's privacy. A Vancouver legal secretary, who left her job with the British Columbia Crown Attorney's office in 2002 following a reprimand regarding her job performance, applied for short-term illness and injury plan benefits on the grounds that she suffered from post-traumatic stress disorder, panic disorder, and major depressive disorder. When the government rejected her application on the basis that there was no evidence that her condition prevented her from working, the employee's union filed a grievance on her behalf and she produced a report from her psychiatrist which confirmed her illnesses and indicated that she could not deal with adversarial and confrontational situations.

The employer applied for pre-hearing disclosure of the psychiatrist's notes and report, in addition to records from her treating physicians and her Government Employees' Health Services file. In balancing the grievor's

---

[12] Privacy Commissioner of Canada, March 16 2003, Summary #143.

[13] Ontario *Labour Relations Act, 1995*, S.O. 1995, c. 1, Sched. A, s. 48(12)(b); British Columbia *Labour Relations Code* , R.S.B.C. 1996, c. 244, s.82(2); Manitoba *Labour Relations Act* , R.S.M. 1987, c. L10 (s. 120(e)); *Canada Labour Code*, R.S.C. 1985, c. L-2 (ss. 60(1)(a), 16(f.1)).

[14] (2002), 109 L.A.C. (4th) 20 (Ont. Arb. Bd.).

right to privacy against the employer's entitlement to a fair hearing, the arbitrator ruled that since the employee put her mental state at issue in a grievance, her medical records should be disclosed but only if relevant to issues of work performance and only pursuant to strict conditions of confidentiality in accordance with the Wigmore rules. Therefore, disclosure was permitted solely to the employer's counsel and medical experts, and only after the union and the grievor had a chance to black out irrelevant material.[15]

An arbitrator of the Prince Edward Island Grievance Arbitration had opportunity to consider whether arbitrators have jurisdiction to order production of an employee's personal information under the P.E.I. *Mental Health Act*.[16] In this case, an employee was dismissed following an investigation based on a residential care patient's complaint that the employee had physically abused the patient. The union grieved the dismissal and requested production of the patient's personal medical information stored in his employer's medical files.

The employer refused to disclose the requested information arguing that it was prohibited from doing so by section 31(13) of the P.E.I. *Mental Health Act*. According to this section, "Except as provided in subsection (9) . . . no person shall disclose in an action or proceeding in any court or before anybody other than the Review Board any knowledge or information in respect of a patient obtained in the course of assessing or treating . . . the patient in a psychiatric facility or in the course of employment in the psychiatric facility, except with the consent of the patient." Subsection 31(9) allows disclosure of patients' clinical records only if the disclosure is "pursuant to a subpoena, order or direction of a judge or provincial court judge with respect to a matter in issue before the judge." However, the union submitted that refusing production of the complainant's medical records would violate the principles of natural justice as well as the grievor's rights under section 7 of the *Canadian Charter of Rights and Freedoms*.

The arbitrator acknowledged that the *Mental Health Act* "is very specific in granting the power to order disclosure only to a judge or provincial court judge, and that section 31 cannot, as a matter of interpretation, be 'read down' to give effect to the power of labour arbitrators to summon and enforce the attendance of witness and to compel them to give oral and written attendance on oath as provided for under the *Labour Code*". The arbitrator also held that the *Mental Health Act* overrides any common-law right to natural justice. Notwithstanding, the requested disclosure was even-

[15] Disability and Accommodation Reporter, September/October, 2004.
[16] *P.E.I.U.P.S.E. v. Provincial Health Services Authority* (2005), [2005] P.E.I.L.A.A. No. 1, 2005 CarswellPEI 100 (P.E.I. Arb. Bd.).

tually ordered as the arbitrator agreed with the union's argument that the Act's ban on disclosure violated the grievor's rights as guaranteed by section 7 of the *Charter*. While it was noted that the Federal Court has ruled that section 7 does not guarantee an individual's interest in maintaining his or her employment, the arbitrator agreed that "the grievor's employment interest is more than merely economic, and in fact involves a 'liberty' component."

At issue in *O.P.S.E.U. v. Ontario Clean Water Agency* [17] was whether an employer could have access to an employee's medical history through the OHIP summary, in relation to an employee's allegation that he had been compelled to leave work in a state of "substantial stress and anxiety" due to workplace harassment. The employer claimed that the situation in which the employee found himself was a result of his pre-existing medical condition.

The Ontario Grievance Settlement Board reviewed the jurisprudence in this respect and found that two tests were developed and used by arbitrators whenever the production of employees' medical records was at issue. One test stems from the decision in *Labourers' International Union of North America, Local 607 v. Municipality of Oliver Paipoonge* [18] and stipulates that disclosure of mental health and psychiatric examinations may only be made "at the point in time when they are in fact necessary or essential for purposes of adjudication of the grievance". The second test was formulated in *Becker Milk Co. v. Milk & Bread Drivers, Dairy Employees, Caterers & Allied Employees, Local 647* [19], and requires the need for disclosure to be "arguably relevant", with a higher onus attached to disclosure of mental health information.

The Board noted that the document requested in this case was not a mental health document, and therefore favoured the "arguably relevant" test. Applying the tests to the facts of the case, the Board ruled in favour of disclosure because both the grievor's mental and physical health and causation, in particular, were very significant issues. However, the arbitrator cautioned that this decision should not be construed as suggesting that in every case, a grievor who alleges that the employer's misconduct caused them to become ill must disclose their entire medical history.

---

[17] (2005), 2005 CarswellOnt 7881 (Ont. C.E.G.S.B.).
[18] (1999), 79 L.A.C. (4th) 241 (Ont. Arb. Bd.).
[19] (1996), 53 L.A.C. (4th) 420 (Ont. Arb. Bd.).

10.3   DISCLOSURE TO OTHER THIRD PARTIES

In balancing access to information against privacy rights, a British Columbia adjudicator has determined that where information from a public record cannot be disclosed but can be reasonably severed, an applicant is entitled to the remainder of the record. The onus is on the body to demonstrate that in the circumstances, it would not be reasonable to sever the record.[20] The mother of a boy who attended school in Nanaimo, British Columbia submitted two requests to the school board for disclosure of records pertaining to the boy's teacher in relation to investigations and hearings, results of a disciplinary hearing and a copy of any discussions from the hearing which the school board had sent to the College of Teachers.

The school board refused to confirm or deny whether the records had been sent to the College, as per section 8(2)(b) of the B.C. *Freedom of Information and Protection of Privacy Act* which permits public bodies to refuse to disclose records containing personal information about a third party if disclosure would be an unreasonable invasion of that party's privacy. The school board agreed to disclose hearing documents in severed form pertaining to personal information of the applicant and her son, but not the named teacher's employment history, in accordance with section 22(3)(d) of the Act, which prohibits disclosure of personal information relating to employment, occupational or educational history of a third party. The school also withheld documents that fell under section 12(3)(b) of the Act, which permits a public body to withhold the substance of deliberations of a meeting of its governing body where the meeting was held in private, and section 13(1), which allows a public body to refuse to disclose information that would reveal advice or recommendation developed by or for a public body or a minister. The applicant argued that the board had no right to sever the records and that the records should be disclosed pursuant to section 25(1) of the Act, which requires immediate disclosure of information where it relates to significant harm to the public and/or its disclosure is clearly in the public interest.

The adjudicator determined that the school board's refusal to confirm of deny whether it had submitted records to the College of Teachers was justified, as disclosure would unreasonably invade the teacher's privacy by revealing whether or not the school board had reported disciplinary action against the teacher under the B.C. *School Act*. The adjudicator also agreed with the board's decision to sever information containing the teacher's

---

[20] Order 04-05, *Re Board of School Trustees of School District No. 68* (Nanaimo-Ladysmith); Office of the Information & Privacy Commissioner for British Columbia, February 16 2004.

employment history, which included information regarding children other than the applicant's son, the teacher's own views and opinions, his work history and past performance, and the investigator's analysis and findings.

However, the adjudicator rejected the board's argument that it could withhold records in their entirety that were generated during *in camera* meetings, and requested that the board sever the brief references to the applicant and her son from the minutes of the meeting and disclose only that part of the document to the applicant. Further, the records that dealt specifically with the applicant and her son were held not to contain any explicit or implicit advice or recommendations to the school board, therefore, disclosure of these documents was permissible. With regard to the applicant's claim that immediate disclosure of information was required where it relates to significant public harm or is clearly in the public interest, the adjudicator held that there is no urgent or compelling need to disclose records without delay which concern an investigation into a teacher's workplace actions and behaviour.

In *Duncanson v. Toronto (Metropolitan) Police Services Board,*[21] the Ontario Divisional Court reviewed a decision by the Information and Privacy Commissioner of Ontario following her refusal of an appeal by two Toronto Star reporters from decisions made by the Metropolitan Toronto Police Services Board and the Ministry of the Attorney General. The reporters had requested from the Board disclosure of the names of all 5,000 police officers employed by the force, and information in relation to public complaints made against individual officers, including their names, ranks, the allegations made, the outcome of the complaints, and the docket sheets of the trials of all officers charged under the *Police Act*. From the Ministry, the reporters had requested disclosure of records of all *Criminal Code* charges laid against officers, including their names, their ranks, the charges and the disposition of the cases. The Commissioner had upheld the refusal to disclose the records and the reporters brought an application for judicial review, seeking orders for disclosure of the records.

The Court dismissed the application for judicial review, upholding the Commissioner's refusal to disclose the names of all officers of the force on the basis that in certain circumstances, such disclosure could reasonably be expected to pose a threat to the health and safety of an officer and others, as per section 13 of the *Municipal Freedom of Information and Protection of Privacy Act*. The reporters had failed to show that the public interest in disclosure outweighed the need to protect police officers and others from serious threat to their health and safety. The Court also rejected the reporters argument that the police should have considered whether some of the offi-

---

[21] (1999), [1999] O.J. No. 2464, 1999 CarswellOnt 2013 (Ont. Div. Ct.).

cers' names could have been disclosed. It was not reasonable to expect the Board to sever the names of officers on the list who would not be endangered by the release of their names from those who would be, and it was within the discretion of the police to refuse the request in light of safety concerns. The Court held that although the Ministry did not provide reasons for refusing disclosure, the reporters were not prejudiced as this had not affected their ability to decide whether to appeal.

The issues in *Canada (Information Commissioner) v. Canada (Commissioner of the Royal Canadian Mounted Police)*[22] were similar and pertained to freedom of information and the right to inspect public documents containing personal information. In connection with litigation against four RCMP officers, an individual had requested information from the RCMP about the officers, including a list of the officers' historical postings, their status and date, the list of ranks and when they achieved those ranks, their years of service, their anniversary dates of service, and any public complaints made against the officers. The RCMP refused the request on the basis that the records constituted "personal information" as defined under section 3 of the *Privacy Act*, and therefore were exempt from disclosure pursuant to section 19(1) of the *Access to Information Act*.

The Federal Court of Appeal held that only information regarding a public servant's current or most recent position had to be released, however, on appeal to the Supreme Court of Canada, the Supreme Court ruled that although the information did qualify as "personal information" pursuant to the Act, the RCMP must disclose all of the information requested by the individual. The exception under section 3(j) of the *Privacy Act* applied, allowing disclosure because the information was directly related to the general characteristics associated with the position or function of a federal employee. The information did not reveal anything about the competence of the officers or divulge any personal opinion given outside the course of employment, rather it provided information relevant to understanding the functions performed by the officers. The Court also held that the information applied retroactively and was not limited to an employee's most recent position.

At issue in *Dagg v. Canada (Minister of Finance)*[23] was whether the information in logs signed by employees entering and exiting the workplace on weekends constituted "personal information" as defined by section 3 of the Privacy Act, and whether the information should be disclosed pursuant

---

[22] (Sub nom. *Canada (Information Commissioner) v. Canada (Commissioner of the Royal Canadian Mounted Police)*) [2003] 1 S.C.R. 66 (S.C.C.) [*Canada v. Commissioner of the RCMP*].

[23] [1997] 2 S.C.R. 403 (S.C.C.).

to section 19(2)(c) of the *Access to Information Act* and section 8(2)(m)(i) of the *Privacy Act*. The logs were kept by security personnel only for safety and security reasons. Dagg filed a request with the Department of Finance for copies of the logs for the purpose of presenting the information to the union to assist them in the collective bargaining process, hoping that the union would be inclined to retain his services. While the logs were disclosed, the names, identification numbers and signatures of the employees were deleted. Dagg filed a complaint with the Information Commissioner, arguing that the deleted information should be disclosed in accordance with the section 3(j)(iii) exception of the *Privacy Act,* which provides for the disclosure of information about a federal employee relation to their position and functions including the classification, salary range, and responsibilities of the their position. The Federal Court, Trial Division ruled that the information did not constitute personal information, however, this decision was reversed by the Federal Court of Appeal.

On appeal to the Supreme Court of Canada, the Court interpreted the *Privacy Act* and *Access to Information Act* together to determine that the number of hours spent at the workplace was information relating to the position or function of federal employees, as it allowed for assessment of the amount of work required for a particular employee's position or function. As such, the information did relate to the "responsibilities of the position held by the employee" pursuant to section 3(j)(iii) of the *Privacy Act* and was accessible to the applicant under *the Access to Information Act.*

In another case involving public body employees, an applicant made a request under Alberta's *Freedom of Information and Protection of Privacy Act* for access to severance arrangements, as well as all employment-related benefits for all managerial employees of the City of Calgary.[24] In response to the request, the City released a number of agreements but refused to provide four supplementary pension agreements, invoking section 17(1) of the Act which requires a public body to refuse to disclose personal information "if the disclosure would be an unreasonable invasion of a third party's personal privacy".

The applicant filed a complaint to Alberta's Information and Privacy Commissioner, and the Adjudicator ordered the City to provide the applicant with the supplementary pension benefit agreements. While acknowledging that all of the information contained in the agreements was "personal information" within the meaning of the Act, the Adjudicator held that the City was obliged under section 17(2) of the Act to disclose all but the names, signatures, and retirement dates of the affected individuals. Section 17(2)

---

[24] Information and Privacy Commissioner for Alberta, Order F2003-002, June 16, 2003.

states that "disclosure of personal information is not an unreasonable invasion of a third party's personal privacy if . . . (e) the information is about the third party's classification, salary range, discretionary benefits or employment responsibilities as an officer, employee or member of a public body . . . or (h) the disclosure reveals details of a discretionary benefit of a financial nature granted to the third party by a public body".

The City argued that section 17(2) did not apply to the supplementary pension agreements because the supplementary pension benefits were not discretionary, as the City had no authority to approve or withhold pension benefits. The Adjudicator did not accept this argument, responding that the City had discretion as to whether, or how, to grant the pension benefit, and City Council had exercised its discretion on behalf of the public body to grant the supplementary pension benefits to the affected retirees.

The Federal Court of Canada issued a similar decision when it dealt with performance bonuses awarded to certain National Research Council ("NRC") employees.[25] An Officer of the Research Council Employees' Association requested a list of recipients under the federal *Access to Information Act* in order to determine how the bonuses were distributed across the NRC's various branches. The NRC refused to provide this information citing section 18 of the Act, which prohibits the head of a government institution from disclosing any record that contains personal information as defined in section 3 of the *Privacy Act*.

The applicant complained to the Office of the Privacy Commissioner of Canada who ordered the NRC to provide a somewhat limited list of bonus recipients. The applicant subsequently applied for judicial review of this decision to the Federal Court. The presiding judge agreed with the applicant that full disclosure must be made and accepted her argument that the names of the employees fell within the exception in section 3(1)(1) of the *Privacy Act*, which provides that "information relating to any discretionary benefit of a financial nature . . . conferred on an individual, including the name of the individual and the exact nature of the benefit", does not constitute personal information.

The Court held that while the employees' names alone were their personal information within the meaning of the *Privacy Act*, the exception in the Act mandating disclosure of discretionary financial benefits applied, given that everything about the awarding of bonuses was discretionary. In addition, the judge ruled that the information requested could be disclosed on the basis of the public interest exception since the information sought

---

[25] *Van Den Bergh v. National Research Council of Canada*, 2003 FC 1116, 2003 CarswellNat 3034 (F.C.).

was of a general nature, and the purpose for which the Officer had requested it was to undertake a legitimate analysis of the expenditure of public funds.

Noteworthy is the fact that unlike the *Privacy Act*, some of its counterpart provincial privacy laws do not distinguish between ordinary individuals and "individuals who [are or were] an officer or employee of a government institution".[26] As a result, public servants are entitled to the same protection of personal information as any other residents of these provinces. This means that disclosure of government employees' names along with their particular salary (as opposed to salary range) and job title constitutes an unreasonable invasion of their privacy. This principle was followed in *MacNeill v. Prince Edward Island (Information & Privacy Commissioner)*,[27] wherein a newspaper publisher made a request to obtain a list of employees, including their names, positions/titles and salary, from the Workers' Compensation Board. The province's Information and Privacy Commissioner rejected the request, ruling that under the provincial *Freedom of Information and Protection of Privacy Act*, an individual's name constituted personal information, the disclosure of which represents an unreasonable invasion of the employee's privacy when combined with their actual salary and job title. The P.E.I. Supreme Court upheld the Commissioner's decision, commenting in particular, that even if public servants were previously thought to forfeit their privacy protection, this was no longer the case after the coming into force of the Act. As such, public employees were entitled to the same protection of their personal information as any other resident of P.E.I.

In *Dickie v. Nova Scotia (Department of Health)*[28] a patient in a provincial treatment facility requested access to information relating to an investigation of a facility employee and the decision taken pursuant to the investigation. The patient had alleged that the employee had engaged in an emotional and sexual relationship with her, thereby breaching his professional duties. Following the investigation, the Department of Health informed her that no disciplinary action could be taken against the employee. The patient then applied for access to information in relation to the investigation and was, per the decision of the Trial judge, granted access to much of the information, including names contained in the report, the employee's work-related conduct, and information communicated in confidence by

---

[26] See for example, *Freedom of Information and Protection of Privacy Act*, S.P.E.I. 2001, c. 37, *Freedom of Information and Protection of Privacy Act*; R.S.A. 2000, c. F-25.

[27] 2004 PESCTD 69 (P.E.I. T.D.).

[28] (1999), [1999] N.S.J. No.116, 1999 CarswellNS 97 (N.S. C.A.).

other employees, as well as their names. The Department of Health appealed the Nova Scotia Supreme Court's decision.

The Nova Scotia Court of Appeal allowed the appeal in part, ruling that while the trial judge was correct in allowing the names to be disclosed, he erred in coming to this conclusion by limiting the definition of personal information instead of interpreting the language in a clear, broad and simple manner. The trial judge also erred in determining that the employee's work-related conduct did not relate to employment history, which constitutes personal information protected by the *Freedom of Information and Protection of Privacy Act*. The Court also held that the judge erred in finding that both the employee and other employees did not communicate their information in confidence. The disclosure of employees' and management's opinions and recommendations regarding the employee, and the employee's response to the allegations were presumed to be an unreasonable invasion of his personal privacy pursuant to the Act. The Court concluded that the types of information which should be disclosed to the complainant were the steps followed in the investigation, the names of employees who provided statements, communications by the patient to them regarding her allegations, and the decision made in relation to the employee over the allegations.

At issue in an application for review filed with the Nova Scotia Freedom of Information and Protection of Privacy Review Office was whether section 20 of the Nova Scotia *Freedom of Information and Protection of Privacy Act* supports the decision of the Department of Education to deny access to the agendas of the Minister and Deputy Minister of Education.[29] The applicant had requested a review of the Department's decision to deny access to all schedules, organizers, planners, agendas, and calendars of the Minister and Deputy Minister over a five-month period from May to September, 2001. The Department claimed an exemption to disclose such information pursuant to section 20(1) of the Act, which obliges a public body to refuse to disclose personal information if disclosure would be an unreasonable invasion of personal privacy, and suggested that it may be unsafe to allow the public to view how these individuals conduct their work throughout the day, including their location and patterns. Further, the Department argued that under section 20(3)(d), the information in the agendas related to employment history in a daily sense, and therefore qualified as personal information which should be exempted from disclosure.

Following previous decisions by both the British Columbia and Ontario Information and Privacy Commissioners, the Nova Scotia review officer noted the widely accepted distinction between personal information and professional information about public servants and individuals holding of-

---

[29]   Report FI-01-138, [2002] N.S.F.I.P.P.A.R. No. 4.

ficial positions in organizations. The review officer accepted that as a general rule, records containing information associated with an individual in the normal course of performing his or her professional or employment responsibilities is not personal information, nor is it personal information when his or her name appears on the record in relation to their functions as public employees.

With respect to the Department's claim for exemption of the agendas under employment history, the officer held that permitting the exemption would allow for too broad a definition of "employment history" and could potentially encompass job position, remuneration, or all employment-related interests, thereby conflicting with section 20(4)(e) which states that disclosure of such information is not an unreasonable invasion of privacy. Further, the officer stated that "employment history" refers only to past employment, rather than aspects of current employment such salary or job position.

While the review officer acknowledged that agendas could include reminders of doctor's appointments and social outings for which disclosure would constitute an unreasonable invasion of personal privacy or involve safety concerns and therefore should not be disclosed, he rejected the Department's assertion that agendas are by definition records of personal information. As such, each document must be considered individually and considered on its own merits regardless of its label, and a careful balancing act between the public's right to access information and the employee's right to privacy is required. The review officer concluded that objective facts recorded in public servants' agenda regarding their activities in the normal course of performing work responsibilities are not personal information about identifiable individuals and therefore must be disclosed to the applicant.

A monetary award of $5,000 was granted to an employee to compensate him for mental distress suffered as a result of the employer's use of unnecessarily intrusive means of ensuring a safe workplace.[30] The employee was suspended following an altercation with his co-worker, and the employer required the grievor to undergo a psychological assessment by a psychiatrist of the employer's choice before returning to work, in accordance with the employer's statutory obligation to ensure violence-free working conditions. The grievor wanted to keep his job and obeyed this requirement. However, he subsequently claimed that the assessment had been conducted in an offensive and improper manner and that the employer

---

[30] *Molson Breweries v. Canadian Union of Brewery & General Workers* (2005), [2005] O.L.A.A. No. 515, 142 L.A.C. (4th) 84 (Ont. Arb. Bd.).

recklessly disregarded his privacy by disclosing the psychiatrist's report to several members of management.

While the arbitrator agreed with the employer that it had reasonable grounds to require the assessment, he nonetheless held that such assessments must be conducted in the least intrusive way possible. The arbitrator further clarified that a much less intrusive approach comprises seeking medical information through the grievor's own doctor or specialist first, and then seeking an independent assessment if the initial medical information is not sufficient, rather than immediately demanding the grievor to undergo a medical assessment by a specialist of the company's choosing. Commenting on the disclosure issue, the arbitrator observed that whenever a company insists upon a psychological evaluation of an employee, it should not forget about its respective duty of confidentiality. Consequently, the arbitrator held that the employer in this case should have sent the report to the company doctor who then could have informed those individuals who had a need to know about the grievor's fitness to return to work.

In another case, a company attempted to argue that the statutory regime designed to protect personal information from unauthorized disclosure infringes on the right of freedom of expression guaranteed by section 2(b) of the *Charter*.[31] This argument was advanced by Canada Safeway Limited, a company that was involved in a dispute with a Calgary Co-op employee, who was detained by the security of one of Safeway's stores for failing to pay for all her store items. At the time of the incident, the detained employee was wearing her Co-op uniform so Safeway contacted the Co-op and advised them of the alleged theft without the employee's consent to this disclosure. The Co-op then terminated the employee. The employee complained to Alberta's Information and Privacy Commissioner alleging that Safeway had wrongfully disclosed her personal information in contravention of section 7(1)(b) of Alberta's *Personal Information Protection Act* ("PIPA"). Section 7(1)(b) prohibits disclosure of an individual's personal information unless the Act provides otherwise or the individual provides his or her consent to the disclosure.

The Portfolio Officer designated by the Commissioner to investigate the complaint found that Safeway was in contravention of the Act. Safeway, in turn, objected to this finding and brought the matter before the Commissioner. It was at this stage that Safeway initiated the *Charter* challenge with respect to section 7(1)(b) of *PIPA*. The Commissioner noted that the imputed privacy legislation was designed to strike a balance between the right of an individual to have his or her personal information protected and the need of organizations to collect, use and disclose personal information when it is

---

[31] *Canada Safeway Ltd. v. Shineton* (2007), 2007 CarswellAlta 1808 (Alta. Q.B.).

reasonable. In the Commissioner's opinion, the right of freedom of information should be placed in this context. As a result, the Commissioner rejected Safeway's argument that section 7(1)(b) of the Act was contrary to section 2(b) of the *Charter*.

The Alberta Court of Queen's Bench upheld the Commissioner's decision, endorsing the Commissioner's position that neither the right to privacy nor freedom of expression is absolute, and adding that he was not satisfied that the disclosure Safeway made to Co-op is the type of expression that section 2(b) of the *Charter* is intended to protect. Further, the judge stated that even if he was wrong about his conclusion and section 7(1)(b) did contradict section 2(b) of the *Charter*, its existence was justified under the section 1 analysis:

> ...I conclude that the restriction in s. 7(1)(d) of *PIPA* is a reasonable and justified limit as contemplated by s. 1 of the *Charter*. In my view, there can be no question that the protection of personal information is an important legislative objective. I am satisfied that, to use Wilson J.'s words from Lavigne, that objective is "logically furthered" by *PIPA*'s restriction. I am also satisfied that *PIPA* represents a reasonable balancing of competing rights and interests and that, while it does impose some limits on expression, those limits are not so severe as to require me to second-guess the balancing the Legislature has chosen to adopt.

In yet another case involving the disclosure by the RCMP of embarrassing personal information about an employee to his employer, the Edmonton Police, the Commissioner held that the RCMP had violated the *Privacy Act* when it failed to seek and obtain the employee's consent.[32] In this case, the employee's son was involved in an altercation with the RCMP, following which the employee was called to provide assistance. The RCMP considered filing obstruction charges against the employee due to his behaviour, but no charges were ever laid; however, the RCMP provided a file of the incident to the Edmonton Police. The Commissioner found that the employee's complaint was well-founded, although no penalty and no remedy was provided for under the Act. On judicial review of the Commissioner's decision, the Federal Court confirmed that the Commissioner's powers were limited to issuing recommendations. Further, the Court determined that it did not have jurisdiction to grant the monetary award sought by the applicant.

---

[32] *Murdoch v. Royal Canadian Mounted Police*, 2005 FC 420, 2005 CarswellNat 800 (F.C.).

(For additional case law regarding disclosure of personal information of employees to third parties, see Chapter 3 – *Personnel Files*, Chapter 4 – *Work Product*, and Chapter 5 – *Personal Opinions*).

11

Storage of and Access to Employee Information

In addition to the legislative scheme aimed at safeguarding employee information from being disclosed other than in accordance with relevant privacy legislation, strict storage and access rules within privacy laws also operate to promote the confidentiality of such information.

In its Order F07-10, British Columbia's Office of the Information and Privacy Commissioner addressed the question of storage of personal information collected by a public organization both within and outside Canada.[1] At issue was whether the "Gallup TeacherInsight Assessment" developed and administered in the United States infringed upon the privacy rights of candidates for teachers' positions. The Assessment was introduced by the Board of Education of School District No. 75 in 2004. Every candidate was required by the Board to take the test as a pre-requisite for being short-listed for the subsequent interviewing process. Various types of personal information, including the names, addresses, and social insurance numbers of job applicants, were collected during the Assessment and stored both in Canada and the United States. The British Columbia Teachers' Federation ("BCTF") and the Mission Teachers' Union ("MTU") took the position that this screening requirement violated the *Freedom of Information and Protection of Privacy Act* (*"FIPPA"*) and filed a complaint with the Office of the Information and Privacy Commissioner of British Columbia.

As the complaint concerned an emerging area of privacy law, the Privacy Commissioner was required to determine and/or clarify a number of substantive issues. These issues included: (1) whether the Board had made reasonable security arrangements with respect to the storage of the collected personal information; and (2) whether the Board had obtained the candidates' voluntary consent to the storage and access of their personal information.

On the question of storing the candidates' personal information in Gallup's database in the United States, one of the the complainant's primary concerns was that such information was not being granted the Canadian

---

[1] June 26, 2007.

level of privacy protection, given that Gallup was subject to the USA *Patriot Act* as well as other laws of the United States. After hearing Gallup's description of the security measures it had implemented, its assurances of taking each and every step to vigorously protect the personal information collected, as well as its assertion that the information in question was not very likely to present data of any interest to authorities enforcing the *Patriot Act*, the Commissioner recommended that once an applicant has submitted his/her personal information to Gallup, the applicant's identifying personal information should be replaced by a numerical number. The Commissioner further suggested that an even more preferable security measure would be to create keys enabling Gallup's clients to associate numerical numbers with applicants' names, and allow the keys to remain in the hands of clients rather than with Gallup.

The Commissioner then reviewed section 30(1), which requires personal information in the custody or under control of a public body to be stored and accessed only in Canada, subject to three exceptions. One of these three exceptions is when consent is provided in the prescribed manner by the individual who has supplied his or her personal information. The Office found in this respect that the data consent page and the introductory page of the Assessment together provided enough information to enable applicants to give their informed consent. The applicants were expressly notified with respect to whom the personal information might be disclosed, how the personal information might be used, and that their personal information would be stored and accessed in the United States.

Lastly, the Commissioner emphasized that a party claiming the existence of informed consent must be able to provide proof thereof. This is of particular importance when consent is given in electronic form. In this case, the evidentiary requirement was satisfied where evidence was provided that an applicant could not proceed with providing personal information to Gallup unless he/she had clicked an "I consent/agree" button on the data consent page.